Applied Science

Science

GCSE

Ken Gadd

Published in 2003 by:
Nelson Thornes Ltd
Delta Place
27 Bath Road
CHELTENHAM
GL53 7TH
United Kingdom

03 04 05 06 07 / 10 9 8 7 6 5 4 3 2 1

A catalogue record for this book is available from the British Library

ISBN 0 7487 7044 5

Illustrations by Arthur Pickering
Page make-up by Florence Production, Stoodleigh, Devon

Printed in Great Britain by Scotprint

Introduction iv

UNIT 1 2
Developing scientific skills

Working safely in science 4

Carrying out practical tasks 18

Handling scientific equipment and materials 23

Recording and analysing scientific data 49

Investigating living organisms 66

Chemical analysis 83

Investigating materials 109

UNIT 2 124
Science for the needs of society

Living organisms 126

Obtaining useful chemicals 167

Materials for making things 194

The importance of energy 211

UNIT 3 240
Science at work

Science in the workplace 242

Making useful products 254

Instruments and machines 286

Monitoring living organisms 312

Index 342

Introduction

This book is written to help students and teachers preparing for a course leading to the GCSE in Applied Science. It's not just about science. It's about scientists as well. I have tried to describe the type of work scientists do and the skills and knowledge they use.

The sections of the book match the units of the GCSE in Applied Science. The features in the book are:

Units

. . . covers the information necessary for this unit of the specification; each unit is broken down into sections

Unit introduction

. . . gives an overview of what's in the unit

You need to

. . . summarise what you need to be able to do by the end of a section

Remember

. . . important things to remember

Technique

. . . how to carry out the technique

Try it yourself

. . . activities to help you learn

Extension work

. . . more advanced work for students aiming to gain higher grades

Questions

. . . to check your learning

About the GCSE in Applied Science

A GCSE in Applied Science is a nationally recognised work-related qualification. This is why it's called 'applied'. It will enable you to choose from a number of routes into further education or employment. This course will appeal to you if you:

- are interested in science and how scientific knowledge is used in the workplace
- want to study a course that is active, with a high proportion of coursework

It is a double award qualification, which means it is equal to two GCSEs – twice the size of most GCSEs.

By taking this course you will:

- gain important scientific skills and knowledge
- find out about people who use science in their work and about the organisations they work for
- carry out activities that show how science is used in the workplace
- develop Key Skills, which are highly valued by employers and further education
- gain confidence by developing the skills to learn things for yourself

About the qualification

The qualification is made up of three units.

Unit 1: Developing Scientific Skills
This unit is about the practical laboratory skills that scientists use to handle equipment, materials and organisms safely and successfully. You will learn about microscopy, working with micro-organisms, chemical analysis and the properties of materials.

Unit 2: Science for the Needs of Society
This unit is about some important underpinning scientific ideas and concepts. It covers four key areas: living organisms and their life processes, chemical processing, properties of materials, and energy conversion and transfer.

Unit 3: Science at Work
This unit is about applying the skills and knowledge from Units 1 and 2 in investigations. There are four areas: science-based organisations, preparation of chemical products, electrical and electronic devices and mechanical machines, and the behaviour of an organism.

It's unlikely that you will be taught the units one after the other. More likely is that your first year activities will combine aspects of Unit 1 and Unit 2. Your second year will probably focus on Unit 3.

About assessment

Unit 1 (Developing Scientific Skills) and Unit 3 (Science at Work) will be internally assessed by teachers at your school. Your work for assessment forms part of your Student Portfolio. You will be asked to follow standard procedures and undertake investigations as part of these units.

Unit 2 (Science for the Needs of Society) will be assessed through external examination.

Acknowledgements

I would like to thank the team at 4 SCIENCE for all their help, and our associates who have made many helpful comments. In particular I would like to acknowledge the support I've received from Jean Scrase and Mike Tingle. Thank you to the staff from Nelson Thornes (especially Jane and Chris) for their patience and understanding and to Helen Roberts for her help during the final stages of manuscript preparation. Thanks too to Peter Borrows for checking issues about safety. Finally thank you to Kacs, a quiet village that provided me with a place of peace and solitude to write the bulk of the book.

Photo credits

Action Plus p. 163, Glyn Kirk p.332; Alamy: Brandon Cole Marine Photography p. 177, Mark Baigent p. 199; Ami Vitale p. 216 top; Maximilian Weinzierl p. 290 bottom; Axon Images p. 17, p. 268, p. 329 top; B&Q p. 19; CPREEC p. 141; Corbis: Lester Lefkowitz p. 1.28; Wally McNamee p. 184 left; Hulton-Deutsch Collection p. 255; Alan Goldsmith p. 314 top; Fisher p. 139; Garden Picture Library: Kathy Collins p. 329 bottom; Getty Image Bank: Gabriel M. Covian p. 207 bottom; Getty Images Stone: Vince Streano p. 14 top; Donovan Reese p. 47; Getty Images Taxi: Benelux Press p. 310 bottom; Holt Studios International: Nigel Cattlin p. 132 right; Rosie Mayer p. 325; ICI: 2.52; Jeyes p. 318; Julian Hill p. 217 bottom; Last Resort Picture Library p. 37 bottom left, right, p. 300 left, right, bottom, p. 302 bottom, p. 333; Martyn Chillmaid p. 5, p. 20, p. 26 top, p. 30, p. 31, p.32 top, bottom, p. 92, p. 93, p. 180, p. 181, p. 173 middle, right, p. 194, p. 221, p. 226, p. 228 right, p. 235, p. 257 top, bottom, p. 267, p. 299, p. 317, p. 320, p. 321, p. 322, p. 324, p.327, p. 339; MFS Fire Extinguishers p. 16; Nortene p. 19; Prosport p. 331; Reckitt Benckiser p. 318; Science Photolibrary: Cordelia Molloy p. 14 middle; BSIP Laurent p. 26 bottom; Jerry Mason p. 92 middle; David Taylor p. 94; Andrew Lambert Photography p. 103, John Durham p. 127, TEK Image p. 195 bottom, Alexander Tsiaras p. 145, David Scharf p. 154 top; Adam Hart-Davis p. 228 bottom left; Corel (NT) p. 291 right; Corel 291 (NT) p. 236; Corel 357 (NT) p. 216 middle; Corel 603 (NT) p. 144, p. 149, p. 164 right, p. 199 bottom, p. 219, p. 222, p. 249 middle, p. 288, p. 313 bottom, p. 332; Corel 745 p. 209; Diamar 7 (NT) p. 144 right; Digital Vision (NT) p. 291 left; Digital Stock 5 (NT) p. 143, p. 250 right; Digital Vision AF/Nat Photos (NT) p. 127; Digital Vision 6 (NT) p. 30, p. 164 left, p. 218 top, p. 232 bottom, p. 269, p. 330; Digital Vision BP/Peter Adams (NT) p. 171; Digital Vision SC (NT) p. 45; House of Commons Information Office p. 245 top right; Image Library/Ingram V2 (NT) p. 184 right; Image Source 2 (NT) p. 146; Imagin/London (NT) p. 268 bottom; Instant Art Signs (NT) p. 6; Photodisc 40 p. 9 top, p. 67 left, p. 168 right, middle and left, p. 205, p. 218 bottom, p. 232 top, p. 245 bottom, p. 245 right, p. 252 middle, p. 252 bottom, p. 340; Rubberball WW (NT) p. 154 bottom, p. 249 bottom, p. 287 bottom, p. 313 top, p. 328; Science Photo Library p. 9 bottom, p.13 top and bottom, p. 14 bottom, p. 24, p. 28, p. 72, p. 73, p. 79, p. 92 bottom, p. 126, p. 132 left, p. 137, p. 139, p. 146, p. 147, p. 153, p. 155 bottom, p. 160, p. 167, p. 169 top, bottom right and left, p. 171 top, p. 172 left, right, p. 173 top left, middle, right, bottom, p. 181 bottom left and right, p. 195 top, p. 196, p. 197, p. 208, p. 212, p. 213 top, bottom, p. 214, p. 216 middle and bottom, p. 220, p. 225, p. 228, p. 229, p. 230, p. 231, p. 232 bottom, p. 243 middle, p. 244, p. 250, p. 264, p. 270, p. 272, p. 276, p. 290 top, middle, p. 305, p. 314 right; Scottish Hydroelectric p. 225 middle; Sheffield City Council p. 155 top; Stanley Tools p. 200, p. 301; T Hill p. 225 top; Topham Picturepoint p. 182; Russ Bishop, Photri p. 226 bottom; UPPA p. 242; Stuart Cohen, Image Works p. 305 bottom; British Library p. 319.

Picture research by johnbailey@axonimages.com

This unit will help you to:

learn about health and safety and the scientific skills used by scientists. Much scientific work is practical and risk assessments must be carried out before this is done. When scientists carry out practical work they often follow standard procedures. To do this well they must know how to handle scientific equipment and materials, and record and analyse scientific data. You will find out how these skills are used in three areas of scientific work:

- investigating living organisms: light microscopy and micro-organisms

- chemical analysis: qualitative chemical analysis and quantitative chemical analysis

- investigating materials: electrical properties and other physical properties.

Developing scientific skills 1

In this unit you will learn about:

Working safely in science 4

Carrying out practical tasks 18

Handling scientific equipment
and materials 23

Recording and analysing
scientific data 49

Investigating living organisms 66

Chemical analysis 83

Investigating materials 109

1.1 Working safely in science

Safety where scientists work

You need to be able to:

- *identify hazard warning signs*

- *identify biological, chemical and physical hazards, including radioactive substances, and their associated risks*

- *follow health and safety procedures.*

You need to be aware of the need to:

- *carry out health and safety checks in the workplace*

- *carry out risk assessments for activities performed in the workplace.*

You need to find out:

- *what can be done to prevent accidents from hazards in a scientific workplace*

- *which emergency procedures to follow if an accident from these hazards happens*

- *about the safety measures employed for handling radioactive materials and the procedures adopted to ensure that people who work with radioactive materials are not exposed to unacceptable risk*

- *about how unwanted or waste materials, including radioactive substances, are disposed of safely.*

Accidents do happen

Everybody in the workplace has a responsibility for health and safety – employers and employees, teachers, technicians and students. So it includes you! Schools, hospitals and factories all have health and safety regulations and codes of practice. Many have health and safety officers. You will be told what the rules are in your school or college. You must respect them. Working together and observing guidance means that accidents remain rare.

However, unfortunately accidents will always occur even if only rarely. When they do everything must be done to minimise their effect. In particular you should know what to do if somebody is injured or if there is a fire. You should know some first aid (you may have the chance to get a first aid certificate). All science-based organisations

Accidents in the places where scientists work are rare. This is because scientists must follow strict regulations and procedures. These are aimed, successfully, at reducing the risk of harming or damaging themselves or people near to them in the workplace.

have an Appointed Person in charge of first aid on site. Who is this in your school or college?

Hazards and risks

There is a difference between hazard and risk!

- A **hazard** is the potential that a substance, equipment or activity has to do harm.
- A **risk** is the likelihood that a hazard will cause harm under the circumstances in which it will be used.

An example will help. Rock-climbing is hazardous. However, it may be of low risk if the proper equipment is used and the rules are followed. Similarly it may be of high risk if done by an inexperienced person with no supervision, but of low risk if done by an expert who is carefully prepared. Think about these other examples: making a cup of coffee or riding a bicycle. Who is at risk? When is the risk high and when is it low?

There are British and European safety standards, for example, the British Standards (BS) kitemark. Equipment that has a British kitemark or European Standards mark has met certain minimum requirements. Equipment without these marks must be rigorously tested before use.

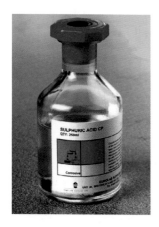

In the laboratory a bottle of concentrated sulfuric acid is a hazard. It is corrosive. The risk is high if it's left without a stopper and near the edge of the bench. The risk is less if the bottle is stoppered and stored out of reach. You can minimise the risk, but only if you recognise the hazard!

Hazards

Hazards in scientific workplaces include:

- careless behaviour
- not using equipment properly
- not using protective and safety equipment
- not following correct procedures
- using chemical substances classified as toxic, highly flammable, corrosive, oxidising, harmful and irritant
- using some micro-organisms
- using utilities, such as gas and electricity.

You have a responsibility to do all you can to reduce the risks from hazards. During the course you will be in situations where there are hazards. You need to be able to identify biological, chemical and physical hazards, including radioactive substances. You must also be able to assess their associated risks.

Corrosive

Dangerous for the environment

Toxic

Highly flammable

Irritant

Oxidising

Radioactive

Harmful

Explosive

Biological hazard

Electrical hazard

Warning

Look out for these hazard symbols. You must be able to recognise them and you need to know what they mean.

The laboratory contains many hazards. However, if you recognise the hazards and their possible dangers you can eliminate or at least minimise the risk.

Risk assessment

You will be asked to carry out many scientific investigations that involve practical work. Before starting any practical work, a risk assessment must be produced to identify possible hazards, assess the risk of using them and decide how the risk can be eliminated or at least reduced to an acceptable level. Somebody experienced in such matters should carry out a risk assessment.

Carrying out a risk assessment

The Management of Health and Safety at Work Regulations, 1999, and the Control of Substances hazardous to Health Regulations, 1999, require employers to *suitably and sufficiently assess the risks to the health and safety of employees to which they are exposed whilst they are at work*. This means risk assessments must be done for every activity carried out.

During the course you will be asked to do some risk assessments. Your teacher **must** check them before you begin work. Here is a checklist for carrying out a risk assessment. You must identify:

- hazards associated with activities or situations, for example, substances and equipment and how they will be used
- associated risks: try to quantify these
    - how likely is that any hazard will be realised?
    - how severe will the consequences be?
    - how often does exposure to the hazard occur?
- who is at risk
- what can be done to eliminate or reduce the risk to a 'reasonable' level
- training that would help
- emergency actions that could be taken
- any remaining risk.

You should record the assessment using a form like this:

RISK ASSESSMENT FORM	
Name of assessor:	Date:
Activity	
Hazards	
Risk	
Those at risk	
Control measures	
Training	
Emergency action	
Remaining risk	
Signature of assessor	

Crossing the road: an example of a risk assessment

Here is a risk assessment for crossing road. It will help you understand what is needed. You can assume that the road is uncontrolled – no lanes, no speed limit and no crossings.

Risk assessment	
Activity or operation	Crossing the road
Hazards	Collision with motor vehicle
Risk	Here we need to estimate the risks from hazards. What kind of person we are talking about, e.g. a five-year old child, a student or a teacher? If an accident does happen, how severe will the injury be (e.g. one or two stitches, a period in hospital or death)? How often is the road crossed (e.g. hourly, daily or more often)?
Those at risk	Pedestrians
Control measures	Impose a speed limit, provide crossings, traffic islands, pedestrian bridges, underpasses, traffic calming
Training	Pedestrians: learn the *Green Cross Code* Drivers: study the *Highway Code*, pass a driving test
Emergency action	Call Emergency Services, give First Aid etc.
Remaining risk	Provided the above measures are implemented, the risk of collision is low. However, any accident that does occur may still be serious.

Here are several useful sources of further information about risk assessment:

ASE (www.ase.org.uk)
- Topics in safety, 3rd edition, 2001
- Safeguards in the school laboratory, 10th edition, 1996

CLEAPSS (www.cleapss.org.uk)
- Hazcards, 1995
- Laboratory Handbook, 2001
- Student Safety Sheets, 1998/2000

SSERC (www.sserc.org.uk)
- Hazardous chemicals CD2: interactive manual for science education, 2001
- Preparing COSHH risk assessments for project work in schools, 1991

Others
- Chemical manufacturers and suppliers catalogues and datasheets

- Microbiology: an HMI guide for schools and further education (HMSO, 1995)
- Safety in biological fieldwork: guidance notes for codes of practice. Ed. D Nichols (IoB, 1990)
- Safety in outdoor education (HMSO, 1989)
- DfEE Safety in science education, 1996

Radioactive material

It is unlikely that you will use radioactive materials. However, you should know about the safety measures employed for handling radioactive materials. These include:

1 Carry out a 'dry run'. This means going through the procedure but without actually using the radioactive material. Check that everything you need, such as waste containers, is at hand.

2 Wear protective clothing, including a lab. coat, disposable gloves and eye protection. Do not take them outside the laboratory.

3 Wear a film badge. Keep it away from extreme heat. Never wear somebody else's badge – only your own.

4 Use a survey meter (for example, a Geiger counter). Be sure you know its sensitivity and, therefore, the limits to which it can detect radiation. Check the area where you are working, passing over it slowly with the meter, before you start work and when you stop for any length of time.

5 Sometimes you may need to use a wipe test for materials that are difficult or impossible to detect with a Geiger counter. Use a piece of filter paper moistened with a water/ethanol mixture to wipe the area where there might be contamination, put it into a scintillation vial and test it with a Liquid Scintillation Counter.

6 Keep a clear record of your work and an inventory of the radioactive material.

7 Wash your hands before leaving the laboratory.

8 Should an accident happen, be sure you know what procedures to follow and who to contact.

The correct protective clothing is essential when working with radioactive materials. The film badge records the levels of radioactivity that the person is exposed to.

Survey meters such as this Geiger counter are used to monitor levels of radioactivity.

How radiation affects the body

Exposure to radiation can cause radiation sickness. The radiation can damage the body's cells. Natural background radiation causes only slight damage that the body can mend. But when it's exposed to artificially high levels of radiation the body can't fight the damage caused.

The first symptoms of radiation sickness include nausea, vomiting, diarrhoea and tiredness. These may be followed by, amongst other symptoms, headache, fast heartbeat, hair loss, bleeding spots under the skin and anaemia. Drugs can be used to relieve some of the symptoms. Blood transfusions may be necessary for patients suffering from anaemia.

Waste disposal

Think about the laboratory where you are working. What do you think happens to any solid material you put in the bin? What happens to things you pour down the sink?

You must dispose of waste safely. Make sure you follow the procedures used in your school or college. The disposal of waste is controlled by government legislation (*The Special Waste Regulations, 1996*).

Anything that goes down the sink ends up in the sewage works. Living micro-organisms are used to clean up the water, so it is vital that they are not poisoned by substances that were disposed of by pouring them down the sink.

All workplaces have their own procedures for the safe disposal of unwanted materials and waste. Some of the categories of waste found in scientific workplaces are: clinical, chemical, radioactive, biological, aqueous. When you are working you need to think about waste

Solids are taken to rubbish tips and, eventually, buried. Sometimes, substances are washed from the tips by rainwater and can end up in rivers and streams. Tips are monitored to ensure that harmful substances are not 'leaking' into public water supplies.

Some solids are incinerated (burnt at very high temperatures). This is common, for example, in hospitals where some clinical waste is disposed of like this. Sometimes the heat generated by burning waste can be used to heat buildings, water and so on. However, the smoke produced may cause problems.

disposal. What should you do when you have finished working with chemicals, micro-organisms or other materials? You must always dispose of waste safely and your school or college will have a procedure for this. Make sure you know what to do before starting any practical work and follow the instructions carefully.

REMEMBER

There are two straightforward things that will help to protect the environment:

- Always use the minimum amount of chemicals, such as reagents, and materials.

- Recycle chemicals and materials where possible. You may be asked to put used chemicals and materials into containers for further treatment.

Questions

1   Your school or college will have safety rules or guidelines for working in the laboratory. Find out what these are.

2   Look around the laboratories, preparation rooms and storage areas in your school or college. Make a list of health and safety precautions that you find and where they are located, e.g. storage of chemicals and equipment, fire alarms, emergency procedures, fire extinguishers, protective clothing, eye wash facilities and so on. If you visit a laboratory in industry or the service sector, make a similar list.

3   Sketch a symbol that shows a product is made to (a) British Standards, (b) European Standards.

    Why are these symbols used?

4   Explain the difference between a hazard and a risk.

5   Give an example and describe how you would reduce risk when:

   (a) using a hazardous chemical

   (b) working with high voltage equipment

   (c) heating to a high temperature

   (d) working with a hazardous biological material.

6   What are the procedures used in your school or college to dispose of waste from the laboratory?

First aid

Common injuries in laboratories are heat burns and scalds, chemical burns, injury from breathing in fumes or swallowing chemicals, electric shock, cuts and damage to the eyes from particles or chemicals. For each of these injuries, **you need to know:**

- *the basic first aid to give*

- *the situations in which it would be dangerous to give first aid.*

You need to find out:

- *why it is useful to have a first aid qualification*

- *the names of organisations which give training for first aid qualifications and how to contact these organisations.*

The importance of first aid

If an accident happens and somebody is injured it's important to treat them as soon as possible. Taking immediate action helps to reduce the possible harm to the person. You should know how to treat some common injuries and, just as importantly, when you should do nothing apart from getting the help of an experienced first-aider.

You will need training in first aid techniques. A number of organisations run courses that will enable you to get a first aid certificate.

Some common injuries in laboratories and how to treat them (and when not to try!)

Heat burns and scalds

Burns are caused by dry heat. Scalds are caused by wet heat. The symptoms are extreme pain, possibly shock, swelling, blistering, redness and, possibly, charred skin.

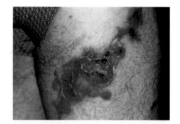

You need to:

- stop the burning by putting plenty of cold water on the burn or scald
- relieve the pain and minimise possible infection by dressing the wound
- treat for the casualty for shock.

Unless the wound is superficial, call 999.

Chemical burns

Chemical burns are caused by acids, alkalis, or other chemicals coming in contact with the skin. They are not usually caused by heat. The 'burn' is a result of the chemical destroying body tissues.

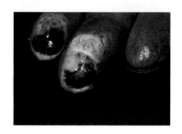

You need to:

- thoroughly wash the area with large amounts of water, for example, under a running tap or shower
- neutralise any chemical remaining on the affected area:
  (a) for acid burns, use a solution of sodium hydrogencarbonate in water, (b) for alkali burns, use a dilute solution of vinegar
- wash the area again with water and gently pat dry with sterile gauze. Do not rub the area.
- take the casualty for professional medical treatment.

For chemical burns to the eye:

- flush the eye(s) immediately with large amounts of water or a sterile saline (salt) solution; wash for at least 10 minutes with at least 2 dm^3 of water. Alkali burns should be washed for at least 20 minutes
- loosely cover both eyes with a clean dressing
- take the casualty for professional medical treatment.

Injury from breathing in fumes or swallowing chemicals

These injuries are difficult to treat. However, anybody who has breathed in fumes should be taken into uncontaminated air as soon as possible. If somebody has swallowed a chemical, rinse the mouth and then they must be taken for professional medical help immediately.

Shock

Shock is a dramatic drop in blood pressure. Shock is often caused by a massive loss of blood. The symptoms are pale, cold skin, sweating, thirst and a feeling of sickness, restlessness, yawning and, possibly, gradual loss of consciousness.

You need to recognise and treat the symptoms and any obvious injuries. You should improve circulation by loosening any tight clothing and reassure the casualty. Lie her or him down with their legs raised. Call 999. Keep the casualty warm with blankets and monitor the casualty's breathing and response to treatment. Prepare to resuscitate if necessary.

Electric shock

Treat in the same way as other types of shock.

Cuts and damage to the eyes from particles or chemicals

You need to be extremely careful when treating damaged eyes. Particles may be flushed from the eyes with water (you should have eye-wash bottles in the laboratory). If the particle cannot be removed like this, you should seek medical help.

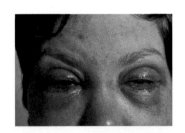

You should NEVER attempt to remove particles that are embedded in the eye. Bandage BOTH eyes and seek professional help straight away. A paper cup held in place over the damaged eye with a bandage is useful for serious injuries while the casualty is being taken to hospital.

Getting a first aid certificate

Perhaps the two best known organisations that offer first aid training are the British Red Cross and the St John's Ambulance. You can find out more about them from their websites. Their web addresses are:

British Red Cross   `www.redcross.org.uk`
St John's Ambulance   `www.sja.org.uk`

A useful way of finding out what courses are available is to look in the telephone directory for the British Red Cross or St John's Ambulance. Alternatively you could go to the BBC health web page (`www.bbc.co.uk/health/first aid action`) and click on *Course Finder*.

1   Find out which people in your school or college are 'first-aiders', in other words people that have first aid certificates.

2   Find out about first aid courses in your area. You may even sign up for one.

Fire prevention

You need to know:

- *what must be done if you hear a fire alarm or smoke alarm*
- *what must be done if you find a fire*
- *how fire doors function*
- *why different types of fire extinguishers (water, carbon dioxide, dry powder, foam, a fire-blanket) are used on different types of fires*
- *about the use of automatic sprinkler systems.*

Don't play with fire!

Fire is dangerous – to people and property. Observing safety regulations will reduce the chance of fire. Observing fire regulations will ensure that the number of casualties in fires is kept to a minimum.

Although many people are killed or injured in fires each year, the vast majority occur in the home and only 6% of deaths and 10% of injuries occur in the workplace. But this safety record will only be maintained (and, hopefully, improved) if everybody takes her or his responsibilities seriously.

Types of fire

There are two possible causes of fire in the laboratory: electrical fires and flammables substances. Fires can be classified as:

Class A	wood, paper, cloth, rubber and some plastics
Class B	flammable liquids such as petrol, paint, paint thinners
Class C	flammable gases
(no class)	electrical equipment, including wiring, fuse boxes, machinery and appliances

The type of fire determines how it should be treated, for example, which fire extinguisher to use.

REMEMBER

For a fire to start there needs to be:

- fuel
- oxygen
- heat.

Take one of these away and

. . . the fire won't start

. . . or it would be put out if it was already going.

What to do if there is a fire

Prevention is the best form of cure! So you should take all possible precautions to make sure a fire doesn't start.

Fire risk assessments must be carried out in the majority of workplaces. Fire and smoke alarms must be tested regularly. Fire exits must be clearly marked and nothing should be put in the way that would stop or slow down people trying to leave. 'Fire drills' ensure that the fire regulations work well, that people know what they must do and buildings are evacuated as quickly as possible. You should always take the drills seriously. They can save lives.

Fire doors

Fire doors prevent the spread of fire and smoke. Many close automatically. Under no circumstances should you wedge or prop open fire doors. Their manufacture must meet strict quality standards (given in the British Standard BS EN ISO 9002).

Fire extinguishers

REMEMBER

Fighting fire with an extinguisher? Remember
PASS:

Pull the pin
And
Squeeze the handle
Sweep side to side

Fires need oxygen to burn. Starve them of oxygen and the fire will go out. Fire extinguishers work by cutting off, or at lease seriously reducing, the supply of oxygen. In effect, they 'smother' the fire. There are a number of types.

Extinguisher	Type of fire
Water	class A
Carbon dioxide	classes B and C and electrical
Foam	classes A and B
Dry powder	classes A, B and C and electrical

Fire blankets

Fire blankets are made from non-flammable materials (ones that don't burn). Just like fire extinguishers, they work by cutting off the oxygen supply. They are used to cover a person whose clothing or hair has caught fire. Some fire blankets contain a gel that absorbs water. The blankets have been soaked in water before being put in their container ready for use. So as well as extinguishing the fire, they ease the pain, cool the burn and protect it to some extent from contamination. The blankets are also used to protect a rescuer from heat and flame.

Automatic sprinklers

Automatic water sprinkler systems turn on when the temperature reaches a pre-set level. Sprinkler heads are spaced, usually on the ceiling, and each directs a spray of water on to a particular part of the room or laboratory. Each sprinkler head is activated separately when its temperature reaches the preset value.

1   Where can you find the fire regulations in your school or college?

Questions

2   Find out what you must do in if you hear a fire or smoke alarm while you are working in the laboratory.

1.2 Carrying out practical tasks

Following standard procedures

When you are given a standard procedure to follow, you must be able to:

- *read the procedure, and check to see if there is anything you do not understand*

- *carry out a health and safety check of your working area*

- *carry out a risk assessment for the activity you are doing*

- *set out your work area and collect together the equipment and materials you need*

- *follow the instructions one step at a time*

- *make accurate observations or measurements, selecting instruments which give the appropriate precision*

- *identify possible sources of error and repeat observations and measurements, when necessary, to improve reliability.*

Why do we need standard procedures?

Much scientific work involves using **standard procedures**. These might be procedures to make a measurement, to prepare and purify a compound, or to monitor a change. For example, standard procedures are used in:

- material science laboratories to determine the properties of materials used in construction
- pharmaceutical laboratories to make medicines
- hospitals to measure pulse, temperature and blood pressure.

A standard procedure usually tells you:

- when and where the procedure can be used
- the scientific principles the procedure is based on
- the equipment and materials that must be used
- how to take a suitable sample, if this is needed
- the procedure
- what results to record and, if necessary, what calculations to carry out
- what to write up in the final report of the experiment.

REMEMBER

Standard procedures tell you exactly how to carry out an experiment. They are often called 'protocols' or 'standard operating procedures'. Companies develop their own standard procedures. Some standards are national or international.

This nurse has been trained to use standard procedures for checking the state of patients' health. Here a patient's blood pressure is being measured. How is it recorded?

The reason for all this detail is simple. The idea is to make sure that when several people carry out the same experiment their results can be compared. For example, if scientists want to compare pollution in different parts of Europe they must use the same standard procedures. This way, any differences they find are due to differences in pollution levels and not equipment, materials or methods used.

Think about choosing land to grow crops. You would need to know about the properties of the soil to be sure of growing healthy plants. For example, you might want to know:

- how well the soil retains moisture, to decide how often it might need watering
- the soil's pH, to decide if lime needs to be added to make it more alkaline
- the nutrients present in the soil, to decide if fertilisers are needed and, if so, how much.

Kits are available from garden centres for some of these measurements. The instructions on the packet are procedures, but they are not given in enough detail to be called standard procedures. You might be surprised to know that there are internationally agreed procedures for determining the properties of soil. Here is an example of an international standard procedure. Just the introduction is given.

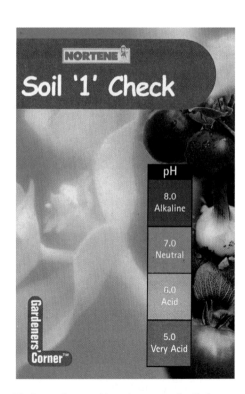

The instructions on this packet are not detailed enough to be called a standard procedure. What further information do you think is needed?

REMEMBER

Using standard procedures ensures that when you see the results of an experiment, you know exactly how the observations and measurements were made, no matter who did it or where it was done.

International Standard **ISO 11465:1993(E)**

Soil quality – Determination of dry matter and water content on a mass basis – Gravimetric method.

1. Scope

This International Standard specifies a method for the determination of the dry matter content and water content of soil samples on a mass basis.

This method can be applied to all types of soil samples. Different procedures are specified for air-dried samples, for example samples pretreated according to ISO 11464, and for field-moist samples.

For the determination of soil water content on a volume basis, refer to ISO 11461.

Sometimes standard procedures need to be 'interpreted'. In other words, they are written for experienced scientists. Here is an example from the British Pharmacopoeia (BP). This contains standard analytical procedures for chemicals used in medicines. Chemicals used in medicines must meet the standards of purity specified in the BP. Here is part of the entry for aspirin.

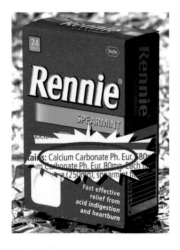

Many indigestion tablets contain calcium carbonate. The letters BP show that the calcium carbonate used in the medicine has been analysed and shown to meet the standards required in the British Pharmacopoeia (BP). Look at the packets or bottles of other medicines. Make a list of ingredients that have BP after them, showing that they have met the British Pharmacopoeia standards for purity.

Aspirin

Assay

Weigh and powder 20 tablets. To a quantity of the powder containing 0.5 g of aspirin add 30 cm^3 of 0.5 mol dm^{-3} *sodium hydroxide VS*, boil gently for 10 minutes and titrate the excess of alkali with 0.5 mol dm^{-3} *hydrochloric acid VS* using *phenol red solution* as indicator. Repeat the operation without the substance being examined. The difference between the titrations represents the amount of sodium hydroxide required. Each cm^3 of 0.5 mol dm^{-3} sodium hydroxide VS is equivalent to 45.04 mg of $C_9H_8O_4$.

No details about carrying out a titration are given. It's assumed that the experienced analyst knows how to do this. The procedure doesn't say how many times the analysis should be repeated. Again it's assumed the analyst knows. Details of the calculation are not given. It's assumed the analyst can work it out from 'Each cm^3 of 0.5 mol dm^{-3} sodium hydroxide VS is equivalent to 45.04 mg of $C_9H_8O_4$'. Finally you will see that some things are in *italics*. These are chemicals that are needed. Details of how to prepare them are given elsewhere in the BP. The letters *VS* tell the analyst these are solutions whose concentration is known accurately.

Techniques and methods

As well as **procedure**, you may also come across the terms **technique** and **method**. There is not really any difference between method and procedure. Scientists often use the two words interchangeably. However, there is a difference between technique and method.

Technique

A technique is a particular way of using scientific equipment and materials. For example, using measuring instruments correctly, carrying out paper chromatography and titrations, using a microscope correctly.

Method

A method is the use of a technique to make a specific observation, measurement or substance. For example, analysing aspirin by titration, identifying the pigments in leaves by paper chromatography, assembling an electrical circuit to measure voltage or current.

In Unit 3 you may well need to develop your own procedures based on techniques. For example, there are many variables you can investigate when looking at the germination of seeds and the growth of the seedlings. The techniques for preparing seeds, sowing them and giving them water, light, carbon dioxide and nutrients are the same. However, you will need to write a procedure when the technique is applied to the particular investigation you are undertaking.

Standard reference materials

You will come across the term 'standard' in another context. Scientists use standard reference materials to check the accuracy of their measuring instruments. For example, if you buy 500 g of cornflakes, how do you know that you are getting 500 g?

There are many cases where 'rogue' traders have cheated their customers. For example, the kilogram mass used to balance the kilogram of potatoes being weighed may have a hole drilled in the bottom so that it doesn't actually weigh 1 kg. When potatoes are added until the weight is balanced the customer ends up with less than 1 kg of potatoes!

The first answer might be, "Well, I would weigh them." But then how do you know the balance is giving an accurate reading? Like all measuring instruments it must be calibrated. This means using a standard reference material to check that it is working properly. So you would take a standard mass and check the balance, making any necessary adjustments if necessary.

Following a standard procedure

In Unit 1 you will follow at least six standard procedures. There must be one or more in each of the following areas:

- using microscopy   see page 67
- working with micro-organisms   see page 72
- qualitative chemical analysis   see page 83
- quantitative chemical analysis   see page 95
- measuring electrical properties   see page 109
- determining other physical properties   see page 115.

In general, when given a standard procedure to follow these are the steps you should take.

1. Read the procedure through slowly and carefully. Check to see if there is anything you do not understand. Always ask your teacher if there is something you don't understand. Never start work before reading through all of the procedure.

2. Carry out a health and safety check of your working area. Make sure your working area is safe and free from obstructions. Make sure you know what the laboratory rules are for fire, first aid and waste disposal. You can read about health and safety on pages 4–17.

3. Carry out a risk assessment for the activity you are doing. You can read how to do this on page 7. You will also find a risk assessment form on the same page.

4. Set out your work area. Make sure the bench surface is clean and clothing, bags and other possible obstructions are stored safely out of the way. Wear protective clothing and eye protection. Make sure equipment and materials are put where they can be easily reached. Collect together the equipment and materials you need. Avoid putting things near the edge of the bench or where you have to reach across other things to get to them.

5. A standard procedure should tell you what equipment and materials to use. However, sometimes you will need to decide what apparatus is required. You may have to select instruments that give the appropriate precision.

6. A standard procedure will give you a step-by-step list of what you should do. Follow these instructions one step at a time. There is no need to copy the procedure, but if you do anything differently you must note the changes in your laboratory notebook or file.

7   Make accurate observations or measurements and record these in your laboratory notebook or file. **Do not** record data on scraps of paper or the back of your hand!

8   If required, carry out any calculations. In a standard procedure you are usually given a formula to use.

9   Identify possible sources of error and repeat observations and measurements, when necessary, to improve reliability. It's much easier to do this if you understand the scientific principles upon which the procedure is based.

Questions

1   Why do scientists use standard procedures?

2   Explain the difference between a technique and a method. Give examples of techniques used in: (a) cookery, (b) gardening.

3   Write a standard procedure for making a cup of coffee from instant coffee granules.

4   Find out what standard procedures are used by the technicians in your school or college.

5   Look at some recipes from a cookery book. Explain whether or not you think these recipes could be described as standard procedures.

1.3 Handling scientific equipment and materials

You need to know how to:

- *recognise and use laboratory equipment and glassware you are given*

- *select and prepare equipment safely for use, including data logging equipment where appropriate*

- *calibrate instruments when necessary.*

Have you got the technique?

Scientists use many scientific techniques regularly. They need to practise them until they are skilled. As you train to be a scientist you also need practice so that you can carry out work with confidence, care and accuracy. You need to be able to use standard **laboratory equipment and glassware**, and to **handle scientific materials**. These basic techniques will also help you when you come to use other, less familiar equipment and materials.

The basic techniques for handling substances and materials include storing, transferring, and mixing substances, stirring and heating them. There are also a number of basic techniques for making measurements. These include measuring mass, length, volume, temperature, time, current and voltage.

Later you will find out more about techniques that are the basis of standard procedures in the six areas where you must carry out practical work for the Unit 1 assessment: using microscopy, working with micro-organisms, qualitative chemical analysis, quantitative chemical analysis, measuring electrical properties and determining other physical properties.

technique

STORING SUBSTANCES AND MATERIALS

These are techniques for storing substances and materials that are bought from a scientific supplier (these should come ready labelled) or samples that have been collected for examination.

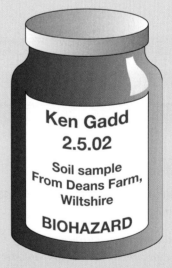

Ken Gadd
2.5.02

Soil sample
From Deans Farm,
Wiltshire

BIOHAZARD

Storage. Substances and materials must be kept in properly labelled, stoppered bottles. The containers might be glass or plastic. The containers must be stored to minimise the risks from hazardous substances, for example, in a fireproof cabinet or in an outside storeroom.

Samples for analysis. If you store a substance that you make or a sample you collect to investigate in the laboratory you should always label it with:

Your name	**Date**
Contents	**Source**
Hazard warnings	

TRANSFERRING SUBSTANCES AND MATERIALS

These are techniques for moving solids and liquids from one container to another.

Transferring solids. You should use a spatula to transfer a solid. A little at a time can be transferred by gently tapping the spatula. You should remember:

- not to try to carry too much on the spatula at one time
- to keep the two containers between which the solid is being transferred as close together as possible
- to wash the spatula before you put it down on the laboratory bench (it is a good idea to lay a sheet of paper towel on part of the bench surface and to put freshly-washed apparatus on it).

Transferring liquids. Liquids are often poured from a beaker into another container. To avoid the liquid going down the outside of the beaker you should pour it down a glass rod. You should remember:

- to hold the glass rod so that it rests in the lip of the beaker.
- to tilt the beaker carefully until the liquid runs down the rod slowly.

If you want a measured volume of a liquid you need to use graduated glassware (see page 41).

Transferring small quantities of liquid. You can transfer small quantities of a liquid (one or more drops or 1–2 cm³) using a dropping pipette. You should remember:

- keep the two containers, between which the liquid is being transferred, as close as possible
- not to overfill the dropping pipette and get liquid in the squeezy bulb
- always keep the dropping pipette upright to avoid liquid going into the squeezy bulb (this is not a problem if all-in-one polythene pipettes are used)
- wash the dropping pipette with distilled water before putting it into a test tube for storage.

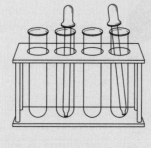

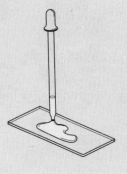

technique

MIXING

Scientists use glassware to put substances and materials in to carry out experiments on them. The experiments might involve making, testing and monitoring changes. You will often need to mix substances in the laboratory, for example:

- to combine them to make formulations such as a medicine, paint and cosmetics
- to carry out chemical tests
- to make substances
- to investigate micro-organisms.

A wide range of glassware is available and it's important to select the most appropriate for the task.

Mixing material. You have a choice of vessels including test tubes (for small quantities), beakers and conical flasks. All of these come in varying sizes. The one you use depends of course on the quantities being used. If the reaction mixture is to be heated, heat-resistant glassware must be used. This is marked 'Pyrex' or an equivalent trade name. Reaction vessels should not be more than a half to two-thirds full. Bear this in mind when choosing your apparatus.

Some reactions involve substances that must not escape into the atmosphere. For example, they may be flammable or hazardous in some other way. You will find glassware with ground glass joints (Quickfit glassware) useful. This type of apparatus may also be assembled and dismantled easily.

technique

STIRRING

It is often necessary to stir a reaction mixture. There are a number of options.

SELECTING A STIRRING METHOD

To select the most appropriate stirring method:

- use a glass rod if the mixture is to be stirred for a short while in an open vessel
- use a paddle stirrer or magnetic flea if the mixture is to be stirred in a vessel where it's not possible to use a glass rod
- also use a paddle stirrer or magnetic flea if the mixture is to be stirred for a longer time.

Stirring. Stirring can be done:
- manually (e.g. using a glass stirring rod)
- with a paddle stirrer driven by a motor (often useful if the liquid to be stirred is quite viscous)
- with a magnetic flea (a small magnet covered in a plastic sheath) driven by a rotating magnet outside the reaction vessel.

In the picture a bioreactor used to convert sugar into ethanol is being stirred with a paddle stirrer.

HEATING

Scientists frequently need to heat substances and materials. There is a range of apparatus that can be used, such as Bunsen burners, ovens, electric hotplates, electric mantles and hot water baths (sometimes called steam baths).

Heating directly with a flame. A glass blower needs very high temperatures to melt glass. A naked flame is used. Different mixtures of fuel gas (for example, natural gas or ethyne) and oxygen give flames of differing temperatures. You may use a Bunsen flame in the laboratory. It isn't hot enough to work with glass, but nonetheless you must be extremely careful if you use a Bunsen in this way.

Heating with a Bunsen burner. Test tubes containing aqueous solutions can be heated directly with a Bunsen burner. The test tube should be held with a test tube holder and not with your fingers! You can also use small Bunsen burners, often called micro-burners, and, where possible, you should do so. The test tube should be gently shaken while being heated.

If possible use wide diameter boiling tubes. Always wear eye protection. Never fill test tubes more than one-fifth full and never heat a mixture in a sealed apparatus, for example, a test tube with a rubber bung in it. NEVER use a Bunsen burner to heat flammable substances!

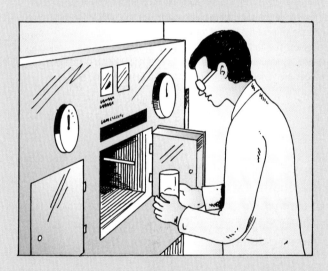

Ovens. Ovens are useful for drying substances and glassware. They are also used to incubate micro-organism cultures.

Beakers and conical flasks can be placed on wire gauze supported by a tripod and heated with a Bunsen burner. A glass rod placed in the reaction mixture will help to avoid uneven boiling which can cause the mixture to 'bump'.

(a)   (b)   (c)

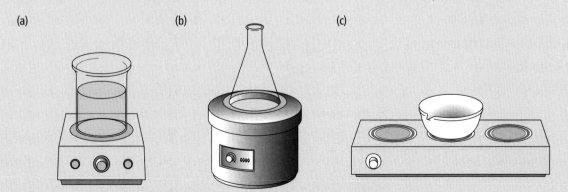

Other methods of heating. Electric hotplates (a), electric mantles (b) and hot water baths (c) (sometimes called steam baths) are all alternatives to Bunsen burners. You should always use them to heat flammable liquids.

Making measurements

Measuring instruments have meters to show the value being measured. There are two types of meters: analogue and digital.

The difference between analogue and digital can be shown if you think about watches. Some watches have hands (one for the hours, one for the minutes and possibly a third for the seconds). The 'time' is marked around the edge of the face of the watch. When you read the watch you look at the position of the hands. The hands move smoothly and we say that it is an analogue output, by which we mean it is continuous. In contrast, the time is shown on a digital watch by a numerical display. The changes are 'jerky'. You don't have to 'read between the lines'.

Analogue

An analogue meter has a display that is continuous. A ruler is a simple example. It is simply a length of wood, plastic or metal that has graduations marked along it. You have to decide where the thing you are measuring comes long the scale. Often what you want to measure will fall between graduations and you have to estimate (see 'Reading between the lines' on page 36). A thermometer is the same. The temperature is marked as graduations and you have to decide where the mercury comes on the scale. The accuracy of an analogue scale is limited by your ability to estimate between the smallest graduations.

Analogue meters have a pointer that moves over a scale. The scale is sub-divided by lines. They are not as easy to use as digital meters (see later). You need to:

- make sure the needle and scale are lined up by looking at them from directly in front. If there is a mirror behind the scale you must be sure that the image of the needle is hidden exactly behind the needle itself

- sub-divide the scale further in your 'mind's eye'. The scale should indicate the precision of the instrument and so it's sensible not to estimate more than the nearest half unit when taking readings.

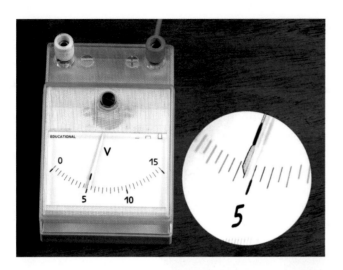

This is one of the problems when reading an analogue meter. Viewed from directly in front you get the correct value (5.0 volts). However, if you read it from the side you get an inaccurate reading of 4.8 volts.

Digital

Digital meters are straightforward to read and are increasingly common. They give a readout in numbers. The number of figures displayed depends on the precision of the instrument. Beware though. Lots of figures in the display may mean high precision, but they do not guarantee accuracy! The instrument should always be calibrated regularly.

Digital meters are used when the measuring device is an electronic probe or sensor.

This pH meter has a digital display. The pH is read directly from the display. The sample of rainwater being tested is very slightly acidic, as the pH is less than 7.

Measuring mass

The balance is one of the most important pieces of equipment in the laboratory. You must know how to use a balance to weigh things. Well, to be correct, we should say 'to measure its mass'. The weight of something is the force it exerts under the pull of gravity. This will vary (slightly) depending upon the altitude of where the measurement is made. A simple example will show the difference. Neil Armstrong, the first man to walk on the moon, had the same mass when he was on Earth as when he was on the moon. Yet when we see pictures of him walking on the moon he seems to be floating. He weighed less on the moon (because its gravity is less than that of earth), but his mass was the same.

Astronauts in space, where there is no gravity, can float freely around their spacecraft (fun for some activities, but more challenging for others!). They seem to be 'weightless'. However, they have the same mass as when they are on Earth. The difference is the gravitational pull.

So in order to make meaningful comparisons (we are back to the idea of standard procedures) scientists all over the world need to be able to compare the mass of objects. What they need to do is take a standard mass and make sure the balance is calibrated correctly. In other words, when a standard 1.0000 kg mass is placed on it, the scale reads 1.0000 kg.

There are many kinds of balances. Some are suitable for weighing very heavy things. Others can be used to weigh very light objects. With some balances you can weigh things more accurately (in other words to more significant places) than with others. When you decide to measure the mass of something you need to choose the most appropriate balance. You need to choose one that has sufficient:

REMEMBER

You may find the words 'weight' and 'mass' confusing! However, just remember: when you 'weigh' something you measure its mass, not its weight.

- range for the object to be measured; for example, you couldn't weigh a car on bathroom scales because the scales only weigh up to around 1000 kg (not to mention the fact that a car wouldn't fit on the scales – but that's a different problem!)
- precision, in other words choose a balance that can measure to the number of decimal places you need; for example, analytical balances need to be able to measure to the nearest 0.001 g (or 0.0001 g in some cases).

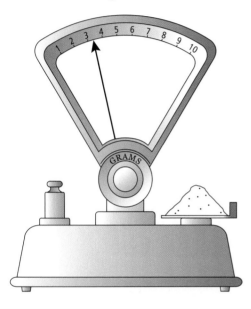

Have a look at the scale on this kitchen balance. What do you think the reading is?

USING AN ELECTRONIC BALANCE

This technique is used to measure the mass of substances and objects.

(A) GETTING THE BALANCE READY FOR USE

You must check that:

1 the balance is level – this can be checked with a bubble level that is often built into the balance; you can level the balance by adjusting the screw feet

2 the balance pan, including the underside, is clean; for example, there are no traces of solids on it (you can use a small brush or paper tissue to clean the pan)

3 the surface is firm (balances are sensitive to small movements)

4 the draught screen is in place for balances which read to ±0.01 g or ±0.001 g.

This balance still needs to be levelled. Its feet must be adjusted until the bubble is in the centre of the red circle.

technique

(B) CALIBRATING THE BALANCE

1 Place a standard mass ('check weight') on the centre of the pan, not at the edge.

2 Read the mass from the digital display and check that it's the correct reading for the standard mass used. If it is not, report the error to your supervisor.

3 Check that the balance returns to zero when the standard mass is removed.

4 Repeat with a number of different standard masses.

REMEMBER

Calibrating an instrument means checking that it is working accurately. Standard reference materials are used to see if the instrument gives the correct accurate measurement.

This standard 20.00 g mass is being used to calibrate the balance. The digital reading shows that the balance is correctly calibrated.

(C) WEIGHING

1 Do not lean on the bench where the balance is.

2 Make sure the object being weighed is dry.

3 (If appropriate, make sure vessels containing liquids are stoppered and glassware that has been dried in an oven is cool before weighing)

4 Check the balance is zeroed.

5 Place the object you are weighing on the centre of the pan, not at the edge.

6 Read the mass from the digital display.

The mass of the beaker is 32.68g.

Quantities and amounts

Counting units

Substances are weighed out on a balance and the mass is recorded. A mass of substance is called **quantity** and the SI unit is the kilogram. In the laboratory you will rarely measure out chemicals in kilogram quantities. The usual units are grams.

Depending upon the balance being used, the mass may be measured with varying accuracy, e.g. to the nearest 1 g, 0.1 g, 0.01 g or 0.001 g. However, scientists are much more interested in the amounts of reacting particles (atoms, ions or molecules) and for this reason they use a counting unit called the **mole** (symbol **mol**). This number is 6×10^{23} chemical particles. It's the same idea as:

a pair of shoes	– 2 shoes
a dozen eggs	– 12 eggs
a ream of paper	– 500 sheets
and similarly	
a mole of chemical	– 6×10^{23} chemical particles.

6×10^{23} particles is an unimaginably huge number. Atoms, ions and molecules are very, very small!

Relative atomic mass

You cannot weigh individual atoms but scientists can measure their relative masses. Relative atomic masses (as the name suggests) tell us how heavy atoms are relative to one another. Hydrogen is the smallest and lightest atom. We take that as the starting point and say its relative atomic mass is 1. A sodium atom is 23 times as heavy, so its relative atomic mass is 23. An atom of iron is 56 times as heavy, so its relative atomic mass is 56. And so we can say that:

- one mole of hydrogen atoms has a mass of 1 g
- one mole of sodium atoms has a mass of 23 g
- one mole of iron atoms has a mass of 56 g.

All of these quantities contain the same number of atoms as one another: 6×10^{23}. This is a really important idea. It means that when you weigh a quantity of a substance you know how many chemical particles you have weighed out.

No element has a relative atomic mass that is a whole number (even though some are very close). At this stage don't worry about why this is. Simply look up the relative atomic mass you need and use this for calculations.

Relative formula mass

You will know that a chemical compound has chemical formula. You can calculate the relative formula mass by adding together the relative atomic masses for the atoms present.

For example:

Sodium chloride has the chemical formula NaCl
Na has the relative atomic mass 23
Cl has the relative atomic mass 35.5
Therefore the relative formula mass of NaCl = 23 + 35.5 = 58.5

Calcium carbonate has the chemical formula $CaCO_3$
Ca has the relative atomic mass 40
C has the relative atomic mass 12
O has the relative atomic mass 16
Therefore the relative formula mass of $CaCO_3$ = 40 + 12 + (16 × 3) = 100

From quantity to amount and back again

Suppose a method says, "weigh out 1 mole of sodium chloride". You know how to work out what quantity is needed. It's simply the relative formula mass in grams (23 + 35.5 = 58.5 g). But what if the method said, "weigh out 2 mol of sodium chloride" or "weigh out 0.5 mol of sodium chloride" or "0.1 mol of sodium chloride"? Well, it's straight-forward. Just multiply the relative formula mass by the amount needed.

For example:

2 mol of sodium chloride = 2 × 58.5 = 117 g
0.5 mol of sodium chloride = 0.5 × 58.5 = 29.25 g
0.1 mol of sodium chloride = 0.1 × 58.5 = 5.85 g

? Questions

1 Find a list of relative atomic masses and complete:
   • one mole of carbon atoms has a mass of ___ g
   • one mole of magnesium atoms has a mass of ___ g
   • one mole of silver atoms has a mass of ___ g
   • one mole of nitrogen atoms has a mass of ___ g
   • one mole of sulfur atoms has a mass of ___ g
   • one mole of zinc atoms has a mass of ___ g
   • one mole of sodium atoms has a mass of ___ g

2 Calculate the relative formula mass of each of the following chemicals:
   • hydrogen chloride, HCl
   • water, H_2O
   • ammonia, NH_3
   • methane, CH_4
   • calcium chloride, $CaCl_2$
   • sodium nitrate, $NaNO_3$

- zinc nitrate, $Zn(NO_3)_2$
- sodium sulfate, Na_2SO_4
- zinc sulfate, $ZnSO_4$
- copper(II) sulfate-5-water, $CuSO_4.5H_2O$

3 Calculate the quantity (in grams) of each of the following amounts of chemicals:

- 5 mol of sodium, Na
- 0.5 mol of copper, Cu
- 0.1 mol of chlorine molecules, Cl_2
- 10 mol of water
- 4 mol of calcium oxide, CaO
- 2 mol of calcium chloride, $CaCl_2$
- 0.01 mol of calcium carbonate
- 0.05 mol of magnesium sulfate-7-water.

?

Measuring length

Look at some rulers and metre rules. You will see that the size of the smallest division varies. For example, some rulers measure to 1 cm; others measure to 1 mm. It depends on the divisions marked on the rulers. This lets you choose the precision you need. For example, you may be measuring:

- the length and breadth of the laboratory
- the length of a piece of electrical wire
- the thickness of a piece of electrical wire
- the length of tiny creature almost invisible to the eye.

The range is enormous. You need to pick the most suitable way to measure each. And with a choice of different sizes of rulers and tape measures, there are many measuring devices to choose from.

You can read more about accuracy and precision on page 63.

technique

READING BETWEEN THE LINES

Often the thing you are measuring will come between two of the smallest divisions on the ruler you are using. In this case you have to be able to estimate the actual value. With practice you will become increasingly confident about your ability to estimate these values. You will come across the same idea with all instruments where you have a scale and a pointer (like the kitchen scales earlier on in the section).

METHOD

1   Look at the scale and see which divisions the pointer falls between.

2   Decide which of these two divisions it's closest to.

3   Estimate the most accurate value you can.

WORKED EXAMPLE

In the picture below the ruler is graduated in 1 cm lengths, in other words the smallest division on the ruler is 1 cm. The piece of wire is somewhere between 9 cm and 10 cm long.

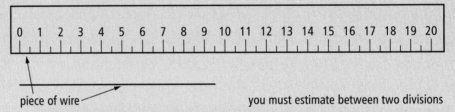

piece of wire   you must estimate between two divisions

Looking closely at where the wire comes, it is clearly a bit nearer to 10 cm. But how much? A reasonable estimate might be 9.6 cm. How certain can you be is the next question – it is only an estimate after all. Well, perhaps if you are practised in making these estimations you may have the confidence to say it is somewhere between 9.55 and 9.65 cm. This means the uncertainty of the measurement is ± 0.05 cm. Remember that this is not an error (the person making the estimate has not done anything wrong that could be corrected). It is an uncertainty.

Measuring length with greater precision

The precision of a ruler is limited by the thickness of the lines drawn on it to show the divisions. You could use a steel ruler with narrow etched lines. It would certainly help, but scientists have more precise instruments they can use. Vernier callipers and the micrometer screw gauge can measure to the nearest 0.1 mm and 0.01 mm, respectively.

It is possible to go one step further. A microscope gives even greater precision when measuring very small objects. There is a measuring scale in the eye piece, called an eye piece graticule. This has to be calibrated by using a very accurate measuring scale on a microscope slide.

You can read more about microscopes on page 68.

VERNIER CALLIPERS

Vernier callipers can be used to measure thin objects such as pieces of wire. They can usually measure to the nearest 0.1 mm. Two types are available, depending on whether internal or external dimensions need to be measured. For example, both the outside diameter and inside of a pipe can be measured.

METHOD

1   Grip the object with the jaws – firmly but lightly being careful not to squash the object at all, in other words, distort it.

2   The numbers on the fixed scale are centimetres; these are divided into millimeters. Read off the number of centimetres and millimetres to the left of the first division of the moving scale.

3   The moving scale has 10 divisions in the space of 9 mm of the fixed scale. Use it to measure to the nearest 0.1 mm by finding the line on the moving scale most closely in line with a line on the fixed scale.

WORKED EXAMPLE

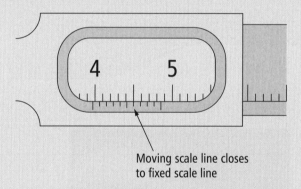

Moving scale line closes to fixed scale line

Reading = 3.9 + 0.06 = 3.96 cm

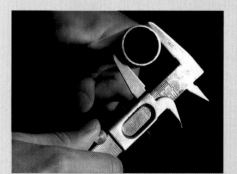

Vernier callipers can be used to measure the outside and inside diameters of tubing to the nearest 0.1 mm. They can also be used to measure the thickness of plastic and metal sheets and many other objects.

technique

MICROMETER SCREW GAUGE

A micrometer screw gauge can be used for the same type of measurements as Vernier calipers. However, it is of greater precision, usually measuring to the nearest 0.01 mm.

METHOD

1 Carefully clamp the object (a ratchet prevents over-tightening).

2 The numbers on the scale are millimetres. Read the number to the left of the moving scale.

3 Use the numbers on the moving scale to find the measurement to 0.1 mm.

4 The small divisions form a Vernier scale with the line of the fixed scale. Count the number of small divisions from the 0.1 mm value to this line.

WORKED EXAMPLE

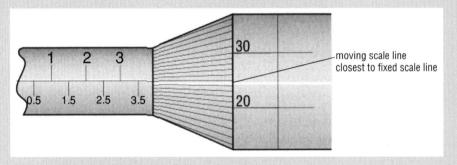

moving scale line
closest to fixed scale line

Reading = 3.5 + 0.24 = 3.74 mm

A micrometer screw gauge can be used to measure the size of objects to the nearest 0.01 mm.

From lengths to areas

The surface area of a simple regular shape can be found by measuring its external dimensions.

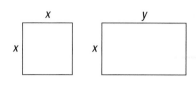

Shape	Perimeter	Area
Square	$4x$	x^2
Rectangle	$2(x+y)$	xy
Right-angled triangle	$x + y + h$	$\frac{1}{2}hx$
Any triangle	$x + y + z$	$\frac{1}{2}hx$

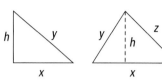

When irregular shapes are involved, the area can be estimated by tracing the outline of an object onto graph paper. All the squares covered by half or more are counted. Alternatively the paper can be cut out and weighed. Paper from the same stock, or even from the same piece, is cut out to a known area and weighed for comparison.

Measuring volume

Solids with regular shapes

You can determine the volumes of simple regular solids by measuring their dimensions and doing the necessary calculations.

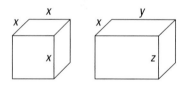

Shape	Surface area	Volume
Cube	$6x^2$	x^3
Cuboid	$2xy + 2xz + 2yz$	xyz
Sphere	$4\pi r^2$	$\frac{4}{3}\pi r^3$
Cylinder	$2(\pi rh + \pi r^2)$	$\pi r^2 h$

Worked examples

Example 1: a cube with sides 5 cm

$x = 5$ cm

Surface area $= 6x^2 = 6 \times 5^2 = 6 \times 5 \times 5 = 150$ cm^2

Volume $= x^3 = 5 \times 5 \times 5 = 125$ cm^3

Example 2: a sphere with radius 14 m

$r = 14$ m

$\pi = \frac{22}{7}$

Surface area $= 4\pi r^2 = 4 \times \frac{22}{7} \times 14^2 = 4 \times \frac{22}{7} \times 14 \times 14 = 2464$ m^2

Volume $= \frac{4}{3}\pi r^3 = \frac{4}{3} \times \frac{22}{7} \times 14^3 = \frac{4}{3} \times \frac{22}{7} \times 14 \times 14 \times 14 = 11499$ m^3

Solids with irregular shapes

Many objects have irregular shapes, for example rocks and stones. You can determine the volume of an irregular solid, provided it is not too large, by measuring the volume of liquid it displaces.

technique

DISPLACEMENT CANS

Displacement cans may be used to determine the density of an irregular shaped object.

METHOD

1 Fill a displacement can with water until it just begins to overflow.

2 Carefully place the object to be measured into the can and collect the displaced water in a beaker that has been weighed.

3 Weigh the beaker and the displaced water to determine the volume of water that was displaced (the density of water is 1.00 g cm^{-3}).

4 The volume of water displaced is the same as the volume of the object.

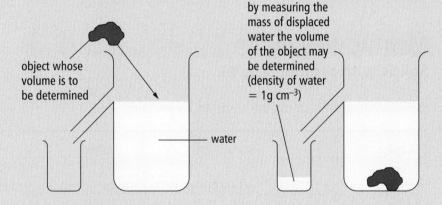

object whose volume is to be determined

water

by measuring the mass of displaced water the volume of the object may be determined (density of water = 1g cm^{-3})

Using a displacement can to determine the volume of an irregular shaped object. Of course the method won't work if the object floats!

WORKED EXAMPLE

A metal screw is carefully place into a displacement can that has been filled with water.

Mass of beaker = 27.82 g

Mass of beaker + displaced water = 30.81 g

Therefore, mass of displaced water = 2.99 g

Since the density of water = 1.00 g cm^{-3}, the volume of water displaced = 2.99×1.00 cm^3.

Therefore the volume of the metal screw is 2.99 cm^3.

Density is an important property of materials. To determine the density of a material you need to be able to measure its mass and determine its volume. You can find out how to determine density on page 120.

Liquids

You will often need to measure volumes of liquids. You can choose from a range of measuring vessels such as graduated beakers, measuring cylinders, pipettes, burettes, volumetric flasks. Each comes in different sizes and each has differing degrees of precision. For example, measuring cylinders may be 10 cm^3, 50 cm^3, 100 cm^3, 250 cm^3, 500 cm^3 or 1000 cm^3 (1 dm^3).

REMEMBER

If you measure the same quantity several times, using the same procedure each time, and get results that are close to one another, we say the measurements are **repeatable**. If other people make the same measurements by the same procedures and they are also close, the measurements are **reproducible**.

technique

CHECKING THE PRECISION OF GRADUATED GLASSWARE

This technique may be used to:

- check the accuracy of graduated glassware such as pipettes and burettes (pipettes and burettes should be checked when they are first bought and regular checks carried out)

- compare the precision of different types of graduated glassware.

A measured volume of water is weighed. As the density of water is 1.00 g cm^3, the actual volume measured out can be found accurately. The technique depends on the fact that a good analytical balance has much greater precision than graduated glassware.

REMEMBER

Graduated glassware has markings on it to show the volume contained. Pipettes have just one mark and so you can only be used to measure a fixed volume. Other glassware such as measuring cylinders and burettes have many graduations. You can use these to measure various volumes of liquids. Their precision varies.

METHOD   For the glassware you are using (for example, measuring cylinder, pipette or burette):

1. Weigh a dry 100 cm^3 beaker to the nearest 0.01 g.

2. Measure out a fixed volume of water and put it into the weighed beaker. If you are using a measuring cylinder, pour the water into the beaker. If you are using a pipette or a burette, let the water run into the beaker.

technique

Note: pipettes and burettes are graduated at a particular temperature. This is because water expands when it gets hot. For very accurate work the water being used should be at the necessary temperature (this is usually written on the glassware).

3   Weigh the beaker with the water to the nearest 0.01 g.

4   Repeat three more times, carefully drying the beaker with paper kitchen towel between measurements.

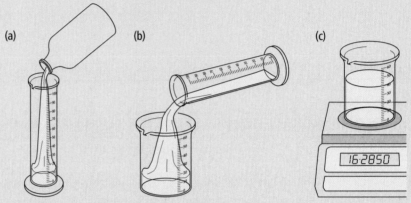

(a)   (b)   (c)

By measuring out a known volume of water and weighing it you can check the precision of a measuring cylinder. The measurement should be done several times. No matter how careful you are it's unlikely you will measure out exactly the same volume each time. This is because the measuring cylinder has an uncertainty associated with its use.

CALCULATIONS

Volume of water measured out = V_x cm³

Mass of beaker = m_1 g

Mass of beaker + water = m_2 g

Therefore, mass of water = $m_2 - m_1$ g

As density of water = 1.00 g cm³

Actual volume of water measured out = $(m_2 - m_1) \times 1.00 = V_y$ cm³

V_y cm³ is the actual volume of water; V_x cm³ is the volume you measured with the glassware

The difference between V_y and V_x tells you how precise the glassware is.

WORKED EXAMPLE

Using a 100 cm³ measuring cylinder, 20 cm³ of water was poured into a dry beaker and its mass measured.

Volume of water measured out = 20 cm³

Mass of beaker = 50.83 g

Mass of beaker + water = 71.02 g

Therefore, mass of water = 71.02 − 50.83 = 20.19 g

As density of water = 1.00 g cm³, actual volume of water measured out = 20.19 cm³

Here are some typical results for the mass of 20 cm³ of water measured out using different graduated glassware.

Graduated glassware	Mass of 20 cm³ water/g				
	Expt 1	Expt 2	Expt 3	Expt 4	Expt 5
500 cm³ measuring cylinder	21.36	17.62	19.02	22.58	18.29
50 cm³ measuring cylinder	19.11	18.98	20.79	21.01	21.16
20 cm³ pipette	19.96	20.05	20.01	20.04	19.99

The smaller the difference between the highest and lowest values (the range) the surer you can be about using the glassware to measure 20 cm³ of water.

	Mass of 20 cm³ of water/g		
	Highest (y)	Lowest (x)	Range ($y - x$)
500 cm³ measuring cylinder	22.58	17.62	4.96
50 cm³ measuring cylinder	21.16	18.98	2.28
20 cm³ pipette	20.05	19.96	0.09

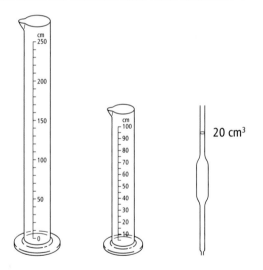

Look at where the 20 cm³ graduation mark is for each of these pieces of graduated glassware. You will see that the smaller the range, the narrower the diameter of the glassware where the graduation is. Can you explain why?

Gases

Volumes of gases can be found by collecting them by displacing water from a graduated vessel such as a burette (if the gases are not too soluble) or by using a gas syringe.

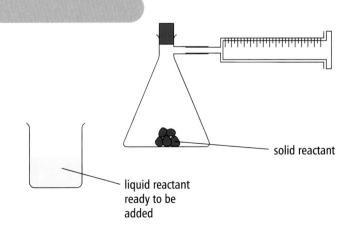

The volume of gas given off is measured using a syringe. As the gas is given off the plunger of the gas syringe moves. The volume of the gas can be measured directly from the graduated syringe. The precision of the gas syringe can be determined in the same way as other graduated glassware.

solid reactant

liquid reactant ready to be added

Measuring temperature

You can measure temperature in a number of ways. Mercury thermometers are often used, but you should use them carefully as glass is fragile and mercury vapour is toxic (poisonous). Another problem is that a mercury thermometer may take a significant amount of heat from a small sample. You will probably have -10–110 °C and 0–360 °C mercury thermometers in your laboratory. You may have others. In hospitals and health centres clinical thermometers, which are also mercury thermometers, are used to measure a patient's temperature.

A clinical thermometer needs to give high precision over a small range. A wider range thermometer is more versatile (it can be used in a wide range of situations), but it is less precise.

Alcohol thermometers can be used to measure lower temperatures. Some dye is added to the alcohol so that is can be seen easily.

You could also use an electronic temperature probe. These contain thermistors. The electrical resistance varies with temperature and this is converted to a scale or digital readout on a meter. Probes can be placed in a wide variety of inaccessible places, such as in opaque objects where glass thermometers cannot be read. You can use an electronic temperature probe with a data logger. This lets you record temperature change over a period of time. The device plots the results for you.

When choosing an instrument to measure temperature you need to think about:

- How precisely do you need to measure the temperature? Remember, the smaller the range the greater the precision.
- What range of temperature do you need to measure? Choose the range carefully, as exceeding the maximum on the scale will cause the bulb to burst if you are using a thermometer.
- Where will the measurements be made? If it is difficult to get to or impossible to see directly you should consider using an electronic temperature probe.

A culture being placed in an incubator (an oven where the temperature is carefully controlled by a thermostat). Controlling temperature is important for many biological and chemical reactions. Ovens and water baths are often used. These should be checked to make sure that they are accurate enough for your work.

- Does the temperature need to be measured over a period of time? If so, you should consider using an electronic temperature probe together with a data logger.

Measuring time

You will often need to measure time. The most common ways in the laboratory are with a stopclock or a stopwatch. These may be digital (with a number display) or analogue (with a scale and pointer). Electronic timers can also be used.

Measuring current and voltage

An analogue ammeter or a multimeter may be used to measure the current flowing. It is connected in series with the sample of material or the component being tested.

An analogue voltmeter or a multimeter may be used to measure the voltage (sometimes called the potential difference) across a sample of material or the component being tested. The voltmeter is connected in parallel.

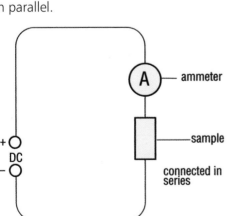

In athletics electronic timing has allowed times for 100 m races to be given to the nearest 100th of a second. Before that hand-held stopwatches could only be relied on to the nearest 10th of a second.

Measuring current using an ammeter.

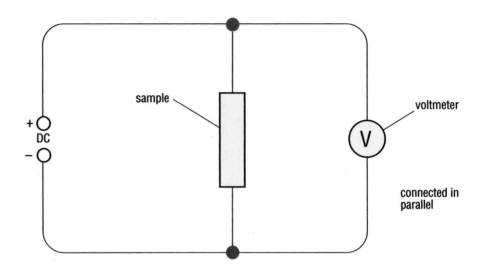

Measuring voltage using
a voltmeter.

You can read more about measuring the electrical properties of
materials on pages 109–114. You will also find out about making and
testing electrical devices on page 291.

Probes and data loggers

There is a wide range of electronic devices that can be used to collect
data automatically. They are called probes (or sensors). These devices
are really useful, both in the laboratory and in the field, for example
when carrying out environmental studies.

Data can be recorded using a data logger. It can be transferred to a
computer later and the data processed automatically, for example,
calculations carried out and graphs or other images produced. This is
especially useful if you want to:

- collect large numbers of measurements in a short time (faster
  than you could take the readings)
- collect data continuously over a long period.

Here are some examples.

Probe	Useful applications
Temperature	• monitoring temperature changes in a bioreactor or chemical reactor
	• recording temperature changes in different parts of a building over the course of a day, a week or even longer
pH	• pH changes in a culture of micro-organisms over a week
	• pH of soil or water samples during an environmental study
	• pH changes during an acid-base titration when an indicator can't be used to 'see' the end point
Oxygen	• oxygen concentration in pond over 24 hours
	• oxygen concentration in a river at various points along it
Light	• electronic timing, for example, in athletics and swimming
	• automatic switches, for example, in electrical hand driers
Movement	• stretching of a wire under tension
	• the flexing of a building in a high wind

Although you don't need to know exactly how these instruments work it helps to have some idea. The more you understand, the more you will be able to make sense of data that you collect.

You can read more about electrical and electronic devices such as sensors on pages 296–304. As part of your assessment for Unit 3 (Science at work) you will need to make and test an electrical or electronic device. You may decide to make a measuring instrument that uses a sensor.

This environmental scientist is using probes to monitor the temperature, pH and dissolved oxygen of the river.

Engineers attach strain gauges to different parts of the building to measure how much the building moves, for example, in wind.

Questions

1 Choose the most appropriate piece of apparatus to measure the diameter of the objects by pairing the letters and numbers of each. Numbers may be used more than once or not at all.

A	A brick	**1**	Tape measure
B	A cell	**2**	Micrometer
C	A field	**3**	Microscope eyepiece graticule
D	A metal wire	**4**	Vernier callipers
E	A round table	**5**	Metre rule

2 List the pieces of apparatus that you can use to measure the volumes of liquids in order of increasing accuracy. Give an example for each of when you might use it.

3 You are asked to prepare a sample of soil for analysis. 10 g of soil is measured out and stirred in gently boiling water for 2 hours. List the apparatus you would use.

4 An electrician wants to check that a piece of wire is satisfactorily insulated. List the equipment that would be used to carry out the test.

5 Describe how the following apparatus may be calibrated:
(a) electronic balance
(b) pipette.

6 Find out how the following apparatus could be calibrated:
(a) stopwatch
(b) pH meter.

7 Calculate the volume of:
(a) a cube with sides of 2.5 cm
(b) a cube with a surface area of 24 cm^2
(c) a table tennis ball with a diameter of 3 cm
(d) polythene rod that is 30 cm long and has a diameter of 0.7 cm

8 Compare the advantages and disadvantages of a glass thermometer and an electronic thermometer (a thermistor).

9 Describe how you would determine (a) the mass and (b) the volume of a piece of gravel that's about 1 cm across. Calculate the density of the gravel.

10 Describe how the temperature of the air could be monitored over a 24-hour period.

1.4 Recording and analysing scientific data

You need to be able to:

- *present data in tables, bar charts, histograms, pictograms, pie charts, graphs and other visual ways, as appropriate*

- *carry out simple numerical calculations*

- *analyse and interpret your results*

- *evaluate your investigation and suggest improvements.*

So you have collected your data . . .

As you have read, a standard procedure tells you what to do with observations and measurements you make in an experiment. However, you need to know about some of the options for recording and presenting data. You should also be able to carry out some straightforward calculations.

To remind yourself about standard procedures have another look at page 18.

It's really important to think about results you obtain. What do they mean? How confident can you be about their meaning? Do some of the data look a bit odd and hard to explain? Should the experiment be repeated? Without this there is little point in collecting the data! We call it **evaluating** your experiment.

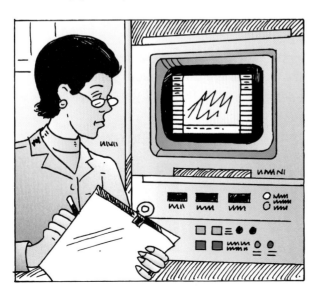

Relatively cheap, high performance computers have made it possible to collect, process and display data in a far more detailed and sophisticated way than was possible before. They are also very fast workers!

Presenting data

There are a number of options for presenting data that you get from an experiment. Reading through the next section will help you choose the most suitable for any work you are doing.

Tables

Data are often displayed in the form of a table. You will see many examples throughout this book. If you produce tables, make sure that each column is headed properly and, if numerical quantities are given, that the correct units are shown.

Drawings

Although data will often be measurements that can be presented in tables, drawings will also be necessary in reporting methods and findings. For example, sketches of electrical circuits you use or chromatograms that have been developed and a number of other purposes. Drawing is particularly useful for microscope work.

Photographs and videotapes

Photographs and videotapes can also be used to record data.

Charts and graphs

Plotting charts and graphs can simplify the analysis of data, for example:

- trends can be seen and measured
- data that are out of step with the rest can be spotted.

Bar charts and pie charts

Bar charts are used for qualitative data. The lengths of bars can be used to show and compare:

- the numbers of different things, for example, the number of fish found in different rivers
- how often (the frequency) something occurs, for example, the number of each species of fish that are found in a river.

The categories do not have any particular order. The bars are separated by clear gaps. We call this a discontinuous scale. You could use colours such as red, green or blue to highlight the categories.

Bar charts are a good way of representing discontinuous data. These are sets of data where there are definite categories in no particular order.

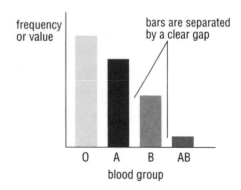

MAKING DRAWINGS OF MICROSCOPE IMAGES

USE   Drawings are a useful way of recording what you can see through a microscope.

METHOD

1. Decide if a drawing is appropriate. Is a simple description in words clear enough?

2. Decide whether to use plain paper or ruled paper. Use feint lines if you need to put text on the same page.

3. Use a good, sharp pencil. HB is usually hard enough to remain sharp, but gives a reasonably dark line.

4. Draw glassware etc. in the standard way as two-dimensional line drawings of sections through equipment.

5. Make large, clear drawings with continuous pencil lines.

6. Leave room for labels/annotations (short explanatory notes). Do not label on the drawing itself.

7. Avoid shading and colour unless absolutely necessary (no 'artistic effects').

8. Arrange label lines neatly around drawing, horizontally or radiating from the centre. Do not cross them. Ensure label lines touch the structure being labelled.

9. Give a suitable title.

10. Indicate magnification, scale or actual size if this is not apparent.

EXAMPLE

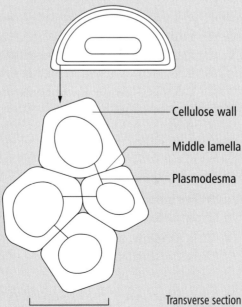

Cellulose wall

Middle lamella

Plasmodesma

50 μm

Transverse section of a pine needle, showing where you can find cells with exceptionally thick walls

technique

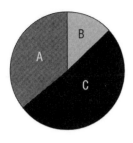

Like bar charts, pie charts are useful for representing discontinuous data. The angle of each segment is proportional to each individual value. Labels and sub-headings should indicate what each segment shows and what units are used.

Pie charts can also be used to compare relative frequencies or sizes. Data are converted to angles. You can choose between bar charts and pie charts – it just depends on what you think looks best.

Histograms

Histograms look a bit like bar charts. However, they are used for quantitative data. The area of the bar indicates the number of individual items in a category. A continuous scale is used (you can see that there are no gaps between the bars). Data are arranged in a regular sequence with measurements occurring at equal intervals.

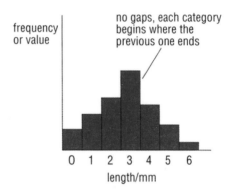

Histograms are useful for representing artificial categories of data in a definite order on a continuous scale.

Graphs

Graphs are an excellent way of recording quantitative data where one quantity varies with another. A continuous scale is used.

Imagine you are carrying out an experiment to see how one factor changes another, for example, how much a nylon rope stretches when different masses are hung on it. You choose one variable to control. In this case it is the mass added to the rope. We call this the independent variable. You then measure the other variable, which in this case is the length of the rope. This is called the dependent variable.

You plot the independent variable (the mass added to the rope) along the horizontal or x-axis. The variable you measure the changes in (the length of the rope) is plotted on the vertical, y-axis.

Straight line graphs are very important in scientific work. Two quantities may be calculated from a straight line graph:

- The **gradient** of the line. This tells you how quickly (the rate of change) the dependent variable changes with the independent variable.
- The **intercept** of the line on either the x-axis or the y-axis.

Graphs often give curves rather than straight lines. You will need to draw the smoothest curve that you can between points so that you can

REMEMBER

The variable that you control is called the independent variable. You plot this along the horizontal or x-axis.

The variable you measure the changes in is the dependent variable. This plotted on the vertical, y-axis.

read off values for points in between the ones that you have plotted. An example of this is in the use of calibration curves. By using samples of known values an instrument may be calibrated.

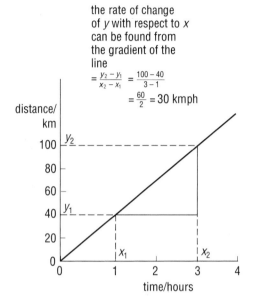

the rate of change of y with respect to x can be found from the gradient of the line

$$= \frac{y_2 - y_1}{x_2 - x_1} = \frac{100 - 40}{3 - 1}$$

$$= \frac{60}{2} = 30 \text{ kmph}$$

An example of using a straight line graph. The gradient of a graph of the distance a car has travelled (y-axis) against the time taken (x-axis) gives the car's speed.

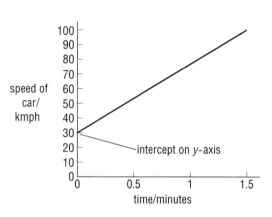

This graph shows the increase in speed of a car with time. The graph shows that timing began when the car was travelling at 30 km p h (the intercept on the speed axis, when time = 0). The gradient of the straight line gives the acceleration.

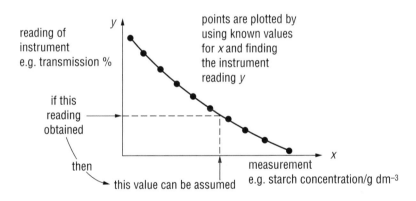

points are plotted by using known values for x and finding the instrument reading y

reading of instrument e.g. transmission %

if this reading obtained

then

this value can be assumed

measurement e.g. starch concentration/g dm⁻³

Calibration graphs may be straight lines or curves. In this graph a smooth curve has been drawn for the calibration of a colorimeter.

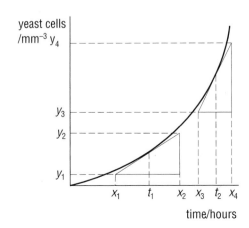

If graphs give curves rather than straight lines, rates can still be estimated by drawing a tangent to the curve. A tangent is a line at right angles to the curve at that point. This graph can be used to measure the rate of growth of yeast cells in glucose solution.

technique

DRAWING GRAPHS

USE This technique is used to represent quantitative data on a continuous scale.

METHOD

1 Decide which variable is independent and which one is dependent. Plot the independent variable on the horizontal (x) axis and the dependent variable on the vertical (y) axis.

2 Choose scales to fit the available space, but avoid awkward multiples (for example, use twos or fives but not threes).

3 If necessary, break scales to avoid crowding points in one corner of the graph paper, but make this clear.

4 Label axes and state units. A forward slash is used, for example, length of rod/cm.

5 Use a sharp pencil to plot points clearly and accurately and to draw lines. If more than one line is plotted on the same axes, label them.

6 Only draw a best straight line (using a ruler) or smooth curves of best fit if the intermediate values are meaningful. You must be able to assume that the values in between your measured ones are an accurate estimate of real values. You need continuous scales for this. If they are not continuous or there is any doubt, rule straight lines between the consecutive points if you wish to show a trend.

7 Give the graph a suitable title.

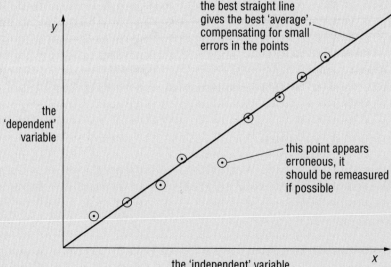

Carrying out calculations

Using formulae

Most standard procedures give a formula for calculating results. The measurements that have been made are substituted into the formula given and the result calculated.

Example: The purity of aspirin can be determined by a standard procedure that involves:

1 Weighing accurately about 0.5 g of powdered aspirin into a 250 cm^3 conical flask and adding 10 cm^3 of ethanol. The contents of the flask are swirled to dissolve the powdered aspirin.

2 2–3 drops of phenolphthalein indicator solution are added.

3 Titrating the solution with 0.100 mol dm^{-3} sodium hydroxide solution until a permanent pink colour remains.

The purity of the aspirin is calculated using the formula:

$$\frac{V}{m} \times 1.802 \ \%$$

where V = difference in burette readings; m = mass of aspirin.

So, if the mass of aspirin used was 0.400 g and the volume of 0.100 mol dm^{-3} sodium hydroxide solution needed was 22.0 cm^3

$m = 0.400$ g

$V = 22.0$ cm^3

The purity of the aspirin $= \dfrac{V}{M} \times 1.802 = \dfrac{22.0}{0.400} \times 1.802 = 99.1 \ \%$ w/w

You will come across many other examples of this later in the book.

Formulae for a straight line graph

You have already read about the usefulness of straight line graphs. The formula for a graph is a mathematical description of it. For a straight line graph that passes through the origin (0, 0) the formula is:

$y = mx$

In this formula m is the gradient. It is a constant (always has the same value). By rearranging the formula, you will see that the gradient is:

$m = \dfrac{y}{x}$

If you look again at the figure on page 53 you can see why the gradient gives you the speed of the car.

m = speed

y = distance moved by the car

x = time it takes for the car to move distance y

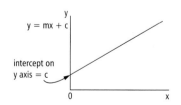

The formula for a straight line graph that intercepts the y axis at c (when x is zero) is

$y = mx + c$

Again, in this formula m is the gradient and is a constant.

Being able to rearrange formulae is very important. It's quite straightforward to do. There is one rule for you to remember: to rearrange a formula, do exactly the same thing to both sides.

If you multiply or divide, you must do it to everything on both sides. A trick that does the same thing is to cross multiply when you want to get rid of fractions:

e.g. $\dfrac{A}{B} = \dfrac{C}{D}$

Multiply the top of each side by the bottom of the other side:

$$\begin{array}{cc} A & C \\ B & D \end{array}$$

And so, AD = BC

(This is the same as multiplying both sides by BD).

This still works if only one side is a fraction, because you effectively treat the non-fraction as being 'over one':

Example 1	Example 2
$A = \dfrac{B}{C}$	$A + B = \dfrac{C}{D}$
$\dfrac{A}{1} = \dfrac{B}{C}$	$\dfrac{A + B}{1} = \dfrac{C}{D}$
$\begin{array}{cc} A & B \\ 1 & C \end{array}$	$\begin{array}{cc} A + B & C \\ 1 & D \end{array}$
	(A + B)D = C
AC = B	AD + BD = C
Try to find the formula for C	Try to find formulae for A, B and D

For electrical circuits, current (I), voltage (V) and resistance (R) can be linked by the formula for a straight line graph. You can rearrange this formula to find any one of these in terms of the other two.

   $V = IR$

   $\dfrac{V}{I} = R$

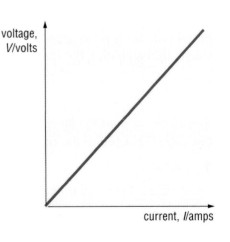

Analysing and interpreting data

Once you have collected your data and done any necessary calculations it's time to look at them closely and see what they tell you. This is what we call **analysing** the data and **interpreting** them. But first let's look at the types of data you might obtain.

Types of data

Qualitative data use categories. Things are grouped by the selection of certain common features (qualities) such as colour or shape. Qualitative data are descriptive and not numerical.

An example of using qualitative data. Experienced zoologists can identify species of birds, butterflies, fish and other animals from their physical features. They can also say whether they are male or female. Botanists can identify plants from their shapes and colours.

Another example of using qualitative data. A geologist might investigate rocks and minerals using a variety of chemical tests. Observations of the reactions provide them with qualitative data from which they can identify a rock or mineral. If you added dilute hydrochloric acid to a small piece of rock and it fizzed, giving off carbon dioxide, you could tell from this qualitative observation that the rock was a carbonate.

REMEMBER

Qualitative data are usually subjective. What may appear to be green-blue to you may be seen rather differently by somebody else. You need to be objective, precise in the words you use, and give as much information as possible.

REMEMBER

With quantitative data you can't rely on a single measurement. Comparing measurements of the same thing allows you to check your:

- instruments – are they calibrated correctly and do they give accurate readings?

- technique – are you working carefully and accurately?

Quantitative data involve measurement. Numerical values (quantities) are given, such as the length and mass of an object. The measurements can also be used to calculate other things, such as the density of a material or the concentration of a solution. When something is worked out by calculation rather than direct measurement we say it has been determined. Accurate and reliable measurements are central to scientific work.

Normally, you expect your instruments to be accurate. To make sure, measure the same thing twice using two different instruments. For example a standard mass can be weighed on two different balances. If they are both accurate, they will give the same reading (within their limits of precision). As an example, look back to pages 41–43 to remind yourself how graduated glassware can be checked.

Comparing your results with those of other people, or repeating your own, is an effective way to detect and eliminate human error. You need to be careful though. An instrument like a balance can give consistent results even if it is not accurate. You can also get consistent values if you do the same thing wrong each time!

Many things that you measure will not give you consistent values because they vary. For example, the diameter of a piece of wire may vary slightly at different points along its length. The water content of soil samples will vary depending on exactly where in a field they have been taken.

When this happens, you will need to get a best estimate by taking a series of measurements and finding the average or mean.

Spotting 'dodgy data'

You should always be on the look out for data that don't seem right. If in doubt, repeat the observation or measurement. You may even think the whole experiment should be carried out again.

Graphs are a good way of spotting dubious data. If you plot a number of data and they make up a straight line graph with the exception of one or two readings, it seems likely something has gone wrong with them. If possible they should be measured again. If this isn't possible, then they should be ignored.

The more you understand about the scientific principles upon which measurements are made, the more likely you are to recognise dubious data.

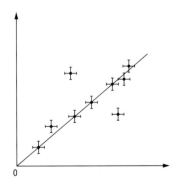

Graphs are a good way of spotting 'dodgy' data. Two of the points here appear to be dubious and so they have been ignored when drawing the graph.

Average and range

You can calculate the **average** of a number of measurements by:

1   adding together all the measurements that were made, and then

2   dividing by the number of measurements that were made.

Sometimes you will measure the same property for a number of different samples, for example, when investigating how tall people are in your group. Other times you may be making several measurements on one sample, for example, when analysing a chemical to see how pure it is.

Suppose you were investigating the growth of wheat. Several weeks after sowing, you visited the field and measured the height of a sample of the wheat. The heights were:

89 cm, 93 cm, 87 cm, 96 cm, 92 cm, 90 cm, 89 cm, 92 cm.

$$\text{Average} = \frac{89 + 93 + 87 + 96 + 92 + 90 + 89 + 92}{8} = \frac{728}{8} = 91\,\text{cm}$$

So the average height of the wheat sample is 91 cm.

The **range** is the difference between the largest and smallest values. It gives you a good idea of how consistent the measurements are. A small range tells you there is little variation in a sample. A large range means values can vary greatly.

The range for the sample of wheat is 96 − 87 = 9 cm.

Mean, mode and median

Often the average (or as it is more correctly called, the **mean**) by itself does not tell you very much. You may need to know more about variation in the thing that we are measuring. Mean, mode, median and range can be useful when looking at how much something varies.

The mean, median or mode can be used as the 'average' of a set of measurements. Choosing the most appropriate one to use depends on how the measurements vary and the use that is made of the 'average' value.

REMEMBER

Mean	the arithmetic average = sum of individual values divided by number of values
Mode	the most frequently occurring value
Median	the central value found by placing all the values in order of magnitude (the average of the central values, if there is an even number of values)
Range	the difference between the maximum and the minimum value in a set of results

Commercial growers need to know about germination rates. They also need to know what's needed for the plants to continue to grow healthily.

The **mode** is the most commonly occurring value in a set of data. It can sometimes be a better 'average' value to use. For example, a few large values can make the mean on the large side.

Imagine you were measuring the germination rates for seeds in a greenhouse. Altogether there are over 100 seeds trays. You take ten as a sample and measure the percentage germination in each. There can be no doubt about the germination rate – you know how many seeds were sown and you can count how many seedlings appear. The percentage germination rate in each case is calculated using the formula:

$$\text{Percentage germination} = \frac{\text{number of seedlings}}{\text{number of seeds sown}} \times 100\ \%$$

Suppose the germination rates were:

85%, 55%, 85%, 90%, 85%, 30%, 95%, 90%, 85%, 90%

$$\text{Mean} = \frac{85 + 55 + 85 + 90 + 85 + 30 + 95 + 90 + 85 + 90}{10} = \frac{780}{10} = 78\%$$

Mode = 85% (the value which occurs the largest number of times)

In this case, the mode would be a better 'typical value' to use. So if you wanted to estimate the germination rate for all the trays in the greenhouse without measuring them individually, it might be better to assume an 'average' of 85% rather than 78%.

The **median** is the central value when all of the measurements have been placed in order of size. For example:

2, 2, 2, 3, <u>3</u>, 4, 4, 5, 5

Median = 3

With an even number of values you take the average of the two central values. For example, for the germination rates above:

30%, 55%, 85%, 85%, <u>85%, 85%</u>, 90%, 90%, 90%, 95%

the median is $\frac{(85 + 85)}{2} = 85\%$

Remember, the mean is 78%. The importance, therefore, of using the median is that it offsets the effect of the two low values (30% and 55%) to give a better estimate of a 'central value'.

Sometimes . . .

- you will not expect much variation in your measurements. For example, if you are measuring the whole of something, such as the mass or length of a piece of wire, repeated measurements should not vary by more than the precision of your instrument. If they do, something is wrong!

- you can only measure part of something, in other words a sample. If the variation is greater than the instrument's precision, this tells you variation is in the thing you are measuring. So then you need to know the range.

Suppose that you are analysing indigestion tablets. They come in a box containing 50 tablets. You need to weigh out samples for analysis. The balance can measure mass to the nearest 0.001 g. You take six tablets for analysis. If you measured the mass of all six tablets several times you would not expect much variation in the total mass. Any differences would be due to the precision of the balance ($\pm$ 0.001 g). However, if you weigh the tablets individually you will probably get a variation. Here are some typical results:

Tablet	1	2	3	4	5	6
Mass/g	0.502	0.510	0.506	0.494	0.498	0.508

The smallest value for mass is 0.494 g and the largest is 0.510 g. The range is therefore 0.510 – 0.494 = 0.016 g. This is well above the precision with which we can measure using the balance ($\pm$ 0.001 g). So we can assume that the variation is due to differences in the tablets, rather than to measurement errors. What is the mean mass of the tablets?

Secondary sources

Often you will need to compare your results with those obtained by other scientists. This can be found in:

- databases
- textbooks
- data books
- the scientific literature.

An experiment used to obtain data is called a primary source. Sources of information that has been collected and recorded by other scientists, and recorded in a suitable form, are called secondary sources.

FIND IT OUT

Find out what secondary sources are in your school library or resource centre that may be of use during your course. Keep a list in the back of your notebook or file. Make a note of what each is particularly useful for.

Most large science-based companies have libraries of paper-based and electronic information sources. University resource centres also have huge stocks of information sources.

And finally . . . how meaningful are the results?

The last part of a scientific investigation is to **evaluate** it and **suggest improvements**.

Reliability, repeatability and reproducibility

These words probably sound much the same. But they have precise meanings in science. **Reliability** is about the confidence you have in the data you have collected (both observations and measurements). It can be judged by seeing if you get the same data when you do the experiments again and again. If it is, the data are **repeatable**. However, it doesn't necessarily mean they are reliable. You may be making the same mistake each time. A good check is to see if somebody else gets the same results. If they do, we say the data are **reproducible**. Data that are repeatable **and** reproducible are said to be reliable.

A combination of repeatability and reproducibility means these scientists can be confident that their data are reliable.

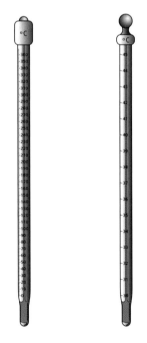

The scale on the clinical thermometer has smaller graduations than the 0–360 °C thermometer. This means it has a higher precision and the uncertainty of the measurement is less. But there is a down side. The clinical thermometer can only be used over a small temperature range and so is less versatile.

Error and uncertainty

There is a difference! **Errors** are caused by faulty equipment or by people using equipment incorrectly (operator error). Both can be eliminated. Equipment should be checked regularly, for example, measuring instruments should be calibrated regularly. Practice, care and patience will make it less likely that the operator uses equipment incorrectly.

Uncertainty is due to the precision of the measuring instruments being used. For example, if you want to measure out 25.0 cm³ of water, you will have a smaller uncertainty if you use a 25.0 cm³ graduated pipette than if you used a 100 cm³ measuring cylinder (see page 43). Simply, the smaller the smallest graduations are on a measuring instrument, the less uncertainty there is in the measurements.

Accuracy and precision

Now these two words really do cause confusion! In fact some dictionaries use one as the definition of the other. Let's try to be clear about the difference when they are used in science. As you have seen, **precision** is about uncertainty of measurements and depends on the precision of the measuring instrument. But mistakes can also creep in due to poor equipment or operator error. The combination of uncertainty and error adds up to the **accuracy** of a measurement. Simply, accuracy is how close a measurement is to the actual value. An analogy might help you.

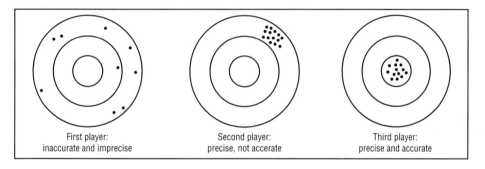

First player:
inaccurate and imprecise

Second player:
precise, not accerate

Third player:
precise and accurate

The dartboard analogy. Think about a game of darts. Three darts players throw their darts. The first player has darts all over the place. The throwing is neither precise nor accurate. The second player has darts clustered closely together but not around the bull's eye. This is precise but inaccurate throwing. The third player has darts clustered closely together close to the bull's eye. This is precise and accurate throwing.

Making improvements

At the end of an investigation, look back over what you did and try to identify sources of uncertainty and errors in measurements. Try to estimate the uncertainties (look at the precision of the measuring instruments you used). Might there be any errors, for example, was the measuring instrument calibrated before being used? Decide how reliable any observations or measurements were, and what the accuracy and precision of measurements you made was.

Then suggest improvements for:

- how the reliability of observations and measurements could be improved, for example, by repeating measurements, taking more frequent readings and so on
- how the accuracy and precision of measurements could be improved, for example, by using more precise measuring instruments.

?
Questions

1   In one week a woman ate various vegetables and fruit. The table below lists the content of some important nutrients in mg per 100 g of the vegetable or fruit that she ate.

	Vitamin A/mg	Vitamin C/mg	Calcium/mg
Broad beans	22	30	30
Brussels sprouts	67	35	27
Cauliflower	5	70	18
Onions	0	10	31
Parsnips	0	15	55
Peas	50	25	13
Potatoes	0	10	4
Apples	5	5	4
Oranges	8	50	41

If a 'good source' of nutrients is defined as one that contains more than 10 mg per 100 g (10 mg for vitamin A), construct a table to show the number of foods that the woman ate that were 'good sources' of three nutrients, two nutrients, one nutrient and no nutrients.

Represent this information in the form of a pie chart.

2   Find the mean, median and mode of the following measurements of the heights of a group of students:

Heights (in m): 1.74, 1.50, 1.83, 1.96, 1.67, 1.78, 1.89, 1.67, 1.67, 1.79

3   Materials that conduct electricity allow an electrical current to flow through them when a voltage is applied across them. The size of the current depends on the size of the voltage and how good a conductor the material is. It will have a certain resistance to the flow of the electrical current.

By measuring the voltage and the current, the electrical resistance can be calculated.

$R = V/I$

where R = resistance (in ohms), V = voltage (in volts) and I = current (in amps).

(a) Rearrange the formula to obtain one for voltage and one for current.

(b) Calculate the voltage when the resistance is 1.70 ohms and the current is 1.88 amps.

(c) Calculate the current when the voltage is 9.4 volts and the resistance is 2.5 ohms.

4   If a rocket accelerates smoothly, the speed at which it's travelling
     for a particular period of time can be found using:

$v = u + at$

where v = final speed (in metres per second, m s^{-1}) after time t
(in seconds, s), u = initial speed (in metres per second, m s^{-1}) and
a = acceleration (in metres per second per second, m s^{-2}).

Calculate the speed of the rocket in kilometres per hour after 10
seconds if it's accelerating at 1 kilometre per second per second.

Calculate the acceleration of the rocket in kilometres per second
per second if it reaches 1800 kilometres per hour after 10 seconds.

Hint: be careful when using units of time in your calculations.

5   The electrical resistance of a material was investigated. The voltage
     was varied and for each voltage used the current was measured.
     The results are shown in the table.

Voltage, V/volts	1.6	3.4	5.3	6.6	8.3
Current, I/amps	2.0	4.1	6.0	7.9	10.1

(a) Plot a graph of voltage (on the y-axis) against current
    (on the x-axis).

(b) Comment on the results that were obtained in the experiment.

(c) The graph is of the form $y = mx$. What does the m in this
    general formula stand for?

(d) Rewrite the formula $y = mx$ for the graph you plotted by using
    R (resistance, V (voltage) and I (current).

(e) Use your graph to calculate the best value that you can for the
    resistance of the sample.

6   The following results were obtained when the speed of an
     accelerating car was measured at 10-second intervals.

Time/seconds	10	20	30	40	50
Speed/kilometres per hours	46	77	109	142	165

Using the formula $v = u + at$, rearrange it so that it is in the
form $y = mx + c$.

Plot a graph of the experimental results. Use it to follow the
following:

(a) Was the car accelerating smoothly? Explain your answer.

(b) Find the initial speed of the car, i.e. when the stopwatch was
    started.

(c) Find the acceleration of the car over the period for which it was
    accelerating smoothly.

1.5 Investigating living organisms

Living organisms

There are probably around 30 million different species of organisms living on Earth. They vary in size and complexity from tiny one-celled organisms that are invisible to the naked eye to huge trees and massive whales. Yet all have important features in common. Understanding these features can be of great practical benefit. It can help, for example,

- farmers to grow crops and keep animals
- scientists to obtain useful products such as medicines from plants and micro-organisms
- ecologists to look after nature reserves.

Microscopy

You need to be able to:

- *set up a light microscope ready to use, choosing a suitable objective lens for the task*

- *prepare samples for investigation, including making a temporary slide, using a staining technique.*

Seeing the invisible

Light microscopes are by scientists to study living organisms that are too small to be seen by the human eye. Microscopes are also used to study cells and tissues that make up living organisms.

Scientists use microscopes to examine and count cells in hospital laboratories, to examine specimens in forensic science and archaeological investigations, by research workers in all areas of natural science and in the research and development and quality control departments of many industries. And there are many other uses. Laboratories where scientists work with microscopes include pathology, haematology, bacteriology, environmental and forensic science.

Comparison microscopy is used in forensic science to compare one sample with another. A comparison microscope is effectively two microscopes side-by-side. The operator can look at the two samples, one with each eye.

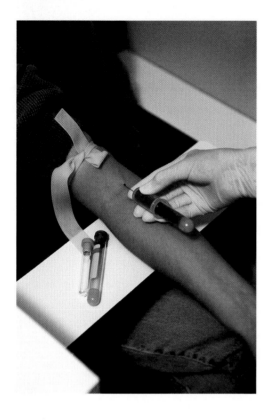

Blood samples are taken to check the state of a person's health. Several tests are carried out in the hospital pathology laboratory. One is to look at the cells present in blood. Abnormal cells can be identified and this helps the doctor to diagnose the problem.

Using a light microscope

You will learn how to use a microscope in the laboratory. Microscopes are expensive instruments and you should take great care when working with them. There are three steps in using a microscope:

- getting it ready to use
- preparing the sample for examination; this usually means you need to make a temporary slide
- looking at a slide (permanent or temporary) and recording the necessary information.

You should learn the basic techniques for each of these stages.

SAFETY

You must take care with biological stains. They should be handled carefully and you must follow the safety instructions that come with them.

Remember, all biological samples are BIOHAZARDS.

As with all scientific work, a risk assessment must be carried out before starting work.

technique

PREPARING THE MICROSCOPE FOR USE

USE This technique is quite general and may be followed when getting any light microscope ready for use. Some may have special requirements and so the instructions that come with them must be followed carefully.

EQUIPMENT • Light microscope, and a lamp if necessary.

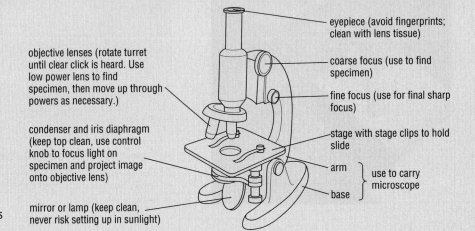

eyepiece (avoid fingerprints; clean with lens tissue)

objective lenses (rotate turret until clear click is heard. Use low power lens to find specimen, then move up through powers as necessary.)

coarse focus (use to find specimen)

fine focus (use for final sharp focus)

condenser and iris diaphragm (keep top clean, use control knob to focus light on specimen and project image onto objective lens)

stage with stage clips to hold slide

arm
use to carry microscope

base

mirror or lamp (keep clean, never risk setting up in sunlight)

The light microscope. Make sure you are familiar with all the parts and what they do.

METHOD

1 Position the microscope so that it is comfortable to use and has a good light source (not the sun).

2 Rotate the nosepiece so that the lowest power (smallest) objective lens is in use.
Note: A compound microscope has an eyepiece lens and several alternative objective lenses.

3 Adjust the mirror (and condenser, if present) so that light is evenly spread across the field of view.

4 Adjust the diaphragm to give a bright, but not dazzling, field of view.

CALCULATIONS To calculate the magnification, multiply the magnification of the objective lens by the magnification of the eyepiece lens:

magnification = magnification of objective lens × magnification of eyepiece lens

$$M_{total} = M_{obj} \times M_{eye}$$

WORKED EXAMPLE Magnification of the objective lens, $M_{obj} = 40$

Magnification of the eyepiece lens, $M_{eye} = 10$

Total magnification, $M_{total} = 40 \times 10 = 400$

technique

PREPARING TEMPORARY SLIDES

USE   This technique may be used to prepare temporary slides of solid and liquid samples. It also outlines the general method for staining samples before examination.

EQUIPMENT AND MATERIALS

- Sample to be examined
- Mounted needle
- Stain solution, e.g. methylene blue or iodine
- Slides and cover slips
- Dropping pipette
- Scissors or scalpel
- Forceps
- Beaker of water
- Marker pen
- Discard pot containing disinfectant

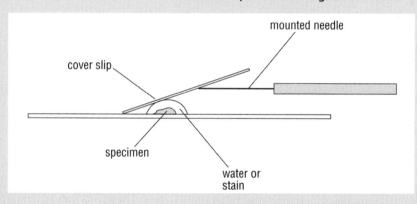

Making a temporary slide

METHOD

1 Place the sample to be examined on the slide.

For liquid samples, e.g. pond water

Using a dropper pipette put a drop of the sample on the centre of a clean slide.

For solid samples, e.g. plant tissue

Using a dropper pipette put a drop of water on the centre of a clean slide. Carefully spread the solid sample out in the drop of water. For example,

- peel a small strip of red epidermis (the thin outer 'skin') from a rhubarb stalk
- peel a small piece of onion epidermis (the thin 'skin' found on the inside of each layer of onion 'flesh')
- pull a leaf from a moss plant.

2 Use a mounted needle to lower a cover slip over the drop of liquid on the slide.

technique

3 Remove any excess water with a paper tissue but do not draw all the liquid out from under the cover slip.

4 If the sample needs to be stained, for example with methylene blue stain or iodine stain, use the stain in place of water in step 1. Alternatively the stain can be added by irrigation.

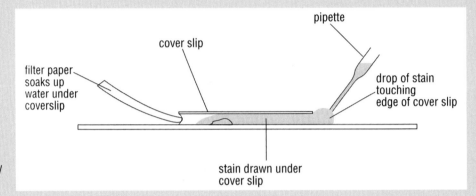

filter paper soaks up water under coverslip

cover slip

pipette

drop of stain touching edge of cover slip

stain drawn under cover slip

Irrigating a temporary slide with a stain

5 Examine the slide under the microscope immediately, starting with the low power objective lens.

6 After examination, dispose of the slide and paper tissues in an appropriate way (this will depend on the nature of the sample).

It is not possible for you to prepare slides of some biological materials. These will have been made for you and are called prepared slides. Other samples you will mount yourself. These are called temporary slides and after looking at them you will dispose of the slide safely.

technique

LOOKING AT A SLIDE

USE This technique outlines the way a prepared slide should be examined with a light microscope.

EQUIPMENT AND MATERIALS
- Light microscope
- Slide with the prepared sample

METHOD

1 Clip the sample slide in place on the stage. Looking at the microscope from the side, use the coarse focus knob to lower the objective lens to close to the surface of the slide.

2 Looking down the microscope, use the same knob to gradually raise the lens until you can see the sample. Bring it into focus by small adjustments of the coarse focus knob followed by the use of the fine focus knob.

technique

Note: The microscope should always be focussed upwards in this way to avoid damaging the slide (and lens).

3 Examine the slide and move it to view different parts, note how it moves in your field of view.

4 To use a higher power objective lens, bring what you want to look at into focus in the centre of the field of view with the low power objective lens. Change to the higher power objective by turning the nosepiece. Then focus with the fine focus knob only and focussing upward. If this does not work, look from the side as you lower the lens with the fine focus knob before trying again. If necessary, adjust the brightness using the diaphragm.

RESULTS The record of the examination should include:

- the name of the sample and where it came from

- how the sample was prepared for investigation

- the magnification used

- notes of what you can see, including any structures that you can identify, for example, using a labelled drawing that includes an indication of scale (keep the labels clear of the drawing) or a photograph.

Questions

1 Calculate the magnification that would be achieved if you used a light microscope with
   an objective lens of magnification 50 and an eyepiece lens of magnification 5
   an objective lens of magnification 20 and an eyepiece lens of magnification 10
   an objective lens of magnification 40 and an eyepiece lens of magnification 5

2 Describe how you should prepare a temporary slide of a yeast suspension taken from a fermenter.

3 Find out why scientists use microscopy and what types of microscopes they use.

4 There are still some things that can't be seen under a light microscope. Scienists use electron microscopes to investigate these. Find out about transmission and scanning electron microscopy and what scientists use these techniques for.

Micro-organisms

You need to:

- *understand the importance of aseptic techniques and be able to use them to culture micro-organisms and dispose of them safely*

- *investigate the effects of anti-microbial agents on the micro-organisms*

- *set up a culture, which will produce a useful product, such as a food substance.*

Some are good; some are bad

Micro-organisms are living organisms that are too small to be seen individually without magnification. They are found almost everywhere on the planet and include bacteria, viruses and some fungi. Some micro-organisms are pathogenic. This means they cause disease, to us or to plants and animals. These must be handled very carefully. Other micro-organisms are extremely useful and can be used to make useful products such as foods and medicines.

So there are many areas of scientific work where it's important to be able detect, identify and manipulate specific micro-organisms. Amongst other places, scientists work with micro-organisms in:

- pathology laboratories, for example in hospitals or public health departments
- the food industry, for example, the production of bread, beer, wine, yoghurt
- horticulture and agriculture, for example, to control pests
- the pharmaceutical industry, developing and manufacturing medicines, for example, antibiotics

Culturing

The number of micro-organisms will increase if they are kept at the right temperature and fed. We say that they multiply, and this process is called culturing. Scientists use culturing in two ways:

- to increase the number of micro-organisms needed in the production, for example, of a food, beverage or medicine

An example: yeast is a micro-organism used in the brewing and baking industries. It converts glucose into ethanol (sometimes simply called 'alcohol') and carbon dioxide. This is called alcoholic fermentation. In baking, the carbon dioxide given off during alcoholic fermentation is trapped within the structure of the dough, causing it to expand. Conditions are chosen so that the yeast can multiply and produce carbon dioxide.

You may have seen mould on stale bread. The mould is actually a clump of micro-organisms. Each micro-organism is too small to see, but when there are enough the clump of them becomes visible. The micro-organisms grow and multiply (increasing in number) if the conditions are right – the temperature is right and they have food. The growth of mould on stale bread is uncontrolled. However, some scientists grow micro-organisms for particular reasons, and they do it in a carefully controlled way. This is called culturing.

Yeast is a useful micro-organism. During baking bread it converts glucose into ethanol, giving off carbon dioxide. This gas causes the dough to expand and the bread to rise. What other substances are used to make bread rise? Try to find out how they work.

REMEMBER

Culturing micro-organisms means keeping them under the right conditions so that they will multiply.

- to increase the numbers of micro-organisms so that they can be identified more easily

An example: doctors take urine specimens to identify micro-organisms such as bacteria that are the cause of you not feeling well. This helps them prescribe the most suitable antibiotic.

The importance of aseptic techniques

Micro-organisms are everywhere almost, for example, on your hands and on the laboratory bench. If you want to isolate a single type of micro-organism, you must:

- make sure that other micro-organisms do not cause contamination
- avoid handling micro-organisms directly as they may be harmful

Using aseptic techniques ensures that both of these needs are fulfilled.

REMEMBER

To culture micro-organisms they must be given food (nutrients) and kept in a warm place (incubated).

One technique for culturing samples is to spread a small amount over the surface of a jelly containing suitable food (nutrient agar) and to keep it in a warm place (usually an incubator). The micro-organisms present multiply to form clumps that you can see. These clumps are called colonies.

It's important that only the organisms present in the sample are cultured. Great care must be taken to avoid contamination and you can do this by using aseptic techniques, in other words using:

- equipment that has been sterilised to kill any micro-organisms present
- standard procedures written to reduce the chances of contamination while you work.

All micro-organisms present in a sample multiply during incubation, including any harmful ones. So it is important that we incubate at a temperature that makes it less likely that pathogenic organisms will grow. It is also very important that after incubation, samples should not be opened and must be disposed of safely.

Culturing micro-organisms

You will learn how to culture micro-organisms in the laboratory. This means knowing how to set up experiments where the micro-organism you want to study is given food and kept at the right temperature. You should learn the basic techniques for each of these stages.

- preparing streak and spread plates using aseptic techniques; this means putting the micro-organism that you want to culture on a suitable nutrient jelly in a Petri dish
- incubating the plates (keeping them at the right temperature) by putting them in an oven set at the appropriate temperature
- looking at the incubated plate for sign that the micro-organism has grown and colonies are visible

REMEMBER

Health and safety

Wear eye protection and protective gloves.

Do not open the Petri dishes after incubation.   BIOHAZARD

Remember, many biological samples are BIOHAZARDS.

As with all scientific work, a risk assessment must be carried out before starting work.

For the streak plate method, a suitably trained teacher or technician could demonstrate this aseptic procedures using wire loop and flaming techniques rather than a disposable inoculation loop. For the smear plate method, a demonstration could also be carried out using a glass spreader and flaming with alcohol rather than disposable sterile swabs.

technique

STREAK PLATES

USE   This technique may be used to prepare streak plates of various micro-organisms using aseptic technique.

EQUIPMENT AND MATERIALS
- Sterile equipment:
  3 × Petri dishes containing nutrient agar
  12 × pre-sterilised inoculation loops
- Sterile water
- Bunsen burner
- Overnight broth cultures of two micro-organisms (for example, *Micrococcus luteus*, *Bacillus subtilis*, *Escherichia coli*)
- Discard pot containing disinfectant
- Marker pen
- Tape to secure Petri dishes

METHOD FOR A STREAK PLATE

1 Arrange a clean workspace so that you have a Petri dish containing nutrient agar, a sterile inoculation loop and a bottle containing the bacterial sample within reach. Loosen, but do not remove, the top of the sample bottle.

If you are right handed, hold the bottle or lid of the Petri dish in your left hand and the inoculation loop in your right hand for this procedure.

Keep the loop as steady as possible and do not put it down until you have completed the procedure in step 4.

2 Hold the inoculation loop like a pen, but at the end furthest from the loop and almost vertical.

3 With the little finger of the hand holding the loop, remove and hold the lid of the bottle (by turning the bottle using the other hand). With the bottle at a slight angle pass the neck of the bottle briefly through the hot part of the Bunsen flame and back. Dip the inoculation loop into the sample, re-flame the neck of the bottle and replace the lid. Put down the bottle. Keep the loop of sample as still as possible.

4 Hold the lid of the Petri dish and lift it just enough to give access (but keep it above the agar). With the loop parallel to the surface of the agar, smear the sample, using forward and backward movements, over the first section of the agar surface as shown in the diagram. Replace the lid of the Petri dish.

5 Discard the loop in disinfectant.

6 Turn the Petri dish through 90° anticlockwise and use a new sterile inoculation loop to make three parallel forward streaks spreading the sample out from the previous area.

7 Repeat step 6 twice more, carrying the last stroke into the centre of the plate, so that the sample is streaked onto the agar surface as shown in the diagram.

8 Discard the loop.

9 Seal the plate by using 4 short strips of adhesive tape to secure the lid to the base. Turn the Petri dish over for incubation (to prevent condensation dripping onto the agar surface).

10 Label the base of the plate. Write your name, the date, the sample and the technique used, but keep it small and near the edge or it will be difficult to examine the plates after incubation.

11 Repeat steps 1–10 for a second micro-organism and for a sample of sterile water.

technique

technique

SPREAD PLATES

USE

This technique may be used to prepare spread plates of various micro-organisms using aseptic technique.

EQUIPMENT AND MATERIALS

- Sterile equipment:
  3 × Petri dishes containing nutrient agar
  3 × dropper pipettes
  3 × sterile swabs

- Sterile water

- Overnight broth cultures of two micro-organisms (for example, *Micrococcus luteus, Bacillus subtilus, Escherichia coli*)

- Bunsen burner

- Discard pot containing disinfectant

- Marker pen

- Tape to secure Petri dishes

METHOD FOR A SPREAD PLATE

1 Arrange a clean workspace so that you have a Petri dish containing nutrient agar, a sterile pipette, a sterile swab, a discard pot and a bottle containing the bacterial sample within reach.

2 Loosen, but do not remove, the top of the sample bottle.

If you are right handed, hold the bottle or lid of the Petri dish in your left hand and the sterile pipette in your right hand for this procedure.

3 Take the sterile pipette from its wrapper or container without touching its dispensing end. With the little finger of the hand holding the pipette, remove and hold the lid of the bottle (by turning the bottle using the other hand). With the bottle at a slight angle pass the neck of the bottle briefly through the hot part of the Bunsen flame and back. Squeeze the bulb of the pipette gently, lower it into the liquid in the bottle and release the pressure on the bulb to draw up a small amount of sample into the pipette, re-flame the neck of the bottle and replace the lid. Put down the bottle. Hold the pipette carefully and as still as possible.

4 Hold the lid of the Petri dish and lift it just enough to give access (but keep it above the agar), drop five drops from the pipette onto the surface of the agar. Replace the lid of the Petri dish.

technique

5 Put the pipette directly into the discard pot.

6 Lift the lid of the Petri dish enough to place the sterile swab onto the surface of the agar. By moving the swab and rotating the dish make sure that the liquid is spread over the entire surface of the agar. Replace the lid of the Petri dish.

7 Put the swab directly into the discard pot.

8 Let the surface of the agar dry.

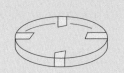

9 Seal the plate by using 4 short strips of adhesive tape to secure the lid to the base. Turn the Petri dish over for incubation (to prevent condensation dripping onto the agar surface).

10 Label the base of the plate. Write your name, the date, the sample and the technique used but keep it small and near the edge or it will be difficult to examine the plates after incubation.

11 Repeat steps 1–11 for a second micro-organism and for a sample of sterile water.

INCUBATING PLATES

USE This technique keeps plates at the right temperature for the growth of micro-organisms. You should check the best temperature for the micro-organism you are using since it can vary slightly. However, 25–30 °C is the most common.

EQUIPMENT AND MATERIALS
- Prepared plates
- Incubator at 25–30 °C

METHOD Incubate the inverted plates in an oven at 25–30 °C for 48 hours. After this time examine each plate (SAFETY: do NOT open the plates).

RESULTS You should note:
- if there are any colonies present
- what the colonies look like
- whether all the colonies on a plate look the same.

technique

Many household cleaners contain substances that kill bacteria such as germs. But how could you test they do what they say?

Anti-microbial agents

Some substances stop or reduce the growth and multiplication of micro-organisms. They are biostatic. Other substances kill the micro-organisms. These are biocidal. Substances may have different effects at different concentrations and towards different organisms.

Antibiotics are anti-microbial agents that work at very low concentrations and can be used in medicines. Pharmaceutical companies are always testing new substances for anti-microbial activity. Hospital laboratories need to test the sensitivity of pathogenic (harmful) micro-organisms to different antibiotics. In both cases a technique is used which involves putting a sample of the substance being tested onto an agar plate spread with the test micro-organisms. After a period of incubation the presence of a clear zone, where micro-organisms have not grown, around the test substance indicates that it has some anti-microbial activity.

SAFETY

Wear eye protection and protective gloves.

Do not open the Petri dishes after incubation. BIOHAZARD

Remember, many biological samples are BIOHAZARDS.

As with all scientific work, a risk assessment must be carried out before starting work.

technique

ANTI-MICROBIAL ACTION

USE   This technique may be used to test the effectiveness of anti-microbial agents.

EQUIPMENT AND MATERIALS

- Sterile equipment: Petri dish containing nutrient agar; filter paper discs (with a diameter in the range 5–15 mm); dropper pipette; 4 × sterile swabs

- Sterile water

- Overnight broth culture of *Micrococcus luteus*

- Samples to be tested

- Sterile forceps

- Bunsen burner

- Incubator at 25–30 °C

technique

METHOD   Use the same aseptic technique as was described for spread plates.

1. Prepare a spread plate of *Micrococcus luteus*. Leave to dry.

2. On the base of the prepared plate label your name, the date and four sectors, for three samples and a control.

3. Remove sterile forceps from their packaging. Use the sterile forceps to take a filter paper disc, dip it into the first test sample, allow it to drain on the side of the container, and place it on the surface of the agar in the appropriate sector on the prepared spread plate.

4. Place the forceps in the discard pot containing disinfectant.

5. Seal the plate and leave for 2 hours.

6. Repeat steps 3 to 5 for each of the remaining samples and for a control disc dipped in sterile water.

7. Incubate the inverted plate at 25–30 °C for 48 hours.

8. Remove the plate from the incubator and examine without opening it.

RESULTS   Note if there is:

- an even growth of micro-organisms over the area of the plate
- any evidence of inhibited growth around the filter paper discs and, if so, record the diameter of the area

Using micro-organisms to make useful products

Micro-organisms are used to make useful products in:

- the food industry, for example, the production of bread, beer, wine, yoghurt
- the pharmaceutical industry, developing and manufacturing medicines, for example, antibiotics.

Here are three examples you can try in the laboratory.

Milk contains a sugar called lactose and a protein called casein. To make yoghurt from milk, the lactose must be converted to lactic acid. 'Lactic acid' bacteria are added to milk to bring about this chemical change. As more lactic acid forms the pH drops. This causes the casein to coagulate and thicken the yoghurt. By cooling the mixture when pH reaches 4.5 the process can be stopped. The yoghurt now has its characteristic flavour. This is because there is just the right balance of chemicals present.

Making beer and wine is a huge business. Glucose is converted to ethanol and carbon dioxide by yeast. This process is called fermentation. It is the basis of the brewing industry and the manufactures of beers and wines.

technique

MAKING DOUGH

USE This technique may be used make dough and, for example, to compare different flours and different yeasts.

EQUIPMENT AND MATERIALS

- Flour
- Fresh and/or dried yeast
- Warm water (about 25 °C)
- Thermometer
- Stop clock
- Scales
- Beakers
- Measuring spoon or spatula
- 100 cm³ measuring cylinders
- Chopstick or dowel to reach to the bottom of the cylinder
- Water bath at about 25 °C (or large container for warm water)
- Stand, boss and clamp
- Plastic board or sheet (for kneading the dough)

SAFETY

Dough prepared in a laboratory should not be eaten. BIOHAZARD

A risk assessment must have been carried out before starting work.

METHOD

1 Wash your hands.

2 Fill a measuring cylinder to about the 100cm³ mark with water at about 25 °C.

3 Weigh out two 75 g samples of flour.

4 Put 2 g yeast (or a 2 cm³ measure) into a small beaker, mix it to a creamy consistency with a little of the warm water.

5 Add 75 g flour and a further 50 cm³ warm water. Mix to absorb the water, turn out onto a clean surface and knead to make a soft ball of dough.

6 Roll the dough into a sausage shape and drop it into the bottom of a clean, dry 100 cm³ measuring cylinder. Gently push it down to the base. Label the cylinder.

7 Repeat steps 5 and 6 with the second sample of flour without using any yeast.

8 Stand both measuring cylinders in a water bath at 25 °C.

9 Record the height of the dough every 10 minutes for an hour and record your results in a table.

10 Bake the dough samples in an oven for 2–3 hours. Remove them from the oven and note their appearance (a) immediately after coming out of the oven, (b) after cooling for 30 minutes.

MAKING ETHANOL

USE

This technique may be used to produce ethanol ('alcohol') by fermentation. It may be sued to compare the effectiveness of different types of yeast. It may also be adapted to see the effect of varying things lime the temperature, glucose concentration and quantity of yeast.

EQUIPMENT AND MATERIALS

- Sterile 500 cm^3 conical flasks containing 400 cm^3 yeast nutrient solution
- Sterile bungs with fermentation traps attached to fit the flasks
- Sterile measuring spoons
- Dried yeast
- Glucose
- Thermometer

METHOD

1. Put 200 cm^3 yeast nutrient solution into each of two sterile 500 cm^3 conical flasks.

2. For each flask:
   - remove and hold the cotton wool plug with one hand
   - quickly tip a 5 cm^3 measure of dried yeast into the flask with the other hand
   - immediately replace the cotton wool plug

3. Label both flasks with your name and the date and indicate which flask will have glucose added (step 4).

4. Using the same technique as in step 2, add three level 15 cm^3 measuring spoonfuls of glucose to one flask only.

5. For each flask:
   - without touching the parts that will go inside the flask, take a sterile bung and fermentation trap in one hand
   - remove the cotton wool plug from a flask with the other hand and replace it with the fermentation trap
   - push the bung firmly into the neck of the flask
   - half fill the fermentation trap with sterile water.

6. Gently swirl the flasks to mix well and keep the two flasks in a warm room.

7. After 30 minutes, and two or three times each day for a few days, count the number of bubbles of carbon dioxide that pass through the fermentation trap in five minutes. Calculate the hourly rate. Check the level of liquid in the fermentation trap daily and top up with sterile water if necessary.

SAFETY

Wear protective clothing and eye protection.

Do not open the flasks during or after incubation. Under no circumstances should the products of fermentation be consumed.   BIOHAZARD

A risk assessment must have been carried out before starting work.

technique

technique

MAKING YOGHURT

USE   This technique may be used to make yoghurt and to investigate the factors that affect its production.

EQUIPMENT AND MATERIALS

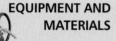

SAFETY

Do not taste any samples that are prepared in the laboratory. BIOHAZARD

A risk assessment must be carried out before starting work.

- Sterile (or very clean!) 100 cm³ beakers, 10 cm³ measuring cylinder and glass rods

- UHT milk

- Live natural yoghurt

- Cling film or aluminium foil to cover beakers

- Water bath or incubator at 40–45 °C

- pH probe and meter (a data logger if pH is to be recorded continuously)

METHOD

1. Set up two test cultures, one with plain UHT milk and one in which you add 10% by volume of live yoghurt.

2. Determine the pH of each at the start of incubation and after 2, 4, 6 and 18 hours. If you have the equipment, record the pH continuously.

3. Record your results in a table or print your recorded data.

Questions

1. Explain what is meant by 'culturing a micro-organism'.

2. Give two reasons why scientists are interested in culturing micro-organisms.

3. Explain what is meant by 'aseptic technique'. Why is this technique so important?

4. Describe how each of the following may affect the growth of colonies of micro-organisms:
   - temperature
   - availability of nutrients.

5. Find out about the jobs done by environmental health officers and how studying micro-organisms forms part of their work.

6. Micro-organisms are used in the pharmaceutical industry to make drugs. Find out about the development of a drug from its discovery until it is available on prescription or over the counter at the pharmacy.

1.6 Chemical analysis

Reasons for analysing substances

Analytical chemists test substances and materials to find out what chemical compounds are present. For example, they test for pollutants in river water or banned substances in athletes. They also determine how much of these compounds is present, for example, their concentration in solutions.

There are two types of chemical analyses that you will carry out. **Qualitative analysis** involves identifying a substance. To do this you will need to know how to use chemical tests to identify various ions and gases, and flame tests to identify certain metal ions. **Quantitative analysis** involves determining how much of a substance is present. One example is an acid-base titration. You will need to know how to carry out such a titration.

Where analytical chemists work

Chemists are employed as analysts in different laboratories. For example, they work in industrial laboratories (undertaking research or quality control), forensic science laboratories and hospital pharmacies. Many analysts collect samples for analysis from the outdoors, for example, rivers, soil and the air. They are said to be working in the field.

Samples for analysis

How you take samples of a substance or material for analysis depends on where they come from and what you want to know about them. Before you start you need to know if the composition depends on where the sample is taken from.

- If you are not sure, you should take samples from different places. You must analyse all of them before you can come to any conclusions.

To check that these cans of cola contain the ingredients claimed on the label, a number of cans should be taken for analysis. We call these 'representative samples'. The contents of any one can are homogeneous, in other words its composition is the same throughout.

- If you are sure the composition of the substance or material is the same no matter where it's taken from, only a single sample is needed for analysis.

You should always take sufficient samples to be able to carry out the analysis several times if necessary. Repeating an analysis is how you check the accuracy of the analysis.

This chemical will be used as a starting material in a chemical manufacturing process. Its purity must be checked before use. It is likely to be of uniform composition and so only one sample needs to be taken for analysis (remembering that there must be sufficient to repeat the analysis 2–4 times). However, if there is any doubt about its uniformity, samples should be taken from different parts of the drum, for example, top, middle and bottom.

Environmental scientists are interested in air quality and pollution. The effects of car exhaust fumes on the air quality in this busy street can be tested. However, the air might vary depending on how far from the road it is taken, the time of the day and so on. The scientist must decide where, when and how many samples to take.

The preparation of a sample for analysis depends on the analytical techniques to be used. A number of things need to be considered:

- how much is needed for analysis?
- does the sample need to be ground into a powder before analysis?
- does the sample need to be dissolved to give a solution and, if so, what concentration?

- if the sample is already a solution, does it need to be diluted before analysis and, if so, what concentration?

Qualitative chemical analysis

You need to:

- *separate mixtures by evaporation, distillation and chromatography to determine their composition*

- *carry out qualitative chemical tests for Na^+, K^+, Ca^{2+}, Cu^{2+}, Pb^{2+}, Fe^{3+}, Cl^-, SO_4^{2-}, CO_3^{2-} ions using reagents and/or flame tests*

- *draw conclusions from your results.*

Many scientists are involved with identification of substances and materials, for example pathologists in hospitals and forensic scientists. Nowadays scientists often use sophisticated and expensive instruments. It is unlikely that you will be able to use this in your school or college laboratory. However, you may be able to visit laboratories where these instruments are in use.

Evaporation

Some substances dissolve in water. They are soluble. The substance that dissolves is called the solute. What it dissolves in is called the solvent. And you end up with a solution. For example, sodium chloride dissolves in water.

Solute: sodium chloride
Solvent: water
Solution: solution of sodium chloride in water

Many substances are not soluble in water. To dissolve them a different solvent is needed. Often organic liquids can be used to dissolve substances that are insoluble in water. For example, nail varnish removers and some paint strippers can be used as solvents.

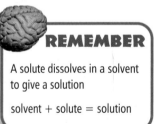

REMEMBER

A solute dissolves in a solvent to give a solution

solvent + solute = solution

You can show that substances are dissolved in a solvent by evaporating the solution. The solution is heated to drive off the solvent. The solvent is changed to a vapour and evaporates. This is how water samples are analysed to see if they contain dissolved solids. There are standard operating procedures for determining the quantity of dissolved solids in water, for example, in rivers, streams and lakes. A measured volume of water is evaporated and any solid that remains is weighed.

(a)   (b)

Sugar dissolves in water to give a colourless solution.
What is the solute and what is the solvent?

technique

EVAPORATION

USE

This technique may be used to obtain a solid from a solution. It may also be used to determine how much solid is in a solution.

EQUIPMENT AND MATERIALS

- Measuring cylinder
- Evaporating basin
- Hotplate or steam bath

METHOD

1 Measure out the required volume of solution using a measuring cylinder.

2 Weigh an evaporating basin (m_1 g).

3 Pour the solution into the weighed evaporating basin.

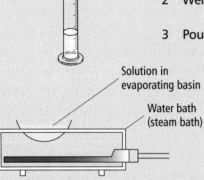

Solution in evaporating basin

Water bath (steam bath)

4 Place the evaporating basin and solution over heat using either steam (from a hot water bath) or electric hotplate.

5 Heat gently. This avoids the solution 'spitting' and splashing out of the evaporating basin.

6 Keep heating until all the water has been driven off.

7 Weigh the basin again (m_2 g).

8 After weighing, carry out tests on the solid to identify it.

CALCULATIONS

Volume of solution = V cm^3
Mass of dissolved solid
= mass of basin and solid after evaporation – mass of basin
= $(m_2 - m_1)$ g
Percentage of solid in solution = $\dfrac{m_2 - m_1}{V} \times 100\%$

WORKED EXAMPLE

A sample of river water was collected for analysis. It was filtered to remove any undissolved solids. 200 cm^3 was measured into an evaporating basin and evaporated to dryness. The mass of the basin was 102.11 g. The mass of the basin and the solid after evaporation was 103.15 g.

Therefore,
Mass of dissolved solid = 103.15 – 102.11 = 1.04 g
Percentage of dissolved solid in the river water
= $\dfrac{1.04}{200} \times 100\% = 0.52\%$

You can't identify the dissolved solids by evaporation alone. You can only show that they are there. To find out what the solids are you need further tests such as flame tests or chemical reactions (you will find out about these on page 94).

REMEMBER

Evaporation is an important technique used in the preparation of chemical compounds. You will probably use it when you are making chemicals in the laboratory. The preparation of chemical compounds is described on pages 267–285.

Distillation

If you have a solution, the solvent can be obtained by distillation. The solution is heated and the solvent changes to a vapour. This is condensed and collected as a liquid. This is an important separation technique, but is not much used to help identify substances.

DISTILLATION

technique

USE   This technique may be used to obtain a solvent from a solution. The temperature at which it distils over is its boiling point. This can be used to help identify the solvent.

EQUIPMENT AND
MATERIALS   Quickfit distillation glassware.

METHOD   1   Put together the distillation apparatus as in the diagram.

2   Remove the distillation head and pour in the solution. Add a few anti-bumping granules.

Water out

3   Warm the flask until the liquid begins to boil gently. Keep heating so that the solvent distils over at about 1–2 drops per second. Use a Bunsen burner for non-flammable liquids or a water bath/heating mantle for flammable liquids.

Water in

4   Take the reading on the thermometer as the solvent is distilling over.

Heat

5   Stop the distillation when there are a few cubic centimetres of liquid left in the flask.

As pure liquids boil at fixed temperatures these temperatures are called **boiling points**. They can be used to help identify unknown liquids. For example:

Liquid	Boiling point
Ethanol	79 °C
Water	100 °C
Propanone	56 °C
Ethanoic acid	118 °C

Rather than distil the liquids it is more usual to reflux them and record the temperature of the vapour above the boiling liquid.

Distillation can also be used to separate a product from a reaction mixture (see Unit 3).

Chromatography

You will probably have done some chromatography before. Perhaps you separated food colourings or ink dyes. It is a really useful way of separating mixtures and identifying what substances are present.

There are two types of chromatography that you can do easily without the need for expensive equipment. They are paper chromatography and thin layer chromatography (usually abbreviated to tlc). They have been largely overtaken by more sophisticated types of chromatography but are still used by scientists. Here are a couple of examples:

- pharmacopoeias give standard procedures for checking the quality of drugs and medicines; tlc is often used to check for the presence of impurities
- the job of some chemists is to make chemical compounds; they can check for unused reactants and any unwanted products by using paper chromatography or tlc.

Other forms of chromatography are more sophisticated, for example gas-liquid chromatography (glc) and higher performance liquid chromatography (hplc). These are used in numerous types of analytical laboratories, for example, forensic, environmental and research.

Quantitative chemical tests

Chemical substances often have at least one characteristic reaction that may be used to identify them. These qualitative chemical tests can be used to identify ions in aqueous solution and gases. Some metal ions can be identified using a flame test.

Standard procedures are given below for:

- chemical tests for ions
- chemical tests for gases
- flame tests.

There are many variations of the procedures and you may find slightly different ways of carrying out the tests in other sources.

REMEMBER

The R_f value (the retention factor) is always the same for a compound provided all conditions (for example, the type of chromatography paper or tlc plate and the developing solvent) are kept the same. This means that the R_f value can be used to identify the substances present in the mixture.

technique

PAPER CHROMATOGRAPHY AND THIN LAYER CHROMATOGRAPHY

USE These techniques may be used to separate and identify the substances present in a mixture.

EQUIPMENT AND MATERIALS

- Suitable solvents (CARE: MANY SOLVENTS ARE HAZARDOUS)
- Chromatography paper or a tlc plate
- Pencil
- Screw top jar

METHOD

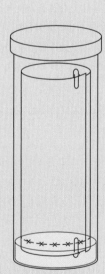

1 Dissolve the samples to be tested in a suitable solvent.

2 On a piece of chromatography paper or a tlc plate, draw a pencil line 2 cm from the bottom and another 1 cm from the top.

3 With the pencil, draw small crosses on the bottom line (as many as there are samples to be tested).

4 Put one drop of a sample on the paper or plate where there is a pencil cross. Repeat until all the samples have been spotted, each a different cross. Label the spots in pencil.

5 Pour the developing solvent into a screw top jar, to about 1 cm depth.

6 Then:
(a) either roll the paper into a cylinder, keeping it in place with two paper clips top and bottom, and stand it in the jar
(b) or stand the tlc plate in the jar (the plates are stiff enough to stand alone), leaning it against the side.

9 Put the top on the jar and leave until the developing solvent reaches the top pencil line.

9 Take the paper or plate out of the jar and leave it to dry.

9 When dry, lay the paper or plate flat and mark the centre of each spot with a pencil.

10 Measure the distances between the bottom line and the centre of each spot, and the distance from the bottom lie to the top line.

CALCULATIONS

Distance from bottom to top pencil lines = x cm
Distance from bottom pencil line to centre of spot = y cm
Retention factor $(R_f) = \dfrac{y}{x}$

CHEMICAL TESTS FOR IONS

SCOPE Ions in solution can be identified by their chemical reactions. In this standard procedure tests are given for:

carbonate, CO_3^{2-}	copper, Cu^{2+}
chloride, $Cl-$	iron(III), Fe^{3+}
sulfate, SO_4^{2-}	lead, Pb^{2+}

You will find tests for other ions in more specialised textbooks.

PRINCIPLE The ions are identified from their chemical reactions:

Carbonate ions react with hydrochloric acid to give a salt, water and carbon dioxide.

Chloride ions react with silver nitrate to give silver chloride.

Sulfate ions react with barium chloride to give barium sulfate.

Copper(II) ions react with dilute aqueous ammonia to give copper(II) hydroxide. This dissolves in more aqueous ammonia to give a complex ion.

Iron(III) ions react with sodium hydroxide to give iron(III) hydroxide. This dissolves in ammonium thiocyanate to give a complex ion.

Lead(II) ions react with sodium hydroxide to give lead(II) hydroxide which dissoves when more sodium hydroxide solution is added.

See pages 267–285 for more information.

EQUIPMENT AND MATERIALS
- Sample tubes
- Test tubes
- Dropping pipette
- Gas delivery tube
- Bunsen burner

REAGENTS

• 1 mol dm^{-3} nitric acid	CORROSIVE
• Concentrated nitric acid	CORROSIVE
• 1 mol dm^{-3} aqueous ammonia	CORROSIVE
• 1 mol dm^{-3} sodium hydroxide	CORROSIVE
• 1 mol dm^{-3} hydrochloric acid	LOW HAZARD
• Calcium hydroxide solution ('limewater')	LOW HAZARD
• 1 mol dm^{-3} silver nitrate solution	LOW HAZARD, STAINS SKIN AND CLOTHING A BLACK COLOUR
• 1 mol dm^{-3} barium chloride solution	LOW HAZARD
• 1 mol dm^{-3} ammonium thiocyanate solution	LOW HAZARD

HEALTH AND SAFETY   Wear protective clothing and eye protection.

A risk assessment must be carried out before work begins.

PROCEDURE   *Sample preparation*
Substances for analysis must be in solution (the test for carbonates is
an exception). If the substance is solid, try dissolving it in distilled water.
If it does not dissolve, try:

- 1 mol dm^{-3} nitric acid (warming if necessary)
- concentrated nitric acid (warming if necessary).

Once a suitable method has been found, take a small quantity of
solid (equivalent to 2–3 grains of rice) and prepare about 10 cm^3 of
stock solution.

Store the solution in a fully labelled sample tube. Also keep a
sample of the original substance.

The following tests for ions should be carried out on 1–2 cm^3
samples of the stock solution.

Carbonate, CO_3^{2-}
Add 1 mol dm^{-3} hydrochloric acid to the sample (which may be
either a solid or an aqueous solution).

Pass any gas given off through calcium hydroxide solution
('limewater').

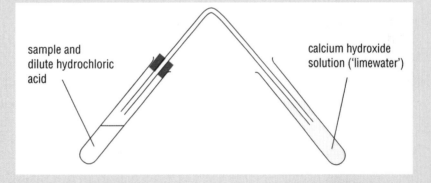

sample and
dilute hydrochloric
acid

calcium hydroxide
solution ('limewater')

Apparatus for testing that a gas
given off in a chemical reaction
is carbon dioxide

Positive result: Formation of a white precipitate (calcium
carbonate) confirms that the gas is carbon dioxide and, therefore,
indicates the presence of carbonate ions in the sample.

Chloride, Cl^-
Add an equal volume of 1 mol dm^{-3} nitric acid (unless nitric acid
was used to dissolve the substance) followed by a few drops of
0.1 mol dm^{-3} silver nitrate solution.

Positive result: Formation of a white precipitate (silver chloride)
indicates chloride ions in solution.

Standard Procedure

The formation of barium sulfate

Sulfate, SO_4^{2-}

Add an equal volume of 1 mol dm^{-3} hydrochloric acid followed by a few drops of 0.1 mol dm^{-3} barium chloride solution.

Positive result: A white precipitate of barium sulfate indicates sulfate ions in solution.

Copper, Cu^{2+}

Solutions of copper ions are usually green or blue. Add 1 mol dm^{-3} aqueous ammonia drop by drop.

Positive result: Formation of a blue precipitate that dissolves to give a deep blue solution when further ammonia is added indicates copper ions in solution.

Identifying copper ions in solution by adding dilute aqueous ammonia.

Iron(III), Fe^{3+}

Solutions of iron(III) ions are usually yellow. Add 1 mol dm^{-3} sodium hydroxide until the solution is alkaline.

Positive result: Formation of a rusty brown precipitate suggests the presence of iron(III) ions. To confirm, add 1 mol dm^{-3} hydrochloric acid until the precipitate just dissolves, followed by 2 drops 0.1 mol dm^{-3} ammonium thiocyanate solution. Formation of an intense red solution indicates that iron(III) ions are present in solution.

The intense red colour formed when iron(III) ions react with ammonium thiocyanate.

Lead, Pb^{2+}

Solutions of lead ions are usually colourless. Add 1 mol dm^{-3} sodium hydroxide until the solution is alkaline.

Positive result: Formation of a white precipitate that dissolves to give a colourless solution when further sodium hydroxide solution is added indicates lead ions are present in solution.

RESULTS   The observations from positive tests are given in the procedure.

CHEMICAL TESTS FOR GASES

SCOPE If a gas is given off at any stage, it can be identified as oxygen, carbon dioxide or hydrogen using the following suitable chemical tests.

PRINCIPLE Oxygen supports combustion (burning). A glowing splint will reignite if it is put into oxygen.

Carbon dioxide reacts with calcium hydroxide solution to give calcium carbonate.

Hydrogen explodes when ignite in the presence of oxygen.

EQUIPMENT AND MATERIALS
- Test tubes
- Wooden spill
- Dropping pipette
- Gas delivery tube
- Bunsen burner

REAGENTS
- Calcium hydroxide solution ('limewater')   HARMFUL

PROCEDURE *Oxygen*
Place a glowing splint into the gas.

Positive result: If the splint begins to burn, the gas is oxygen.

Testing for oxygen

Carbon dioxide
Pass the gas through calcium hydroxide solution ('limewater').

Positive result: Formation of a white precipitate (calcium carbonate) confirms that the gas is carbon dioxide.

Hydrogen
Hold a burning splint in the mouth of the test tube containing the gas.

Positive result: If there is a small explosion (a 'popping' sound), the gas is hydrogen.

RESULTS The observations from positive tests are given in the procedure.

FLAME TESTS

SCOPE Flame tests can be used to identify metal ions in compounds. Many metal ions, but not all, give coloured flames. The colours are used to identify the metal ion.

PRINCIPLE Heating metal ions in a hot flame causes electrons to jump to higher energy levels. As they fall back the energy is often given out as visible light.

EQUIPMENT AND MATERIALS
- Watch glass
- Nichrome wire
- Bunsen burner

REAGENTS
- Concentrated hydrochloric acid   **CORROSIVE**

SAFETY Wear protective clothing and eye protection.

A risk assessment must be carried out before work begins.

PROCEDURE 1 Place a small sample of the solid on a watch glass.

2 Using a dropping pipette, add a few drops of concentrated hydrochloric acid.

3 Moisten a piece of Nichrome wire with the mixture and hold it in a Bunsen flame. Note the colour.

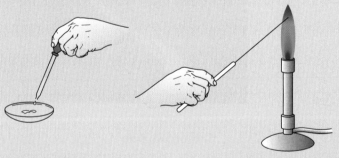

RESULTS

Colour of flame	Indicates the presence of:
Bright yellow	Sodium ions
Lilac (still visible through blue glass)	Potassium ions
Green	Copper ions
Brick red	Calcium ions

A positive test for calcium ions.

Questions

1   Describe how you would separate a mixture of dyes dissolved in water using paper chromatography.

2   What is the importance of the retention factor, R_f, in chromatography?

3   Why would you use standard reference materials when using chromatography to identify substances in a mixture?

4   Describe a chemical test to identify each of the following ions:
    (a) chloride
    (b) sulfate
    (c) carbonate
    (d) copper
    (e) lead

5   Describe how you would carry out a flame test. What colour flame would you expect to see for compounds of each of the following metals:
    (a) copper
    (b) sodium
    (c) potassium
    (d) calcium

Quantitative analysis

You need to:

- *prepare solutions of specified concentrations using the units: g dm^{-3} and mol dm^{-3}*

- *carry out titrations*

- *carry out calculations to determine the concentration of a substance in solution.*

Qualitative analysis is about what substances are in a mixture. Quantitative analysis is about how much of each substance is preset. Like qualitative analysis, quantitative tests involve chemical reactions.

Standard solutions

Standard solutions are the basis of quantitative analysis. You may have read elsewhere in this book about the British Pharmacopoeia. In this, standard solutions can be recognised by the use of the letters *VS* after the solution. This means 'volumetric standard'.

Standard solutions are solutions where the concentrations are known accurately. In contrast, concentrations of reagent solutions only need to be approximate. Standard solutions are usually made up in smaller quantities than reagents solutions and only when needed. Their concentrations are given as:

g dm^{-3}   the quantity of solute (grams) in 1 dm^3 of solution (<u>not</u> water). For example, 1.70 g dm^{-3} silver nitrate solution means there is 1.70 g of silver nitrate, $AgNO_3$, in 1 dm^3 of solution.

mol dm^{-3}   the amount of solute (mol) in 1 dm^3 of solution (<u>not</u> water). For example, 0.200 mol dm^{-3} sulfuric acid means there is 0.200 moles of H_2SO_4 in 1 dm^3 of solution.

It is much more common to use the units mol dm^{-3}.

REMEMBER

You need to be more accurate when making standard solutions and also use substances of higher purity. Always use distilled water.

REMEMBER

You will often come across the expression 'weigh out accurately about'. This may sound confusing! However, 'weigh out accurately about 5 g of sodium chloride' means that you should accurately weigh between 4.95 g and 5.05 g of sodium chloride. It doesn't matter if the mass is not exactly 5.00 g, but you do need to know the exact mass used.

technique

PREPARING A STANDARD SOLUTION USING WEIGHING BY DIFFERENCE

USE This technique can be used to prepare standard solutions for quantitative analysis. It's the most commonly used technique. However, it cannot be used to make a standard of solution of a specified concentration.

EQUIPMENT AND MATERIALS
- Top pan balance (able to weigh to 0.001 g if possible)
- Small beaker
- Volumetric flasks (100 cm^3, 250 cm^3)
- Pipettes (10 cm^3, 20 cm^3, 25 cm^3, 50 cm^3)
- Safety pipette filler
- Solid substance for making standard solution
- Distilled water

METHOD
1. Weigh a small beaker.
2. Add approximately the mass of solid that's needed.
3. Weigh the beaker and the solid, m_1.
4. Tip the solid into the funnel and weigh the beaker again, m_2. There will be some small quantity of material left in the weighing vessel but this doesn't matter. You know how much solid is in the funnel and this is what will be used to make up your solution.

technique

5 Wash the funnel into the flask.

6 Add distilled water until the flask is about three-quarters full.

7 Swirl the contents and check that the solid has dissolved.

8 Add more water to take the solution up to the graduation mark on the flask. You can use a teat pipette to do this.

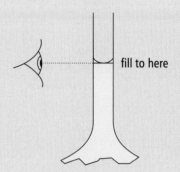

fill to here

9 Place the flask on a level surface and view the graduation mark and bottom of the meniscus horizontally.

10 Shake the solution before using it. Keep your thumb over the stopper while you shake the solution.

Make sure your eye is level with the graduation mark.

NOTE For solids that are difficult to dissolve the weighed quantity can be dissolved in distilled water in a beaker and warmed if necessary. After cooling, the solution is poured into the volumetric flask (using a funnel) and anything left in the beaker is washed in with distilled water.

CALCULATIONS The concentration of the solution in g dm^{-3} may be calculated from the formula

$$c = \frac{(m_1 - m_2) \times 1000}{V} \text{ g dm}^{-3}$$

where c = concentration of the solution, g dm^{-3}
m_1 = mass of beaker + solid to be weighed out, g
m_2 = mass of beaker + any remaining solid, g
V = volume of volumetric flask used

To calculate the concentration of the solution in mol dm^{-3}, divide by the relative formula mass of the solid, M.

$$\text{concentration} = \frac{c}{M} \text{ mol dm}^{-3}$$

WORKED EXAMPLE   *Preparing a standard solution of sodium chloride*
Mass of beaker + sodium chloride, m_1 = 55.24 g
Mass of beaker + any remaining sodium chloride, m_2 = 51.82 g
Made up with distilled water in a 250 cm^3 (V) volumetric flask
The concentration of the solution in g dm^{-3}

$$= \frac{(m_1 - m_2) \times 1000}{V} \text{ g dm}^{-3}$$

$$= \frac{(55.24 - 51.82) \times 1000}{250} \text{ g dm}^{-3}$$

$$= 13.28 \text{ g dm}^{-3}$$

The relative formula mass of sodium chloride = 58.5

Therefore the concentration = $\frac{13.28}{58.5}$ = 0.227 mol dm^{-3}

technique

PREPARING A STANDARD SOLUTION USING DIRECT WEIGHING

USE This technique can be used to prepare standard solutions for quantitative analysis. It is used to make standard solutions where the concentration has been specified.

EQUIPMENT AND MATERIALS

- Top pan balance (able to weigh to 0.001 g if possible)
- Small beaker
- Volumetric flasks (100 cm³, 250 cm³)
- Pipettes (10 cm³, 20 cm³, 25 cm³, 50 cm³)
- Safety pipette filler
- Solid substance for making standard solution
- Distilled water

METHOD

1 Place a short stem funnel in the neck of the volumetric flask.

2 Weigh the substance in a small beaker and tip it into the funnel.

3 Using a wash bottle containing distilled water wash the funnel/weighing boat into the volumetric flask. This makes sure all the solid goes into the volumetric flask. Add distilled water until the flask is about three-quarters full.

4 Swirl the contents and check that the solid has dissolved.

5 Add more water to take the solution up to the graduation mark on the flask. You can use a teat pipette to do this.

6 Place the flask on a level surface and view the graduation mark and bottom of the meniscus horizontally.

7 Shake the solution before using it. Keep your thumb over the stopper while you shake the solution.

CALCULATIONS The concentration of the solution in g dm⁻³ may be calculated from the formula

$$c = \frac{(m_1 - m_2)}{V} \times 1000 \text{ g dm}^{-3}$$

where c = concentration of the solution, g dm⁻³
m_1 = mass of beaker, g
m_2 = mass of beaker + solid, g
V = volume of volumetric flask used

To calculate the concentration of the solution in mol dm⁻³, divide by the relative formula mass of the solid, M.

$$= \frac{c}{M} \text{ mol dm}^{-3}$$

Worked example

Preparing a standard solution of silver nitrate
Mass of beaker, m_1 = 60.44 g
Mass of beaker + silver nitrate, m_2 = 62.14 g
Made up with distilled water in a 100 cm³ (V) volumetric flask
The concentration of the solution in g dm⁻³

$$= \frac{(m_1 - m_2) \times 1000}{V} \text{ g dm}^{-3}$$

$$= \frac{(62.14 - 60.44) \times 1000}{100} \text{ g dm}^{-3}$$

$$= 17.0 \text{ g dm}^{-3}$$

The relative formula mass of silver nitrate = 170
Therefore the concentration $= \dfrac{17.0}{170} = 0.10$ mol dm⁻³

PREPARING A STANDARD SOLUTION FROM A SOLUTION OF KNOWN CONCENTRATION

USE   This technique can be used to prepare standard solutions for quantitative analysis. It is useful for substances that are impossible or very difficult to obtain as pure, dry solids. Examples are hydrochloric acid, sulfuric acid and sodium hydroxide.

EQUIPMENT AND MATERIALS

- Beaker
- Volumetric flasks (100 cm³, 250 cm³)
- Pipettes (10 cm³, 20 cm³, 25 cm³, 50 cm³)
- Safety pipette filler
- Solution of known concentration to be diluted
- Distilled water

Method

1 Rinse a beaker with the solution to be diluted. Then pour in sufficient for your needs.

2 Use a pipette and safety pipette filler to transfer the volume needed into a volumetric flask.

3 Add distilled water until the flask is about three-quarters full.

4 Swirl the contents.

5 Add more water to take the solution up to the graduation mark on the flask.

6 Place the flask on a level surface and view the graduation mark and bottom of the meniscus horizontally.

7 Shake the solution before using it. Keep your thumb over the stopper while you shake the solution.

technique

technique

technique

CALCULATIONS

The following formula may be used:

$$V_s = V_f \times \frac{c_f}{c_s}$$

where

Vs = volume of solution to be diluted
V_f = final volume of diluted solution
c_f = concentration of diluted solution
c_s = concentration of solution being diluted

WORKED EXAMPLE

You are given a bottle containing 1 mol dm^{-3} hydrochloric acid. You need to prepare 100 cm^3 of 0.1 mol dm^{-3} hydrochloric acid.

Using

$$V_s = V_f \times \frac{c_f}{c_s}$$

where

Vs = volume of solution to be diluted
V_f = 100 cm^3
c_f = 0.1 mol dm^{-3}
c_s = 1 mol dm^{-3}

Therefore, $V_s = 100 \times \dfrac{0.1}{1} = 10$ cm^3

Volumetric analysis and titrations

Chemicals react with one another in definite proportions. This is where we get the idea of **balanced chemical equations**. These equations tell you not only what the reactants and products are but also how much is reacting and being produced. You will use them to calculate yields in Unit 3 (page 261).

It is really useful to be able to 'read' chemical equations. It's a bit like somebody reading out shorthand. So, for example, the balanced chemical equation for the reaction between sodium hydroxide and hydrochloric acid is:

$$NaOH\ (aq) + HCl\ (aq) \rightarrow NaCl\ (aq) + H_2O\ (l)$$

This is chemical shorthand for:

One mole of sodium hydroxide dissolved in water reacts with one mole of hydrogen chloride dissolved in water (i.e. hydrochloric acid) to give one mole of sodium chloride dissolved in water and one mole of water.

Here's another example:

$$AgNO_3\ (aq) + NaCl\ (aq) \rightarrow AgCl\ (s) + NaNO_3\ (aq)$$

This is chemical shorthand for:

One mole of silver nitrate dissolved in water reacts with one mole of sodium chloride dissolved in water to give one mole of solid silver chloride (i.e. a precipitate) and one mole of sodium nitrate dissolved in water.

As we know that one mole of a substance has the same mass as its relative formula mass (you can read about this on page 33), we can write these in terms of the masses of reactants and products.

For example, the relative formula masses of silver nitrate, sodium chloride, silver chloride and sodium nitrate are:

silver nitrate, $AgNO_3 = 108 + 14 + (16 \times 3) = 170$
sodium chloride, $NaCl = 23 + 35.5 = 58.8$
silver chloride, $AgCl = 108 + 35.5 = 143.5$
sodium nitrate, $NaNO_3 = 23 + 14 + (16 \times 3) = 85$.

And so we can say:

170 g silver nitrate dissolved in water reacts with 58.5 g sodium chloride dissolved in water to give 143.5 g solid silver chloride (i.e. a precipitate) and 85 g sodium nitrate dissolved in water.

Volumetric analysis makes use of reactions like these. Suppose you have:

- a solution of silver nitrate and you know its concentration (let's say it's 1.70 g dm^{-3}), i.e. a standard solution
- 20 cm^3 of sodium chloride solution whose concentration you want to find.

All you need to do is find out how much silver nitrate is needed to react completely with the sodium chloride. If 30 cm^3 of the silver nitrate solution is needed, the calculation goes as follows:

1   The concentration of the silver nitrate solution is 1.70 g dm^3, i.e. 1.70 g of silver nitrate in 1 dm^3 (1000 cm^3) of solution.

2   So in 1 cm^3 there is $\underline{1.70} = 0.0017$ g silver nitrate
    1000

3   And in 30 cm^3 there is $0.0017 \times 30 = 0.051$ g silver nitrate

4   From the chemical equation we know that 170 g silver nitrate react with 58.5 g sodium chloride.

5   So 1 g of silver nitrate reacts with $\underline{58.5} = 0.344$ g sodium chloride.
    170

6   And 0.051 g of silver nitrate reacts with $0.344 \times 0.051 = 0.0175$ g sodium chloride.

7   Therefore, in the 20 cm^3 of sodium chloride solution whose concentration you want to find, there is 0.0175 g sodium chloride.

8   Therefore in 1 dm^3 (1000 cm^3) there is $\underline{0.0175} \times 1000 = 0.583$ g sodium chloride
    30

9   So the concentration of the sodium chloride solution is 0.583 g dm^{-3}

The trick is to be able to know when the two solutions have just reacted completely.

What usually happens is that a **titration** is carried out. This means that the standard solution is added to the one of unknown concentration until the **end-point** is reached, i.e. the reaction has just gone to completion. Often an **indicator** is used to show the end-point.

Acid–base titrations are one important example. We will use this to illustrate more about the technique of volumetric analysis and titrations.

About acids

Acids dissolve in water to give a solution of **hydrogen ions**, H$^+$(aq). The other ions present depend on the acid. For example, hydrochloric acid contains hydrogen ions, H$^+$(aq), and chloride ions, Cl$^-$(aq):

$$HCl(g) + aq \rightarrow H^+(aq) + Cl^-(aq)$$

In equations like this, 'aq' is used to represent an excess of water.

Name	Formula	Name of salt
Mineral acids		
Hydrochloric acid	HCl	chloride
Nitric acid	HNO$_3$	nitrate
Sulfuric acid	H$_2$SO$_4$	sulfate
Phosphoric acid	H$_3$PO$_4$	phosphate
Carboxylic acids		
Methanoic acid	HCOOH	methanoate
Ethanoic acid	CH$_3$COOH	ethanoate
Lactic acid	CH$_3$CH(OH)COOH	lactate
Oxalic acid	(COOH)$_2$	oxalate
Citric acid	CH$_2$COOH.COH(COOH).CH$_2$COOH	citrate

Don't worry about the chemical formulae for carboxylic acids. You will find out much more about them if you study biology and chemistry further.

About bases

A **base** is a compound that neutralises an acid to give a salt and water only. Bases that dissolve in water are called **alkalis**. Metal oxides and hydroxides are bases.

Alkali	Ions in solution	
Sodium hydroxide, NaOH(aq)	Na$^+$ (aq)	OH$^-$ (aq)
Potassium hydroxide, KOH(aq)	K$^+$ (aq)	OH$^-$ (aq)
Calcium hydroxide, Ca(OH)$_2$(aq)	Ca^{2+} (aq)	OH$^-$ (aq)
Ammonia, NH$_3$(aq)	NH$_4^+$ (aq)	OH$^-$ (aq)

Alkalis dissolve in water to give **hydroxide ions**, $OH^-(aq)$. The other ions depend on the alkali. For example, sodium hydroxide dissolves in water to give sodium ions, $Na^+(aq)$, and hydroxide ions, $OH^-(aq)$:

$$NaOH(s) + aq \rightarrow Na^+(aq) + OH^-(aq)$$

Indicators

You have probably seen before that acids and alkalis change the colour of an acid–base indicator differently. This can be used to decide if a solution is acid or alkaline.

Methyl red is a typical acid–base indicator. It's red in acids and yellow in alkalis.

Acid–base titrations

Putting all the ideas you have just read about together, we can begin to see how these reactions can be used in quantitative analysis.

CARRYING OUT AN ACID–BASE TITRATION

USE   This technique can be used for any acid–base titration. The technique is much the same for other types of titration.

METHOD   *Sample preparation*

1   Transfer a measured quantity of substance to a volumetric flask.
   - For a *solid*: weigh the required quantity of sample in a weighing bottle. Use a glass funnel to transfer the powdered solid into a volumetric flask. Ensure all the solid has been transferred by using a squeezy bottle containing distilled water to wash out the weighing bottle and funnel. Make sure the solid has dissolved before making the solution up to the volume of the volumetric flask with distilled water.
   - For a *liquid*: use a pipette to measure a precise volume of the liquid that needs to be diluted (remember to use a pipette safety filler). The pipette should be held vertically and the bottom of the meniscus should be level with the graduations used.

technique

technique

2 Make the solution up to the required volume with distilled water. The bottom of the meniscus must be level with the graduation mark on the flask. The final few drops must be added carefully. A dropping pipette provides a good way of doing this.

Preparing the burette

1 Clamp the burette and make sure it's vertical.

2 Use a funnel to fill it with the standard solution, but make sure that you remove the funnel before you start the titration.

3 Rinse the burette with distilled water. Let it drain thoroughly and then rinse three times with the standard solution (about 10 cm^3 each time).

4 Fill the burette until it's just above the 0.00 cm^3 graduation. Carefully run out the solution until the bottom of the meniscus is just level with the 0.00 cm^3 graduation.

5 Check for air bubbles between the tap and the tip of the burette after you have filled the burette for the first time.

6 Make sure you line up your eye with the bottom of the meniscus and take burette readings. A white card held behind the burette helps you to see the meniscus.

Carrying out a titration

1 Use a pipette to transfer a known volume of the solution to be analysed into a conical flask. Remember:
   - use a pipette safety filler
   - slightly overfill the pipette, remove from the solution and wipe the outside of the pipette with a tissue

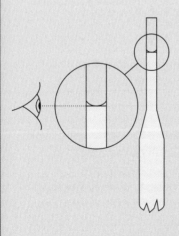

   - allow the liquid to drain until the bottom of the meniscus is touching the calibration line on the pipette, then touch the pipette on a clean glass surface; the bottom of the meniscus must be level with the graduation mark on the pipette, as shown
   - now allow the liquid to run freely into the conical flask; it's often easier to do this if you remove the pipette filler from the pipette first
   - when all the solution has been drained, touch the pipette tip on the inside of the conical flask (do not blow out any remaining solution).

2 Add 2–3 drops of a suitable acid-alkali indicator.

3 Titrate with a standard acid (if the sample is an alkali) or a standard alkali (if the sample is an acid) from a burette.

4 The end-point is when the solution permanently changes colour. Stand the conical flask on a white tile so that you can see this clearly.

technique

5　Carry out a rough titration (do not worry if you slightly overshoot the end-point).

6　Repeat with another volume measured by pipette (the same conical flask can be used provided it has been thoroughly rinsed with distilled water).

7　Add the acid or alkali from the burette 1 cm^3 at a time until 1–2 cm^3 from the approximate end point.

8　The solution in the burette should then be added drop by drop, mixing the contents of the flask thoroughly by swirling it between additions.

9　There is often a drop at the end of the burette at the completion of the titration. Touch the end of the burette with the inside of the neck of the flask to collect the drop and wash the drop down into the flask using distilled/distilled water from a wash bottle.

RESULTS　Record your results in a table like this (of course, you may need to only carry out three titrations).

Titration of . . . . with . . . .

Titration:	1	2	3	4
1st burette reading/cm^3				
2nd burette reading/cm^3				
Difference/cm^3				

(rough)

CALCULATIONS　In a standard procedure you will usually be given a formula to calculate the result.

WORKED EXAMPLE　Titration of 20.0 cm^3 portions of sodium hydroxide solution with 0.100 mol dm-3 hydrochloric acid

Titration:	1	2	3
1st burette reading	1.0	22.1	0.00
2nd burette reading	22.2	43.0	20.7
Difference	21.2	20.9	20.7

(rough)

Average (of 2 and 3) titration = $\dfrac{20.9 + 20.7}{2}$ = 20.8 cm^3

Let's look again at the reaction between sodium hydroxide and hydrochloric acid:

$NaOH \, (aq) + HCl \, (aq) \rightarrow NaCl \, (aq) + H_2O \, (l)$

If the hydrochloric acid has been standardised, i.e. its concentration is known accurately, we can use it to determine the concentration of a sodium hydroxide solution. It's impossible to 'see' the end-point – the solution is colourless to begin with and is still colourless after the reaction. However, we can use an acid–base indicator to tell us.

Extension Work

As you have read, most standard procedures give a formula for you to use to calculate the result from a titration. However, you may be interested to find out where these come from.

From the balanced chemical equation for the reaction you can identify the number of moles of acid and alkali involved:

number of moles of acid = n_a
number of moles of alkali = n_b

Suppose that the following data are obtained from a titration:

V_a cm³ of m_a mol dm⁻³ *acid* reacts with V_b cm³ of m_b mol dm⁻³ *alkali*

You will know three of these four values. Your aim will be to work out the concentration of either the acid or the alkali, whichever is the unknown.

The formula you need for your calculations is:

$$\frac{m_a V_a}{n_a} = \frac{m_b V_b}{n_b}$$

1 mole of acid reacts with 1 mole of alkali

For example, 20.0 cm³ of 1 mol dm⁻³ hydrochloric acid reacted with 25.6 cm³ of 0.100 mol dm⁻³ sodium hydroxide.

Equation for the reaction:

$$HCl(aq) \quad + \quad NaOH(aq) \quad \rightarrow \quad NaCl(aq) \quad + \quad H_2O(l)$$

Therefore, 1 mole of hydrochloric acid reacts with 1 mole of sodium hydroxide.

Using

$$\frac{m_a V_a}{n_a} = \frac{m_b V_b}{n_b}$$

$n_a = 1$
$n_b = 1$
$V_a = 20.0$ cm³
$V_b = 25.6$ cm³
$m_b = 0.100$ mol dm⁻³

Substituting in the formula:

$$\frac{m_a \times 20.0}{1} = \frac{0.100 \times 25.6}{1}$$

Therefore, $m_a = 0.128$ mol dm⁻³
Concentration of hydrochloric acid is 0.128 mol dm⁻³

1 mole of acid reacts with 2 moles of alkali

For example, 20.0 cm³ of m_a mol dm⁻³ sulfuric acid reacted with 24.2 cm³ of 0.200 mol dm⁻³ sodium hydroxide.

Equation for the reaction:

$$H_2SO_4\,(aq) \quad + \quad 2NaOH(aq) \quad \rightarrow \quad Na_2SO_4(aq) \quad + \quad 2H_2O(l)$$

Therefore, 1 mole of sulfuric acid reacts with 2 moles of sodium hydroxide.

Using

$$\frac{m_a V_a}{n_a} \quad = \quad \frac{m_b V_b}{n_b}$$

$n_a = 1$
$n_b = 2$
$V_a = 20.0$ cm³
$V_b = 24.2$ cm³
$m_b = 0.200$ mol dm⁻³

Substituting in the formula:

$$\frac{m_a \times 20.0}{1} \quad = \quad \frac{0.200 \times 24.2}{1}$$

Therefore, $m_a = 0.121$ mol dm⁻³
Concentration of sulfuric acid is 0.121 mol dm⁻³

2 moles of acid reacts with 1 mole of alkali

For example, 20.0 cm³ of 1 mol dm⁻³ nitric acid reacted with 12.8 cm³ of 0.150 mol dm⁻³ calcium hydroxide.

Equation for the reaction:

$$2HNO_3(aq) \quad + \quad Ca(OH)_2(aq) \quad \rightarrow \quad Ca(NO_3)_2(aq) \quad + \quad 2H_2O(l)$$

Therefore, 2 moles of nitric acid reacts with 1 mole of calcium hydroxide.

Using

$$\frac{m_a V_a}{n_a} \quad = \quad \frac{m_b V_b}{n_b}$$

$n_a = 2$
$n_b = 1$
$V_a = 20.0$ cm³
$V_b = 12.8$ cm³
$m_b = 0.150$ mol dm⁻³

Extension Work

Substituting in the formula:

$$\frac{m_a \times 20.0}{1} = \frac{0.150 \times 18.8}{1}$$

Therefore, $m_a = 0.192$ mol dm^{-3}

Concentration of sulfuric acid is 0.192 mol dm^{-3}

Once you have found the concentration of an acid by titration against an alkali of known concentration, the quantity of acid present in the sample can be determined as follows:

Volume of sample containing the acid $= v$ cm^3

Concentration of acid $= m_a$ mol dm^{-3}

Relative formula mass of the acid $= M$

Then, mass of acid in v cm^3 of the sample $= v \times \dfrac{m_a}{1000} v M$ g

Don't forget that you may have diluted your sample of acid before analysis. You must take this into account.

Similarly for an alkali:

Volume of sample containing the alkali $= v$ cm^3

Concentration of alkali $= m_b$ mol dm^{-3}

Relative formula mass of the alkali $= M$

Then mass of alkali in v cm^3 of the sample $= v \times \dfrac{m_b}{1000} \times M$ g

Again, do not forget that you may have diluted your sample before analysis. You must take this into account.

?
Questions

1 Write word and balanced chemical equations for the following reactions:
   (a) hydrochloric acid and sodium hydroxide
   (b) nitric acid and sodium hydroxide
   (c) hydrochloric acid and calcium hydroxide
   (d) sulfuric acid and sodium hydroxide
   (e) sulfuric acid and ammonia.

2 Describe how you would make 1 dm^3 of a standard solution of 0.100 mol dm^{-3} hydrochloric acid starting with 2.000 mol dm^{-3} hydrochloric acid.

3 Describe how you would make 1 dm^3 of a standard solution of 0.200 mol dm^{-3} sodium chloride solution starting with pure sodium chloride.

?

4 Describe how you would determine the exact concentration of a solution of nitric acid that is about 0.5 mol dm^{-3}. You have a standard solution of sodium hydroxide (0.100 mol dm^{-3}) and the usual apparatus for a volumetric analysis.

5 Calculate the concentration of the acid in each of the following titrations:
   (a) 20.0 cm^3 of hydrochloric acid reacted with 25.0 cm^3 of 0.100 mol dm^{-3} sodium hydroxide solution
   (b) 25.0 cm^3 of ethanoic acid reacted with 22.5 cm^3 of 0.500 mol dm^{-3} potassium hydroxide solution
   (c) 20.0 cm^3 of sulfuric acid reacted with 30.4 cm^3 of 0.150 mol dm^{-3} sodium hydroxide solution.

6 Calculate the concentration of the alkali in each of the following titrations:
   (a) 20.0 cm^3 of sodium hydroxide solution reacted with 30.0 cm^3 of 0.500 mol dm^{-3} hydrochloric acid
   (b) 20.0 cm^3 of ammonia solution reacted with 26.8 cm^3 of 0.100 mol dm^{-3} hydrochloric acid
   (c) 25.0 cm^3 of potassium hydroxide solution reacted with 15.5 cm^3 of 0.200 mol dm^{-3} sulfuric acid.

1.7 Investigating materials

Electrical properties

You need to investigate how:
- *the nature, length and thickness of materials influence electrical resistance*
- *current varies with voltage in a range of devices.*

At the flick of a switch

It's almost impossible to imagine a world without electricity. Our homes and the places where we work are full of electrical gadgets and appliances. Examples include:
- heating and lighting
- domestic appliances such as cookers, washing machines, televisions, CD players

- security equipment such as fire alarms, sprinkler systems
- computers and control systems, both in the home and in industry
- medical equipment.

The list is never-ending.

Whether at home or at work, electrical appliances and gadgets have made life easier in many ways.

The design and construction of electrical and electronic devices, fittings and circuits requires knowledge of the electrical properties of materials. Many scientists use this knowledge in areas such as electrical engineering, telecommunications and computer technology.

Resisting the flow

Some materials conduct electricity. We call them conductors. Others don't. We call these insulators. However, it will probably come as no surprise to you that it isn't quite as simple as that! All materials conduct electricity to some extent. It's just that some are much better than others. And this is really important.

Different materials have different electrical resistance. This can be measured directly with a multimeter set on 'resistance'. The resistance of an object is a measure of the current that will flow when a certain voltage is put across it. It can also be calculated using the equation:

$$R = V/I$$

where R is the resistance in ohms (Ω), V is the voltage in volts (V) across the object and I is the current in amps (A).

Think about the electrical fittings you see every day, things like plugs, plug sockets and light sockets. They connect electrical appliances and gadgets to the mains electricity. They all have some parts that conduct electricity and other parts that do not. Materials that are electrically insulating have many uses.

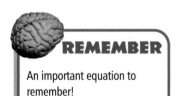

REMEMBER

An important equation to remember!

$R = V/I$

where
R is the resistance in ohms (Ω)
V is the voltage in volts (V)
I is the current in amps (A)

REMEMBER

Electrical conductors have low electrical resistance (high electrical conductivity)

Electrical insulators have high electrical resistance (low electrical conductivity)

Domestic electrical fittings use 230 V and currents up to 13 A. It's essential that the conducting parts like the wires be well insulated from each other. The fitting must also be insulated to prevent the user getting electric shocks. You could see which parts of each fitting are conductors and which are insulators by dismantling them and testing each component with a multimeter.

Determining resistance

You may need to determine the resistance of a material or of a component, such as a light bulb or an electric motor, in an electrical circuit. For convenience we shall simply call these 'objects'. You determine resistance directly with a multimeter or indirectly using a voltmeter and an ammeter.

Resistance of a material or component

SAFETY

ELECTRICAL HAZARD
Handling electrical equipment connected to a power supply is always hazardous. A risk assessment must be carried out before starting work.

REMEMBER

All metals are electrical conductors. Most other materials are insulators, though some are better than others.

ELECTRICAL RESISTANCE USING A MULTIMETER

USE   This is a very quick way to check if an object is an electrical conductor or insulator. It can also be used to measure electrical resistance.

EQUIPMENT AND MATERIALS
- Multimeter set on resistance
- Object to be tested

METHOD
1 Set the multimeter to *resistance*. The range will need adjusting depending on the sample being measured.
2 Check the contact resistance of the connecting wires by touching them together when they have been connected to the multimeter.
3 Place the connecting wires across the object and decide whether it is a conductor or insulator. If required, record the resistance.

technique

technique

ELECTRICAL RESISTANCE USING AMMETERS AND VOLTMETERS

USE

If a multimeter is not available, this technique can be used to calculate the electrical resistance of an object. The resistance of a sample depends on its size and shape. Short fat samples have lower resistance than long thin ones. If the resistances of two materials are being compared it's important to make sure each sample has the same size and shape, for example, wire of the same diameter.

EQUIPMENT AND MATERIALS

- Analogue ammeter (0–5 A)
- Analogue voltmeter (0–2 V)
- 1.5 V battery in holder
- Connecting wires
- Crocodile clips
- Sample to be tested

METHOD

1 Use a sample of the material in the form of a strip or wire.

2 Set up the circuit as shown.

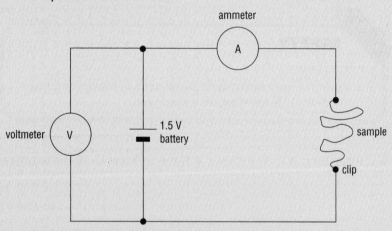

3 Record the ammeter and voltmeter readings.
Note: if the ammeter reading is very small, sue a more sensitive ammeter.

RESULTS AND CALCULATIONS

Use the formula $R = V/I$ to calculate the resistance
where V = voltage, V
I = current, A
R = resistance, Ω

WORKED EXAMPLE

Ammeter reading (current) = 0.48 A
Voltmeter reading (voltage) = 1.2 V
Resistance of sample = $\dfrac{1.2}{0.48}$ = 2.5 Ω

Resistance of a material: length and thickness

The resistance of a material depends on its length and thickness or diameter. You can use the techniques described above to investigate this.

Length

You can carry out an experiment to determine the resistance of different lengths of the same wire using the technique described above. A graph of *length of wire*/m (*x*-axis) against *resistance*/Ω (*y*-axis) is a straight line passing through the origin (0,0). This shows that resistance, *R*, is proportional to length, *l*. We can write this in the form of an equation:

$$R \propto l$$

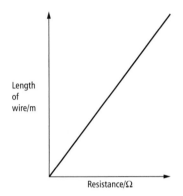

Instead of wire you could use strips or tubes.

Diameter

You can carry out an experiment to determine the resistance of different thicknesses of the same wire using the technique described above. You can measure the diameter of the wire and calculate its area. A graph of *area of wire*/m² (*x*-axis) against *resistance*/Ω (*y*-axis) is a curve. This shows that resistance, *R*, is inversely proportional to area, *A*. We can write this in the form of an equation:

$$R \propto \frac{1}{A}$$

Of course, you don't need to use wire. A bar or strip could be used. In this case you would measure the lengths of its sides and calculate the area.

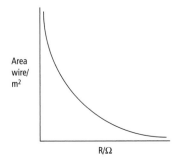

REMEMBER

If you want to compare the resistance of different materials you must use a fair test. This means writing a standard procedure that describes exactly what size and shape samples must be used.

This graph shows how the electrical resistance of a wire varies with length.
- You can see that the resistance is greater for longer wires.
- The straight line tells you that resistance is proportional to length. So, for example, if you double the length of the wire the resistance also doubles.

REMEMBER

The resistance of a sample is:
- greater the longer the sample
- smaller the thicker the sample.

This graph shows how the electrical resistance of a wire varies with diameter. You can see that the resistance is less for thicker wires. The curve tells you that resistance is inversely proportional to area.

Electrical resistivity

You have seen that resistance depends on size and shape. But can we give a value of resistance that doesn't depend on size and shape? The answer is 'yes' and the name we give it is **electrical resistivity**. The idea is straightforward. We know that resistance is proportional to length and inversely proportional to area:

$$R \propto l \quad \text{and} \quad R \propto \frac{1}{A}$$

Bringing these together, we can write the equation:

$$R \propto \frac{l}{A}$$

A graph of R against l/A is a straight line passing through the origin. The gradient tells you the electrical resistivity of the material being tested.

Questions

1   Different jobs need different electrical cables. If you look at the electrical wiring available in a DIY store you will see that it comes in many sizes and types. Try to find out what each type is used for and what the differences between them are.

2   Describe how you could determine whether a material conducted electricity or was an insulator.

3   Copy and complete the following table:

Ammeter reading/amps	Voltmeter/volts	Resistance/ohms
10	1.5	
6		10
	4.5	0.01
0.001	1.5	
5	12	

4   Draw a circuit diagram that may be used to investigate how the resistance of a light bulb changes as the current through it increases. Draw a graph to show how the resistance of the bulb changes as the current through it increases.

Other physical properties

You need to compare:

- *the thermal conductivities of a range of materials*
- *the densities of a range of materials*
- *the strengths of materials of different size, shape and composition.*

As well as electrical properties . . .

Materials are used in buildings, bridges, clothing, cars, boats, aircraft, sports equipment and for many other things. Electrical properties are not the only properties a scientist needs to think about. Engineers and technologists must know about other physical properties. For example, if you were asked to select materials to build a house, some of the material properties you would consider would be thermal conductivity, density and strength.

Choosing the most appropriate material for a design or modifying a design to allow for the properties of a material is vital. Engineers, materials scientists and technologists need to predict how the material will behave in different conditions, how long its 'working life' might be, what tools are required to work it and so on.

You can find out about the properties of materials, their structures and uses on pages 195–210.

Thermal conduction

Heat flows. Things cool down and something else warms up. A fridge cools food inside it and heats the air around it (try feeling behind a fridge). Technologists and engineers often want to control how quickly heat flows. We want to reduce heat losses from our houses and so we insulate them. Outside on a cold winter's day we usually try to reduce our heat loss by wearing the appropriate clothing. Thermal conductance is a measure of how fast heat energy is transferred through a material.

REMEMBER

Conductance or conductivity?

Thermal conduction depends on the size and shape of the sample. Thermal conductivity does not. It's the same reason as electrical resistance and electrical resistivity (see page 114).

technique

COMPARING THERMAL CONDUCTIVITIES OF SOLIDS

USE This technique may be used to compare the thermal conductivity of flat sheets of material. It has limited accuracy, but it's a useful way of comparing materials.

EQUIPMENT AND MATERIALS
- Suitably sized beaker (it depends on the size of the samples under test)
- -10 – 110 °C mercury thermometer
- Electronic thermometer
- Stopclock or stopwatch
- Sample to be tested (it must be flat)

SAFETY Care when using boiling water. Wear safety glasses.
A **risk assessment** must be carried out before you start work.

METHOD 1 Set up the apparatus as shown in the diagram.

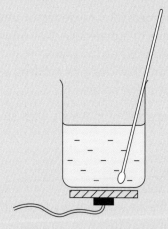

2 Stand the beaker on the test piece and pour about 200 cm³ of boiling water into it.

3 When the mercury thermometer reads 85 °C start the stopclock. Record the temperature every 30 s for five minutes of the bottom of the test piece and the water in the beaker.

RESULTS Record the results in a table like this:

Time/s	Mercury thermometer reading/°C	Digital thermometer reading/°C
0	85	
30		
etc.		

Draw two graphs:
(a) *Time/s* against *Mercury thermometer reading/°C*
(b) *Time/s* against *Electronic thermometer reading/°C*.

The techniques described to compare thermal conductivities are not very accurate. Can you explain why and suggest how they could be made more accurate?

Using the technique described, a material with high thermal conductivity will show a rapid change of temperature. You could investigate different types of plastics, metals and ceramics, each about 2 mm thick. Alternatively you might use some objects that are found in kitchens, such as plates, saucepans and storage containers. If you try it, put the three types of materials (plastic, metal and ceramic) in order of increasing thermal conductivity. Try to find the thermal conductivities of the materials you used. Compare your own findings with the data you find from other sources.

COMPARING THERMAL CONDUCTIVITIES OF SOLIDS: AN ALTERNATIVE TECHNIQUE

technique

USE This technique may also be used to compare the thermal conductivity of flat sheets of material. Again, it has limited accuracy, but is a useful way to compare materials.

EQUIPMENT AND MATERIALS
- 15 ohm resistor rated at 11 watts
- Electronic thermometer
- Connecting leads
- 12 V d.c. supply
- 1 A full-scale ammeter
- Six square sheets of the material to be tested

SAFETY **ELECTRICAL HAZARD**
A **risk assessment** must be carried out before you start work.

METHOD
1 Make a small box out of six identical square sheets of the material. It must be large enough to fit a 15 Ω resistor rated at 11 W and have a hole for the probe of an electronic thermometer.

2 Suspend the box in mid-air by the leads that deliver current to the resistor.

3 Connect the circuit.

4 Record the initial temperature of the air in the box.

5 Switch on the d.c. supply. The ammeter should read about 0.8 A.

6 Wait until the temperature inside the box reaches a steady value. This may take some time.

technique

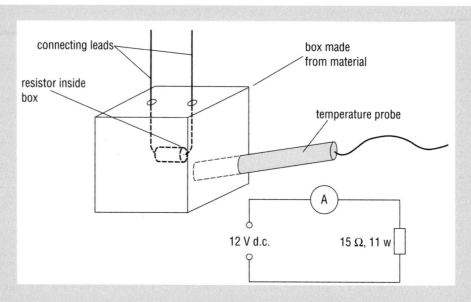

RESISTER For a box made of a higher thermal conductivity material, the steady temperature will be lower than one with a lower thermal conductivity. In other words, the lower the thermal conductivity of a material, the better thermal insulator it is.

RESULTS

Determining density

Engineers and designers need to know about the densities of materials. An aircraft designer can estimate the mass of an aircraft if the densities of the materials used to build it are known. A bridge must support its own weight as well as that of the traffic going over it. This can be calculated if the densities of the construction materials are known.

REMEMBER

The unit of density is kg m^{-3}. However, g cm^{-3} is often used. To convert

- kg m^{-3} to g cm^{-3} divide by 1000

Example: the density of aluminium is 2700 kg m^{-3} or 2.7 g cm^{-3}

- g cm^{-3} to kg m^{-3} multiply by 1000

Example: the density of low-density poly(ethene) is 0.92 g cm^{-3} or 920 kg m^{3}

technique

CALCULATING THE DENSITY OF UNIFORM OBJECTS

USE This technique can be used to determine the density of uniform objects, in other words ones with a regular shape whose dimensions can be measured.

EQUIPMENT AND MATERIALS

- Metre rule
- Electronic balance
- Blocks and rods of glass, Perspex, steel, aluminium and copper

SAFETY Care if you are handling heavy objects.
A **risk assessment** must be carried out before starting work.

METHOD 1 Make the necessary measurements to calculate its volume. For example, the length of the sides of a block and the length and diameter of a cylinder. Remember that the measurements must be in metres (m). If you take measurements in centimetres (cm) you will need to divide by 100 to convert to metres.

2 Measure the mass of the sample in kilograms (kg).

RESULTS AND CALCULATIONS Determine the volume of the sample using the appropriate formula (see page 39).

Calculate the density of the sample using the formula:

$$\text{density} = \frac{\text{mass}}{\text{volume}}$$

The units of density are kilograms per cubic metre ($kg\ m^{-3}$). Sometimes grams per cubic centimetre ($g\ cm^{-3}$) is used.

WORKED EXAMPLES (a) Aluminium block

Dimensions: 5 m by 2 m by 1 m
Therefore, volume = $5 \times 2 \times 1 = 10\ m^3$
Mass = 27,000 kg
Density = $\frac{27,000}{10}$ = 2700 kg dm^{-3}

(b) High density poly(ethene) rod

Dimensions: length = 28 cm (0.28 m); diameter = 2 cm (0.02 m)
Therefore, radius = 0.01 m and cross-sectional area = $\pi\ (0.01)^2$
volume = $0.28 \times \frac{22}{7} \times (0.01)^2 = 0.000088\ m^3$
Mass = 8.45 g = 0.0845 kg
Density = $\frac{0.0845}{0.000088}$ = 960 kg m^{-3}

technique

CALCULATING THE DENSITY OF IRREGULAR OBJECTS

USE

This technique can be used to determine the density of irregular objects, in other words ones with an irregular shape whose dimensions cannot be measured. Pebbles, coins, screws and bolts are all examples. It cannot be used for materials that have a density less than that of water. They would not sink and, therefore, would not displace their own volume of water.

EQUIPMENT AND MATERIALS

- Displacement can
- Measuring cylinder
- Object to be measured

SAFETY

Care if you are handling heavy objects.
A **risk assessment** must be carried out before starting work.

METHOD

1. Fill the displacement can until the water is just level with the overflow spout.

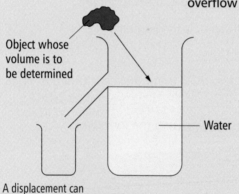

Object whose volume is to be determined

Water

A displacement can

2. Weigh the object being investigated and carefully place it into the displacement can. It is sometimes easier to tie a thin piece of thread to the object and use this to lower it into the can.

3. Collect the displaced water in a measuring cylinder and measure its volume.

RESULTS AND CALCULATIONS

The volume of the displaced water equals the volume of the sample.

Calculate the density of the sample using the formula:

$$density = \frac{mass\ of\ object}{volume\ of\ water\ displaced}$$

The units of density are kilograms per cubic metre ($kg\ m^{-3}$). Sometimes grams per cubic centimetre ($g\ cm^{-3}$) is used.

WORKED EXAMPLE

A large steel bolt with a mass of 79 g displaces 10 cm^3 of water.

Therefore density of steel $= \frac{79}{10} = 7.9\ g\ cm^{-3}$

To convert to $kg\ m^{-3}$, multiply by 1000

Therefore density of steel $= 7900\ kg\ m^{-3}$

Strength of materials

There are two types of strength you should know about: compressive strength and tensile strength. **Compressive strength** tells you how much a material can be **squashed** before it breaks. **Tensile strength** tells you how much a material can be **stretched** before it breaks. They are not the same. For example, a sheet of glass can support a huge weight before it cracks, provided the weight is placed carefully and not dropped. On the other hand a sheet of glass breaks quite easily if you try to bend it.

You will only compare the tensile strengths of materials in the laboratory. There are two techniques you can use.

COMPARING TENSILE STRENGTHS

USE	This technique may be used to compare the tensile strength of wires and thin strips of material.
EQUIPMENT AND MATERIALS	• Two identical strips or wires of the material to be tested • Laboratory stand and clamp • Wooden clamps • Wooden dowel • Mass holder and selection of weights • Floor or bench protecting mat/box of crumpled paper for weights to fall into.
SAFETY	Care if you are handling heavy weights. The sample may snap suddenly – wear safety glasses. A **risk assessment** must be carried out before starting work.
PROCEDURE	1 Clamp the ends each strip or wire so that it forms a loop, as shown in the diagram.

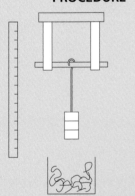

2 Slide a wooden dowel into the lower loops and hang a mass holder from it.

3 Add weights to the mass holder until the strips or wires break. Record the total mass needed to break the sample (mass holder plus weights added).

RESULTS	Calculate the force required to break the material: • total mass needed to break the sample = m kg (**not** in g) • multiply the total mass by 9.8 to give the force in newtons (N).
WORKED EXAMPLE	A sample of paper broke when a mass of 1150 g was hung from it. Total mass needed to break the paper = 1.15 kg Force needed = $1.15 \times 9.8 = 11.27$ N

technique

technique

COMPARING TENSILE STRENGTHS: AN ALTERNATIVE TECHNIQUE

USE This technique may be used to compare the tensile strength of threads, filaments and wires of material.

EQUIPMENT AND MATERIALS

- A length of wire of the material to be tested
- Laboratory stand and clamp
- Mass holder and selection of weights
- Floor or bench protecting mat/box of crumpled paper for weights to fall into.

Safety Care if you are handling heavy weights. The sample may snap suddenly – wear safety glasses.
A **risk assessment** must be carried out before starting work.

PROCEDURE 1 Clamp the end of the wire sample, as shown in the diagram.

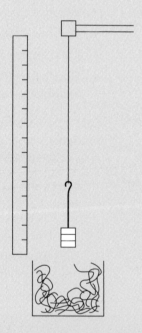

2 Attach a mass hanger to the other end of the wire.

3 Add weights to the mass holder until the wire breaks. Record the total mass needed to break the sample (mass holder plus weights added).

RESULTS Calculate the force required to break the material:

- total mass needed to break the sample = m kg (**not** in g)
- multiply the total mass by 9.8 to give the force in newtons (N).

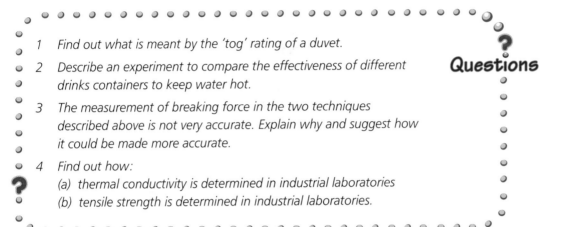

1   Find out what is meant by the 'tog' rating of a duvet.

2   Describe an experiment to compare the effectiveness of different drinks containers to keep water hot.

3   The measurement of breaking force in the two techniques described above is not very accurate. Explain why and suggest how it could be made more accurate.

4   Find out how:
    (a) thermal conductivity is determined in industrial laboratories
    (b) tensile strength is determined in industrial laboratories.

Scienc

This unit will help you to:

Understand how science is applied to the needs of society. Scientists work to improve the quality of our lives – from health to creature comforts. They harness the resources of the Earth, both living and non-living, and obtain useful products from them. To do this effectively they need to understand the world we live in – why things are the way they are.

This knowledge helps scientists, working with others, to:

- obtain products such as medicines, fibres and dyes from living organisms

- take care of plants, animals and ourselves

- obtain raw materials from the ground and convert them into useful chemicals

- produce products that are carefully formulated mixtures of chemicals

- manufacture materials, such as metals, polymers, ceramics and composites, for making things

- make effective use of energy resources.

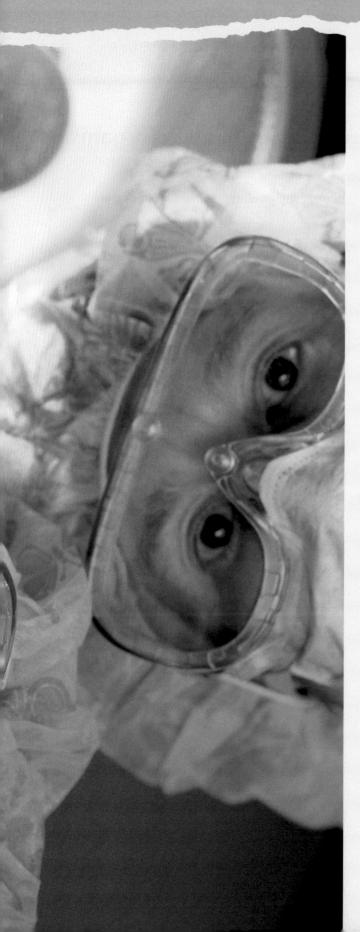

2

In this unit you will learn about:

Living organisms   126

Obtaining useful chemicals   167

Materials for making things   194

The importance of energy   211

2.1 Living organisms

Useful products from living organisms

You need to:

- *be able to identify useful products that can be made from living things*

- *know that wool, silk, cotton, leather, pharmaceutical products and dyes are all obtained from living organisms.*

Agriculture and horticulture are concerned mainly with the production of food. However, many other useful materials can be obtained from plants and animals. These include wool, silk, cotton, leather, pharmaceutical products and dyes.

Plants, animals and micro-organisms must be cared for and nurtured to ensure healthy growth. Scientists may help to achieve this by understanding how living organisms function. The things that you learn in this unit will help you to carry out your investigation of a living organism in Unit 3.

From plants

Everyday you use products obtained from plants, for example, food, fibres and medicines. In most cases the plants are grown especially for these purposes. We call these **cultivated plants**. The useful products we get from plants can be divided into two main categories: natural products and derived products.

We get many useful products from plants. But they are important in other ways as well. Plants affect the weather. They also prevent soil erosion. Forests often act as natural sponges, absorbing rain and then slowly releasing it. If forests are cut down, floods and soil erosion may result.

Natural products

Natural products are obtained directly from the plant and require little or no processing. Most, but not all, are food. Wood, for example, is used for making things and as a fuel. Foods include:

- vegetables (e.g. potatoes, onions, carrots, peas and cabbages)
- fruit (e.g. apples, oranges, strawberries, tomatoes and nuts)
- cereals (e.g. wheat and rice).

Derived products

These need processing before they can be used. For example:

Food and beverages	Sugar, jams, flour, coffee, tea
Clothing	Cotton, linen
Medicine	Digitalis from the foxglove
Fragrances	Rose water, jasmine
Paper	Conifer or eucalyptus trees
Rubber	Rubber ball, car tyres

Many derived plant products have been replaced, to a greater or lesser extent, by synthetic materials. For example, many medicines are made in the pharmaceutical industry using petrochemicals as the raw materials. You can read about this in 'Obtaining useful chemicals', on page 178.

From animals

As well as giving us food and other useful products, plants provide food for domestic herbivores such as sheep, pigs, cattle, horses and goats. We get wool, leather and food from such animals. Most animal products need processing. Even fresh meat, poultry, eggs and fish are usually cooked before we eat them. More complicated processes are used to produce pre-prepared food such as 'ready meals' for the microwave.

Some examples of useful products from animals are:

Food: natural (e.g. meat, poultry, eggs, milk and fish) and derived (e.g. cheese and yoghurt)

Clothing: leather and wool

Medicines: serums for snake and insect bites

From micro-organisms

Micro-organisms are used to make useful products in the food industry (e.g. bread, beer, wine, yoghurt) and the pharmaceutical industry (developing and manufacturing medicines, e.g. antibiotics). You can read about this in Unit 1, in the section 'Micro-organisms', on pages 72–82.

You are fortunate. You have choices. However, some people in the world have very limited resources. They must learn to make the best use of them. Animals are killed and every part of the beast is used – for food, shelter, weapons for hunting, string and rope.

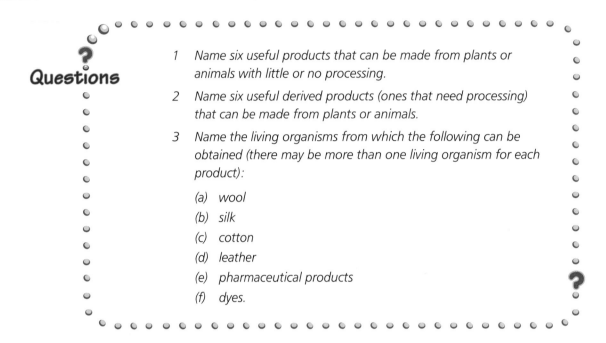

?
Questions

1   Name six useful products that can be made from plants or animals with little or no processing.

2   Name six useful derived products (ones that need processing) that can be made from plants or animals.

3   Name the living organisms from which the following can be obtained (there may be more than one living organism for each product):

(a) wool

(b) silk

(c) cotton

(d) leather

(e) pharmaceutical products

(f) dyes.

Cells, organs and organisms

You need to be able to:

- *describe living organisms as being made up of chemical compounds, and the cell as the common feature of all organisms*

- *describe the similarities and differences between plant and animal cells*

- *explain how substances enter and leave cells by diffusion and osmosis*

- *describe how cells divide by mitosis during growth*

- *describe how cells divide by meiosis to produce gametes*

What is a cell?

Living organisms are made up of chemicals – some simple, others more complicated and many that are very complicated. They can be grouped into:

- inorganic chemicals:
  - **water**: a solvent from some of the reactions and carries substances around the organism
  - **salts** containing ions such as potassium, calcium ions and chloride: makes tissues and organs work properly

- organic chemicals:
  - **carbohydrates** such as sugars, starch and glycogen (sources of energy)
  - **fats and oils (lipids)**: sources of energy
  - **proteins**: form muscles and tendons, for example, and many are important as enzymes (biological catalysts).

Although well over 100 elements are known only about 12 or so elements are needed to make these chemicals. The four most common in your body are carbon, hydrogen, oxygen and nitrogen.

Virtually all living organisms are made up of cells, clumped together to make tissues. In animals, the tissues combine to make organs like the heart, kidneys and liver. But what is a cell? Well, on the simplest level it is a sack of the types of chemicals we talked about earlier.

Your body consists of about one hundred million million cells. If you put 500 of them in a line it would be about 1 cm long. So we can't see cells except with the help of a microscope. You can see quite a lot with a light microscope, but even more with an electron microscope.

However, when cells get together and are organised they add up to a living organism. Countless chemical reactions take place and are responsible for all the actions of organisms.

Animal and plant cells

Animal and plants cells are not quite the same. Look at the drawings below and you will see the differences.

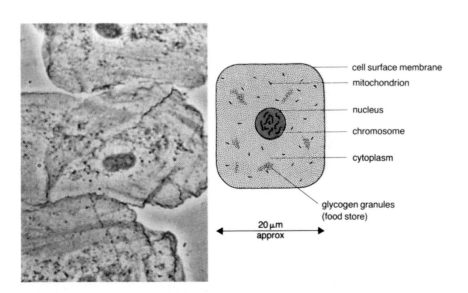

cell surface membrane
mitochondrion
nucleus
chromosome
cytoplasm
glycogen granules
(food store)
20 μm
approx

Some cheek cells seen through a light microscope and a drawing of a typical animal cell.

REMEMBER

There are many different types of cells. They differ in shape, form and the job they do. In your body there are more than 20 different types, for example, smooth muscle cells, nerve cells and white blood cells.

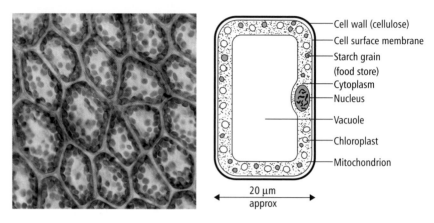

Cell wall (cellulose)
Cell surface membrane
Starch grain (food store)
Cytoplasm
Nucleus
Vacuole
Chloroplast
Mitochondrion

20 µm approx

Some leaf cells seen through a light microscope and a drawing of a typical plant cell. You will see some features that are the same as an animal cell – the cell surface membrane, nucleus, cytoplasm and mitochondria. They have the same purpose as described for animal cells.

TRY IT YOURSELF

Techniques for using a light microscope – setting it up, preparing slides and looking at them – are described in Unit 1. Use these techniques to look at some animal cells and plant cells under the microscope.

1   Set up the microscope.

2   Prepare temporary slides of the following (or you may be given prepared slides to look at):

    (a) Cheek cells – an example of animal cells from a human

    (b) Onion cells – an example of plant cells

    (c) Moss cells – an example of plant cells

3   Look at the slides under a microscope. Compare your observations with the pictures and descriptions of animal and plant cells given above.

    (a) What features of the cells can you identify? Label these clearly on your drawing or image.

    (b) You should be able to see chloroplasts in one of the plant cells, but not the other. Which one? Is that what you observed?

    (c) What were the differences, if any, in the three slides you prepared using moss leaves?

Chemical reactions in the cell

We call the reactions that take place in the cell **metabolism**. In all reactions chemical bonds between atoms in the reacting molecules must be broken. This takes energy. New chemical bonds form to make the products of the reaction. This gives out energy. You can read more about this on pages 190–193.

There are two types of reaction that take place in the cell: building up and breaking down.

Building up

Building up reactions are called **anabolism**. Small molecules join together to make much larger ones. For example, amino acids join together to make proteins. Glucose molecules can join together to make glycogen or starch, both of which store energy in the cell. Anabolic reactions use up energy – they are **endothermic**.

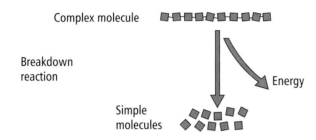

Making big molecules from small ones in the cell.

Breaking down

Breaking down reactions are called **catabolism**. Large molecules are broken down into smaller ones. Respiration (where glucose breaks down to form carbon dioxide and water) is an example. This happens in almost all living cells and releases energy. Catabolic reactions give out energy – they are **exothermic**.

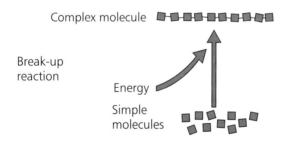

Making big molecules from small ones in the cell.

Enzymes

Many of these reactions are very, very slow. They must be speeded up and this is where **enzymes** play their part. Enzymes are proteins that act as very powerful catalysts. In fact they are sometimes called **biological catalysts**. Not only can they speed up a reaction, but they can also direct it. So if a reaction could give more than one product, the enzyme makes sure only the one wanted is made.

Getting in and out of the cell

The cells need chemicals from the outside and need to get rid of waste products from reactions that take place inside them. For substances to get in and out of the cell they must pass through the cell surface membrane and, if the organism is a plant, the cell wall.

Diffusion

Oxygen gets into the cell by diffusion and carbon dioxide (a product of the chemical reactions during respiration) leaves by **diffusion**. The cell membrane in animal and plant cells is **partially permeable**, which means is has very small holes that small molecules can pass through but not large ones.

There are four main features of diffusion:

- diffusion only takes place if the concentration of the substance is different on either side of the membrane (we call this a concentration gradient)
- the substance moves from the more concentrated side to the less concentrated side
- the higher the concentration difference, the faster the rate of diffusion
- small molecules diffuse more quickly than large ones.

(a) oxygen diffuses in

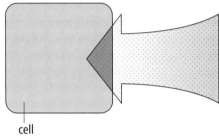

cell

Cells get energy by respiration. Food is broken down into carbon dioxide and water and energy is released. Cells need oxygen for this process. It gets into the cell by diffusion since its concentration outside the cell is greater than inside. The waste product, carbon dioxide, leaves by diffusion because its concentration is greater inside the cell than outside.

(b) carbon dioxide diffuses out

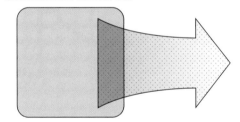

The leaves in these plants are firm because they are well watered. Water flows through the cell surface membranes into the cells (osmosis). This makes the vacuole swell. But it doesn't burst the cells because of the strength of the cell wall. The effect is the same as blowing up a long balloon. The leaves become quite rigid and stand upright.

If plants are not watered enough their leaves begin to droop. We call this wilting. The vacuoles in the leaf cells are not fully swollen because there is not enough water. This causes them to droop. It's the equivalent of letting air out of a balloon.

Osmosis

Osmosis is a special form of diffusion. It's how water enters and leaves a cell. Imagine two solutions, one with more solute in it than the other.

Usually we say the solution with most solute is the more concentrated. For example, 100 cm³ of solution containing 20 g of sugar in water is more concentrated than 100 cm³ of solution containing 1 g of sugar in water.

But we could look at it in a different way. There is less water in the concentrated sugar solution than the dilute one. Using the idea of diffusion, we would expect water to move from the side where it is more concentrated to that where it is less concentrated. In other words, the water passes from the more dilute sugar solution to the more concentrated sugar solution. This process is called **osmosis**.

Salt is sprinkled over some vegetables and fruit to remove some of the water. This happens by osmosis. Try it and see. You will see the same effect if you sprinkle sugar on fruit such as strawberries and raspberries.

Visking tubing is cellulose. It is a partially permeable membrane. You can use it to study osmosis.

TRY IT YOURSELF

Procedure

1. Cut a 10 cm length of Visking tubing. Soak it in water for several minutes.
2. Tie one end with thread to seal it. Then open the other end (a good technique is to rub the sides together r- like trying to open a plastic shopping bag in the supermarket) and fill it with 20% sugar solution.
3. Put a 15–20 cm length of capillary tubing in the open end and tie it firmly with thread.
4. Carefully lower the Visking tubing bag into a 400 cm³ beaker of distilled water (about 1 cm from the top).
5. Clamp the capillary tubing in an upright position and mark the position of the sugar solution.
6. Measure the rate at which the level of the sugar solution changes. Plot a graph of *Distance moved by sugar solution in the capillary tubing/cm* (on the *y*-axis) against *Time/s* (on the *x*-axis).

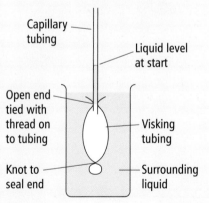

And now . . .

Try to explain your observations.

What differences would you predict if 15%, 10% and 5% sugar solutions had been used? If you have time you could try to set up a suitable experiment.

What difference would you expect if the beaker had contained 15% sugar solution rather than distilled water?

Mitosis and meiosis

Every cell in an organism contains genetic material. It is found on chromosomes. For a particular organism it's identical no matter which cell you are looking at. For example, a muscle cell in your body contains the same chromosomes as a hair cell. Similarly, a plant root cell will contain the same chromosomes as a plant leaf cell.

Each human cell contains 46 chromosomes. Chromosomes are present in matching pairs, called **homologous chromosomes**. In humans there are 23 pairs, 22 are called **autosomes** and one pair are **sex chromosomes**. Other species have different numbers of chromosomes. For example, a dog has 78 (39 pairs) and a cabbage has 18 (9 pairs).

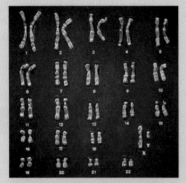

Human chromosomes sorted out and arranged in matching pairs. Each pair of chromosomes is given a number for identification purposes. The **X** and **Y** chromosomes are sex chromosomes, which make this person a male. A female would have two **X** chromosomes.

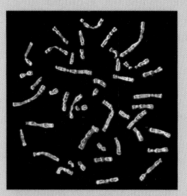

The full set of chromosomes from a cell of a human.

Did you know it takes about 1×10^{11} cells each day to replace skin, blood cells and gut and lung linings in your body?

REMEMBER

Cells make new cells by dividing. They divide by mitosis and meiosis.

- Mitosis is used for growth and repair of cells.
- Meiosis is used to produce eggs and sperm (gametes).

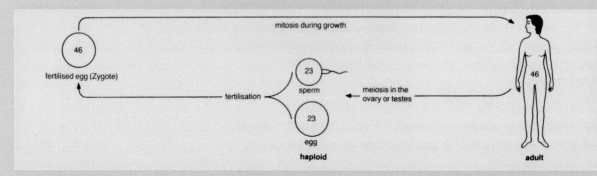

The human life cycle. Cells in the female ovary divide by meiosis. Each egg has 23 chromosomes. Cells in the male testes also divide by meiosis. Each sperm has 23 chromosomes. As a result of fertilisation each cell once again has 46 chromosomes.

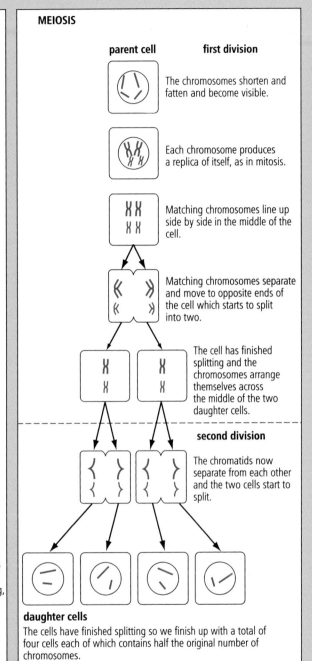

MITOSIS

parent cell

The chromosomes shorten and fatten and become visible.

chromatids

centromere

Each chromosome produces a replica of itself. The original chromosome and its replica are called chromatids. They are held together at a point called the centromere.

The chromosomes line up in the middle of the cell.

The chromatids separate and move to opposite ends of the cell and the cell starts to split into two.

The chromatids become the chromosomes of the two daughter cells. The cell has finished splitting, and we now have two cells each of which contains the same number of chromosomes as the parent cell.

daughter cells

MEIOSIS

parent cell   **first division**

The chromosomes shorten and fatten and become visible.

Each chromosome produces a replica of itself, as in mitosis.

Matching chromosomes line up side by side in the middle of the cell.

Matching chromosomes separate and move to opposite ends of the cell which starts to split into two.

The cell has finished splitting and the chromosomes arrange themselves across the middle of the two daughter cells.

second division

The chromatids now separate from each other and the two cells start to split.

daughter cells

The cells have finished splitting so we finish up with a total of four cells each of which contains half the original number of chromosomes.

Just before a cell is about to divide it is possible to see the chromosomes. Imagine a cell with two pairs of chromosomes, two long ones and two short ones. If the cell divides by mitosis, each daughter cell will also have two long and two short chromosomes.

Imagine a cell with two pairs of chromosomes, two long ones and two short ones. If the cell divides by meiosis, each daughter cell will have one long and one short chromosome, in other words half of what the parent cell had.

When an organism grows, it's making cells. It also needs to replace dead, damaged or worn out cells. Cells need to be able to replicate.

Cell division by **mitosis** results in two new 'daughter' cells that have identical chromosomes to the original or 'parent' cell. It's called the **diploid number**. This ensures genetic stability, in other words that each new cell contains the same information as the old one.

Mitosis also happens during **asexual reproduction** (reproduction without sex). Bacteria, mosses, ferns and fungi reproduce in this way and it ensures that their offspring are clones of their parents with a full set of chromosomes.

Meiosis occurs during the production of eggs and sperm. The daughter cells end up with half the original number of chromosomes – one member of each matching pair. In the case of humans this is 23 chromosomes (the **haploid number**). Both egg and sperm have 23 chromosomes. So the fertilised egg cell contains the complete set of chromosomes again (46).

Because eggs and sperm come from different individuals, they contain slightly different information, which leads to variation in offspring.

? Questions

1 Name the main types of chemicals that are found in living organisms.

2 List the similarities and differences between plant and animal cells.

3 Describe how substances enter and leave cells by diffusion.

4 What would you observe if salt were sprinkled on a piece of cucumber? Explain what happens.

5 Describe how cells divide by mitosis during growth.

6 Describe how cells divide by meiosis to produce eggs and sperm (gametes).

Growing healthy plants

You need to:

- *understand how plants make food by photosynthesis, and know that plants use the process of respiration to release energy*

- *know that plants need, among others, the minerals nitrates, phosphates, potassium and magnesium, which they obtain from soil, for healthy growth*

- *know that nitrates are required for proteins, which are needed for cell growth, and that magnesium is required for chlorophyll.*

Seeing the light

Plants cannot eat like you and me. They have to get their food in a different way. They use **photosynthesis**. At first sight it looks quite simple. The plant gets carbon dioxide from the air and water from the soil. These get into the cell and with some help from sunlight react to give glucose (the simplest sugar) and oxygen.

$$\text{carbon dioxide} + \text{water} \xrightarrow{\text{sunlight}} \text{glucose} + \text{oxygen}$$

Some of the glucose is converted into starch for storage. As you saw earlier, this is an example an anabolic reaction in the cell, in other words a building up reaction that uses energy.

The rate of photosynthesis and, therefore, plant growth depends on:

- light
- temperature
- carbon dioxide
- water.

Photosynthesis only occurs if the leaves are green, and you can show by experiment that green leaves contain a chemical called **chlorophyll**. This is found in the cytoplasm of [plant cells in chloroplasts. You can find out more about photosynthesis on page 213.

REMEMBER

As a result of photosynthesis, plants release oxygen into the atmosphere. Without plants, there would be no oxygen for us to breathe.

Food for growth

Living things need energy. Plants can get this from sunlight through the process of photosynthesis as we have just seen. The energy is stored in cells as starch, the product of photosynthesis.

But plants, like all living things, also need **nutrients**. Nutrients are chemicals that an organism needs to grow and remain alive. They are the raw materials cells use for the hundreds of chemical reactions that take place in them.

Plants get carbon dioxide from the air. They also get water and ions dissolved in water from the soil. Quite large amounts of the following ions are needed:

- nitrate (NO_3^-)   a source of nitrogen, N
- phosphate (PO_4^{3-})   a source of phosphorus, P
- potassium (K^+)   a source of potassium, K

Smaller amounts of magnesium (Mg^{2+}), calcium (Ca^{2+}) and some other ions are also required.

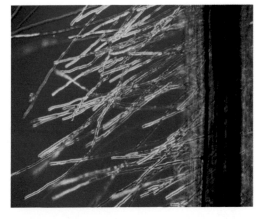

The large number of root hairs on a plant root can be seen using a scanning electron microscope. The structure of the root hairs ensures high surface area and maximum contact with the soil. This helps the uptake of water and ions dissolved in it.

In a plant different elements are needed for different aspects of growth:

Nitrogen, N	for growth of stems and leaves
Phosphorus, P	for healthy roots
Potassium, K	for healthy leaves and flowers
Calcium, Ca	for healthy growth of new stems
Magnesium, Mg	for making chlorophyll.

Fertilisers are used by farmers and gardeners to improve the growth of plants. Most fertilisers contain large quantities of nitrate ions, phosphate ions and potassium ions. They are called NPK fertilisers. You will find out more about this on page 327.

Information from a bottle of tomato fertiliser. A number of ions are nutrients needed by plants to grow and stay alive. The label tells you how much of each is in this particular fertiliser.

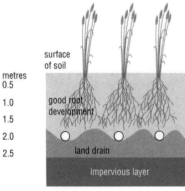
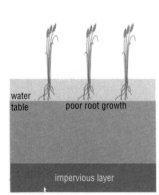

Plants need water to grow, but too much! Good drainage encourages root growth. Soil that has been walked on becomes compacted. The particles are pressed closer together and it's more likely to become waterlogged. Less air is trapped in the soil. Water logging is bad for most plants so farmers and gardeners often drain soils and plough or dig them up. Worms can help!

A Well-drained soil

B Badly drained soil

pH

Many plants are affected by the pH of the soil. Vegetables usually prefer a slightly alkaline soil. This is why lime (calcium carbonate) is spread over soil that's slightly acidic. Some trees are sensitive to the soil pH as well.

The pH makes a difference to which trees will grow well. A soil with a low pH, round about pH 3, is an acid soil. Sitka spruce and birch grow well on such soils. A soil with a lot of chalk in it may have a pH of about 7.5. Corsican pine and beech grow well on such soils.

Determining the pH of soil

You can use kits from garden centres to test the pH of soil. The kits consist of a narrow range indicator that changes colour with pH.

Obtain a test kit and investigate soils from gardens. In each place you decided to test you should take several samples and test each one. Also, make a note of what is growing in the soil being tested. Can you find any relationship between the pH of the soil and the types of plants that are growing well?

TRY IT YOURSELF

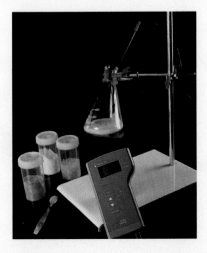

A pH probe gives more accurate values for soil pH than the test kits that can be bought in garden centres. There is a British Standard procedure based on using such probes.

Nitrates, proteins and cell growth

Proteins are essential for growth. To make proteins in a cell, a source of nitrogen is needed. Plants have two sources of nitrogen: nitrogen gas, N_2, from the air and nitrate ions, NO_3^-, from the soil.

Plants can't use the element nitrogen directly. However, certain bacteria can absorb nitrogen from the air and use it for making protein. Some 'nitrogen-fixing' bacteria are in the soil, others are in the roots of plants (for example, peas, beans and clover). The other source of nitrogen is nitrate ions. These are absorbed by plants and turned into amino acids. Amino acids are used to make proteins.

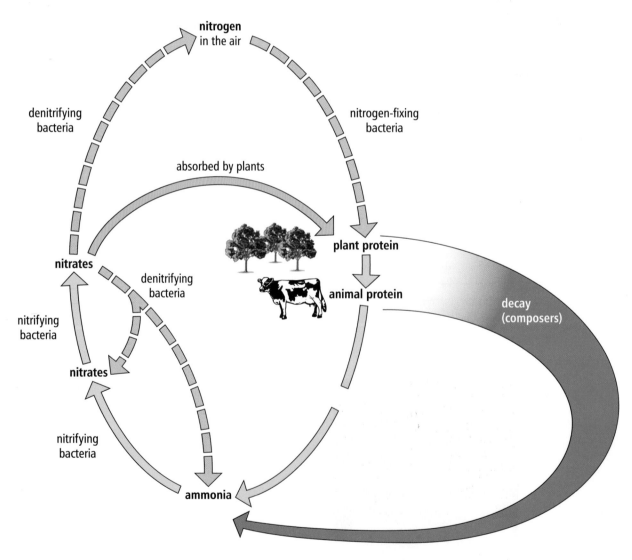

The nitrogen cycle.

Determining nitrates and other available nutrients

You can use kits from garden centres to test for nitrates in the soil. These use a chemical reaction that produces a distinctive colour if nitrates are present. The intensity of the colour tells you roughly how much nitrate is present.

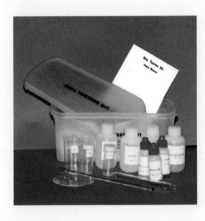

Soil testing kits. Although they are not very accurate, these kits can be used to usefully compare one soil with another and to decide if fertilisers are needed.

Get a test kit and investigate soils from different parts of your neighbourhood. In each place you decided to test you should take several samples and test each one.

A more accurate way to determine the nitrate content is to use a nitrate probe. This is an electronic sensor. If you can, check the values you obtained using a soil testing kit with values measured using the probe.

Other ions, such as phosphate and calcium, can be determined using similar kits and probes.

At the heart of chlorophyll is magnesium

Chlorophyll is the substance that 'traps' sunlight so that its energy can be used in photosynthesis. Chlorophyll is a complicated organic molecule, built around an inorganic ion. That ion is a magnesium ion, Mg^{2+}. This is why magnesium ions are such important nutrients. Without them there would be no chlorophyll. And without chlorophyll there would be no photosynthesis. And without photosynthesis there would be no plants. You can continue the story yourself!

Separating chlorophyll by paper chromatography

Substances found in leaves can be extracted with propanone. The solution you get contains, amongst other chemicals, chlorophyll. Some of these chemicals can be separated and identified by paper chromatography.

Procedure

1   Chop some leaves very finely and put about 2 cm depth in a mortar.

2   Add a spatula measure of sand and grind the mixture for 2–3 minutes.

3   Use a teat pipette to add 2 cm^3 of propanone (FLAMMABLE) and grind for a further 2–3 minutes. Pour the extract into a small, labelled sample tube and stopper. You may need to squeeze the mixture by pressing gently with the pestle.

4   Separate the mixture by paper chromatography (see page 89). Use propanone as the developing solvent.

And now . . .

Each 'spot' is a different chemical in the extract. What colours are they? How many substances appear to be in the extract? Try to find out what these substances are.

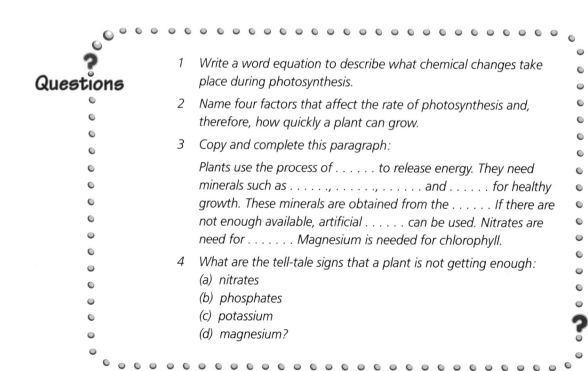

Questions

1   Write a word equation to describe what chemical changes take place during photosynthesis.

2   Name four factors that affect the rate of photosynthesis and, therefore, how quickly a plant can grow.

3   Copy and complete this paragraph:

   Plants use the process of . . . . . . to release energy. They need minerals such as . . . . . ., ..., ... and . . . . . . for healthy growth. These minerals are obtained from the . . . . . . If there are not enough available, artificial . . . . . . can be used. Nitrates are need for . . . . Magnesium is needed for chlorophyll.

4   What are the tell-tale signs that a plant is not getting enough:
   (a) nitrates
   (b) phosphates
   (c) potassium
   (d) magnesium?

Inheritance, selective breeding and genetic engineering

You need to:

- *know the mechanism of monohybrid inheritance where there are dominant and recessive alleles*

- *understand that selective breeding involves selecting the parents with desired traits, crossing them, selecting from their offspring, and then repeating the process over several generations*

- *understand that genetic engineering involves the transfer of 'foreign' genes into the cells of animals or plants at an early stage in their development so that they develop with desired characteristics.*

Inheritance

You are unique. Every cell on your body can be recognised as yours because of the genetic information it carries. This information comes in the form of **genes** on **chromosomes** in the nucleus of your cells. Each gene on our chromosomes controls how a particular part of your body develops.

People **inherit** genetic information from their father and mother. We get half from our mother and half from our father.

Let's take the example of eye colour to show how we get our genes and how we pass them on to our children. Genes that control eye colour may exist in different forms, called **alleles**. Each gene has two alleles, one inherited from the mother and the other from the father.

Helen has brown eyes and Mark has blue eyes. Their daughter, Jean, has brown eyes. Each member of the family has a gene in every cell of their body that controls eye colour.

Suppose **B** is the allele for brown eyes and **b** is the allele for blue eyes. One of these alleles (**B**) is **dominant** and the other (**b**) is said to be **recessive**. This means that brown eyes are dominant to blue eyes. Helen has two **B** alleles in her cells and so she has brown eyes. We can label her **BB**. Mark has two **b** alleles in his cells and so he has blue eyes. We can label him **bb**.

Now, when:

- Helen produces eggs containing half her genetic information, this is a **B** allele

- Mark produces sperm, containing half his genetic information, this is a **b** allele

Genes control how our bodies develop. For example, some genes control the colour of eyes, hair and skin. Others control facial features, height and so on.

REMEMBER

All genes can exist in several forms, called alleles. These are the key to similarities and differences between grandparents, parents and children in the same family. They explain similarity and diversity in nature.

- Mark's sperm fertilises Helen's egg and the fertilised egg has one **B** and one **b** allele
- Jean grows as the fertilised egg divides and divides, with every cell in her body containing one **B** and one **b** allele.

B is dominant to **b** and so Jean has brown eyes. However, her genes still carry the allele for blue eyes and this will be passed on to her children.

> **REMEMBER**
>
> A person's outward appearance is called the **phenotype**, e.g. brown eyes or blue eyes.
>
> A person's allele make-up (responsible for appearance) is called the **genotype**, e.g. **BB**, **Bb** or **bb**.

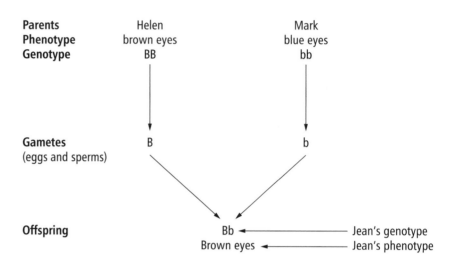

Parents	Helen	Mark
Phenotype	brown eyes	blue eyes
Genotype	BB	bb
Gametes (eggs and sperms)	B	b
Offspring	Bb ◄──────── Jean's genotype	
	Brown eyes ◄──────── Jean's phenotype	

Selective breeding

Plants and animals have been bred by **selective breeding** for thousands of years. For example, the largest seeds from crop plants were planted and smaller seeds thrown away. Cows that produced the most milk were used to produce calves. You can probably think of many other examples. This process was carried on generation after generation, always choosing the seed or animal that had the desired characteristics for breeding.

Many dogs are 'working dogs'. They need the right temperament for the job. Those with the best temperament are chosen for breeding. This is selective breeding and it has been going on for thousands of years.

Harvesting crops with machines is easier if each plant is about the same size. It is even more desirable if they give high yields and are resistant to pests and diseases. Selective breeding has helped farmers to get closer to all of these ideals.

Genetic engineering

People have used selective breeding to modify their food for thousands of years. But this method takes a lot of effort and is a little hit-and-miss. **Genetic engineering** lets scientists modify plants and animals in a way that no amount of traditional breeding could.

Genetic engineering is the science of altering the genes of a living organism. 'Foreign' genes are put into the cells of animals or plants early in their development. The 'foreign' genes carry different information and as the cells develop they take on new characteristics. These characteristics are determined by the nature of the 'foreign' gene.

Making useful products

Diabetes is a disease caused by too little or too much insulin being produced in the body. If you developed diabetes fifty years ago, the insulin used to treat you would have come from an animal, probably a pig. But there were only limited amounts of insulin available and difficulties also arose because animals' insulin was slightly different from human insulin.

In genetic engineering a gene is taken from one organism and put into another. Because the genetic code is the same in all organisms, the gene for human insulin should work just as well if it's put in a bacterium. A bacterium that will produce human insulin has been engineered. Genetically engineered insulin was tried out in 1980 and is widely used today.

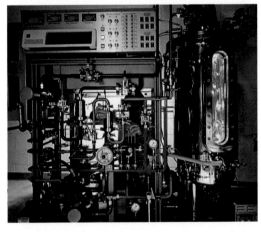

Human growth hormone has been produced by genetic engineering and can be used to treat children with specific growth defects.

Genetic engineering is also used for all sorts of purposes. Scientists can genetically engineer plants to make their own insecticides, bacteria to produce the enzymes used in cheese making, and sheep to produce proteins used to treat haemophilia.

GM foods

The first genetically modified (GM) food, a tomato designed to stay firmer for longer after picking, could be bought in US shops in 1994. In 1996 the first GM tomato paste went on sale in the UK. However,

The first GM food appeared in American shops in 1994. The Flavr Savr tomato was genetically engineered to keep it firm for longer.

many environmentalists were concerned about the safety of the technology. Throughout Europe many people are still unsure about GM food. The UK is carrying out trials of GM crops to assess their safety.

Frost resistant tomatoes

Scientists have developed a frost-resistant tomato plant by adding an antifreeze gene to it from a flounder (a fish that lives in very cold water). This is how it was done, but before you read further it might be useful to remind yourself about cells (pages 128–136).

- The flounder's antifreeze gene was cut out of the chromosomes in a flounder cell.

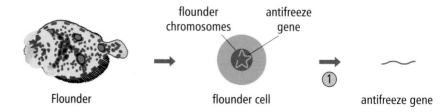

Flounder   flounder cell   antifreeze gene

- The antifreeze gene was put into another piece of DNA (called a plasmid). The result is a piece of recombinant DNA, which is then put into a bacterium.

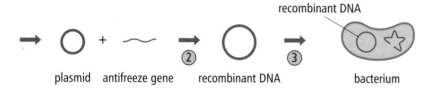

recombinant DNA

plasmid antifreeze gene   recombinant DNA   bacterium

- The bacterium reproduces many times (see page 317). This gives lots of copies of the recombinant DNA.
- Tomato plant cells are infected with the bacteria. The antifreeze gene becomes part of the tomato plant cells. These cells are put in a growth medium and grow into plants.

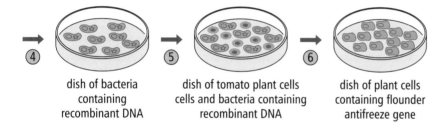

dish of bacteria containing recombinant DNA

dish of tomato plant cells cells and bacteria containing recombinant DNA

dish of plant cells containing flounder antifreeze gene

- The tomato plants are grown. And, yes, the tomatoes are frost resistant.

Cloning

In the 1970s scientists took a single cell from a frog and used it to create a tadpole. The tadpole was genetically identical to the frog. Scientists had cloned the first living organism. But cloning first hit the headlines when news of Dolly the sheep broke. It was the first time a mammal had been cloned. Since then several other animals have been cloned from adult cells:

1996	Sheep
1997	Mouse
1998	Cow
2000	Pig
2002	Cat

The question remains, when will we see the first cloned human?

Dolly the sheep, the first mammal to be cloned by scientists.

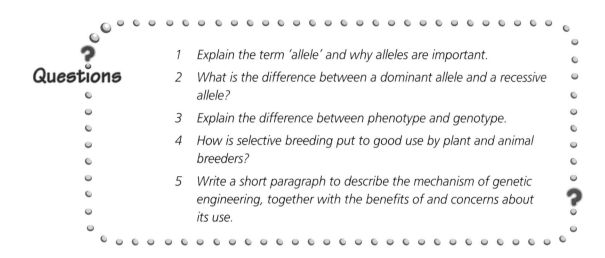

Questions

1   Explain the term 'allele' and why alleles are important.

2   What is the difference between a dominant allele and a recessive allele?

3   Explain the difference between phenotype and genotype.

4   How is selective breeding put to good use by plant and animal breeders?

5   Write a short paragraph to describe the mechanism of genetic engineering, together with the benefits of and concerns about its use.

Agriculture and horticulture

You need to:

- *describe how intensive farming increases crop yields by using artificial fertilisers, pesticides, herbicides and fungicides, and increases meat production by using controlled environments*

- *describe how organic farming uses the alternative methods of natural fertilisers, natural pesticides and mechanical elimination of weeds in crop production, and keeps animals under more natural conditions*

- *compare the advantages and disadvantages of each type of farming.*

Successful farming

Choosing the right crop

Some crops grow better in certain conditions than others. For example, grape vines need plenty of warmth and sunshine for the grapes to ripen properly. You find vineyards on sunny, south-facing slopes in countries like France and Italy. You don't see them in Norway or Scotland. So the first thing to think about is the location of the farm.

Having decided on the crop, you need to choose the best cultivar. A **cultivar** is a commercial variety of a plant. Suppose you decide to grow apple trees. What variety should you choose? A farmer must select a cultivar suitable for the growing conditions. It must give good yields of quality products cost-effectively.

Healthy growth

Once the cultivar has been chosen, you must do your best to look after it and encourage it to produce quality fruit, vegetables or flowers.

Many things affect the growth of plants. A farmer needs to think about the soil, the climate and pests and diseases.

Soil. It's important to know about the soil. Some soils hold water and nutrient ions well, but others do not. Some soils dry out quickly, others tend to get waterlogged. The pH of the soil makes a big difference to what crops will grow well. And, of course, the nutrient and organic matter content must be sufficient for healthy plant growth.

Climate. Climate describes the more regular changes from season to season in such things as rainfall, temperature, wind and hours of sunlight. The climate varies around the UK. For example, Cornwall and the Scilly Isles are rainier, windier and have fewer extremes of temperature during the year than the east of England. This makes a big difference to the plants that can be cultivated there.

What can the farmer do to beat the weather? Greenhouses can be used to extend the growing season. Crops can also be protected from the weather by cold frames or cloches.

Pests and diseases. There are many pests and diseases that can reduce the yields of plants, for example, weeds, fungi, viruses, insects and other animals. A **weed** is a plant that grows where it is not wanted. It competes with the crop for water and nutrients. Examples of fungi that attack crops are mildews and rusts. One of the most important diseases of potatoes is caused by an organism usually classified as a fungus. It causes the disease potato blight. Many **insects** attack crops. You may have seen the holes in cabbage leaves where caterpillars have been eating them. Many **other animals,** such as grey squirrels, damage crops. **Viruses** also damage crops, for example, Tobacco mosaic and Potato leaf curl.

Methods of farming
Improving growing conditions
The structure of soil can be improved. Digging helps to break up solid lumps of soil and puts air into it. Organic matter can be added to improve the structure and make sure that soil retains water better. The pH can also be changed. Some plants prefer slightly acidic soils (pH less than 7) while others prefer slightly alkaline soils (pH greater than 7). The pH can be increased by adding lime (calcium oxide) or limestone (calcium carbonate) to the soil. As you read earlier, greenhouses, cold frames and cloches can be used to protect delicate crops from the weather.

These methods are used by all farmers. However, there are two distinct approaches to adding nutrients and dealing with pests and diseases: intensive farming and organic farming. The table outlines the differences between these two approaches.

Genetic engineering is being used increasingly to enable a more rapid development of varieties resistant to pests and diseases. For example, a gene for disease-resistance can be moved rapidly from one crop to

	Intensive farming	Organic farming
Adding nutrients	Use artificial fertilisers These may be multi-purpose NPK or fertilisers providing a single nutrient	Use 'natural' fertilisers such as manure
	Advantages: Ample supplies Cheap Easy to distribute Easy to control quantities Easy to add different nutrients in the required proportions	Advantages: Not using up natural resources
	Disadvantages: Finite resource; and the effect extraction has on the environment Come in concentrated form and so too much can be added. Often water soluble and so can be washed out into neighbouring streams, rivers and lakes. This can cause eutrofication.	Disadvantages: None
Controlling pest and diseases	Use herbicides, pesticides and fungicides. These are manufactured using crude oil as the raw material. Herbicides are used to kill weeds. Insecticides are generally sprayed onto crops when insect numbers build up. Fungicides are either sprayed onto crops when weather conditions suggest that a fungal outbreak is about to happen or put onto the seeds as a seed dressing Soil sterilisation is only feasible for greenhouse crops. It is useful against pests that live in the soil, such as certain nematodes (round worms)	Removal of weeds by hoeing. Biological control. Increasingly, predators such as lacewings (carnivorous insects) and parasitic wasps are being used in greenhouses to control pests such as aphids and caterpillars Traditional plant breeding can result in new varieties resistant to certain pests and diseases. However, each new variety typically takes 10–12 years to develop, and the pest may soon develop resistance
	Advantages: Not labour intensive	Advantages: None
	Disadvantages: Insecticides are rarely selective. This means that they usually kill a range of useful insects such as predators as well as the pest species.	Disadvantages: None

another. This raises a number of ethical issues and, along with other genetic engineering applications, continues to be a matter of fierce debate.

Questions

1. Summarise the different approaches of intensive farming and organic farming to:
   (a) providing plants with sufficient nutrients
   (b) controlling pests and diseases
   (c) providing suitable living environments for livestock.

2. Make a list of the advantages and disadvantages of each type of farming, intensive and organic.

Micro-organisms

You need to be able to:

- *describe the use of bacteria, yeasts and other fungi in food (yoghurt, bread, beer, wine, protein) and medicine (antibiotics) production*

- *know that diseases may be caused by micro-organisms and name some examples (measles, mumps, rubella, polio, tuberculosis (TB), foot and mouth, athlete's foot and skin infections due to Staphylococcus aureus)*

- *give examples of a range of methods of protecting against infection by harmful micro-organisms in food production (personal hygiene, sterilisation, disinfectants, antiseptics)*

- *understand the use of immunisation to protect humans and other animals from infection by specific micro-organisms (MMR, TB, foot and mouth, polio)*

- *know that antibiotics may kill some bacteria, but not viruses.*

Using micro-organisms to make useful products

Micro-organisms, such as bacteria, yeasts and other fungi produce many things that are useful to us. These include:

- food, for example, bread, yoghurt and cheese
- beverages, for example, ginger beer, wine and beer
- medicines, for example, insulin and antibiotics such as penicillin
- biogas, a fuel that can be obtained from animal and plant waste
- other products, for example, washing powder enzymes.

You can read about how some of these can be made in the laboratory on page 74.

To make these products in large quantities, micro-organisms must be grown on a large scale. This is done in an **industrial fermenter**. The drawing below shows you the important features of a typical fermenter.

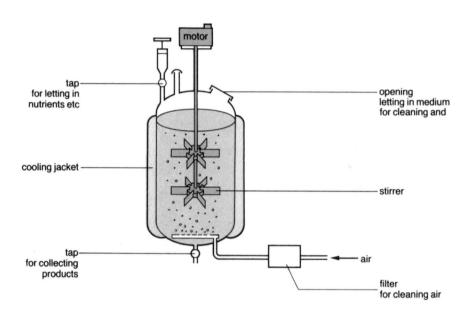

A typical fermenter.

Micro-organisms can cause diseases

Many micro-organisms cause diseases to plants and animals (including us). They are called **pathogens**. The micro-organisms might be bacteria, viruses or fungi. Pathogens work in one of two ways:

- by attacking and destroying cells
- by releasing poisons (toxins) into the bloodstream.

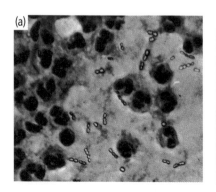
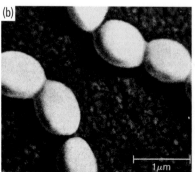
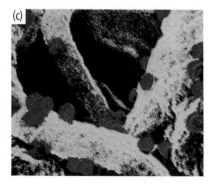

Bacteria can just be seen with a light microscope (a). Under an electron microscope the same type of bacteria can be seen much more clearly (b). Viruses are much smaller than bacteria and can only be seen with an electron microscope. The AIDS virus shows up as red objects (c).

Here is a list of some diseases you may have heard of and their causes.

Micro-organism	Disease
Viruses	Common cold, influenza ('flu), measles, chicken pox, hepatitis B, AIDS, yellow fever, poliomyelitis (polio), mumps, rubella
Bacteria	Salmonella food poisoning, impetigo, tuberculosis (TB), pneumonia, diphtheria, whooping cough, typhoid, tetanus, bacterial dysentery, cholera, syphilis, gonorrhoea
Fungi	Athlete's foot, thrush, foot and mouth

If you feel unwell the doctor will ask what your **symptoms** are. These help the doctor to identify the cause (**diagnosis**) and **prescribe** a suitable medicine (or other treatment). You take the **prescription** to a pharmacist's to get the medicines.

Germs are bacteria and viruses that do us harm. Diseases spread because germs get passed from one person to another. Sometimes they get passed to a person from an animal. Diseases that can be passed from one person to another are called **infectious**. When many people get ill with the same disease in a short space of time we call it an **epidemic**.

Germs can be spread in different ways including:

- droplets in the air caused by coughing or sneezing
- dust (germs stick to the dust particles and get blown around)
- touch (these germs are said to be **contagious**)
- faeces (so you should always wash your hands after going to the toilet)
- animals (rats, mice, cockroaches and flies are some of the culprits)
- blood (which is why sports people with bleeding wounds must leave the field for treatment)
- sexual contact (sexually transmitted diseases such as syphilis, gonorrhoea and AIDS spread like this; treatment is available is special clinics in some hospitals).

Protecting against infection

Protection against harmful micro-organisms is essential in many places, for example, where food is prepared, in a hospital operating theatre and in a hairdresser's. There are a number of steps you can take. Personal hygiene is the starting point. You should always wash your hands before starting work and then at regular intervals. For example, if you change from handling one type of food to another (such as preparing raw meat to handling vegetables), you should wash your hands. The work surface and tools must also be thoroughly washed.

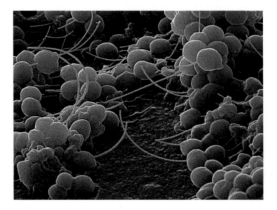

This image, taken with an electron microscope, shows the bacteria living in the crevices of human skin. Personal hygiene helps to reduce the risk of transferring them to somebody else.

Instruments and equipment should be **sterilised**. This can be done by heating them. Heating to 120 °C for 15 minutes is sufficient to kill most germs. For higher temperatures you would have to use a pressure cooker or an autoclave.

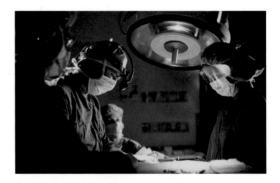

A patient being operated on is particularly vulnerable to infectious diseases. Every precaution is taken to keep germs out of an operating theatre. The surgeons and nurses 'scrub-up' and put on sterilised disposable gloves. The gowns, head covers and face masks worn in operating theatres are also sterilised before use, as are scalpels and other equipment.

Some items will not tolerate this amount of heat. In a hairdressing salon the plastic combs might melt. Instead they are soaked in a **disinfectant**. You have probably seen Dettol. Like other disinfectants it is a chemical that kills germs (just as the label claims). Disinfectants are particularly useful for cleaning surfaces and floors in places such as kitchens and toilets.

All places where food is processed, cooked or served must meet strict hygiene standards. Environmental health officers check that they meet the regulations. Swabs are taken to test for micro-organisms. To detect the number and type present in a specimen a sample is taken and cultured. You can read about culturing on page 72.

An open cut is like an open invitation to germs. The cut may turn septic. You can prevent this by using an **antiseptic**. This is a chemical that kills germs. Look in a first aid box; you should find some antiseptic. One of the early ones, still used today, is *Tincture of iodine*. This is a solution of iodine in surgical spirit (mainly ethanol). It works well, but really stings! Antiseptic creams and ointments, such as Germoline and Savlon, are gentler – but still work well.

Immunisation

Dead germs can be useful. Your body produces **antibodies** when you get a disease. These attack and destroy germs. It's a form of self-defence. The antibodies are specific to the germs that caused the disease. **Antigens** on the surface of the germ make certain white blood cells produce these antibodies. What's interesting is that even dead germs have antigens and they also trigger the production of antibodies.

So suppose some dead germs are put into your body before you get ill. Your body will respond by making antibodies. As you are not ill they have nothing to attack, so they remain in your body ready and willing in case you do get the disease later. This is how **immunisation** works. Quite simply, a small amount of dead germs (called the **vaccine**) is put into your bloodstream. Antibodies form and lie in wait for live germs to appear.

Immunisation is used to protect against specific diseases such as MMR, TB, foot and mouth, and polio.

There are regular immunisation programmes available for babies and young adults. Babies are immunised against various serious diseases such as diphtheria and polio. Teenagers are immunised against tuberculosis. Not all immunisations last for life. Sometimes a **booster** is needed.

But remember, vaccines don't cure disease, they simply help to prevent you getting it.

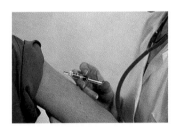

Immunisation is used to protect humans and other animals from infection by harmful micro-organisms. Doctors immunise you by putting a small amount of dead germs (called the **vaccine**) into your bloodstream. This is usually by injection using a hypodermic needle (inoculation) or by scratching the skin. Some vaccines can be taken by mouth.

Antibiotics

Antibiotics are prescribed by doctors to treat diseases caused by bacteria. One of the reasons urine samples are taken is to identify the harmful bacteria so that the most suitable antibiotic can be prescribed. Penicillin was one of the first antibiotics. Antibiotics are examples of **therapeutic drugs**. However, doctors will not prescribe them unless it's absolutely necessary. This is because new bacteria appear all the time that are resistant to our arsenal of antibiotics.

There are two ways in which antibiotics can work. They either kill the bacteria or stop them growing. Unfortunately antibiotics have no effect on viruses.

Some antibiotics, like penicillin, are made using micro-organisms. Others are manufactured on a huge scale by pharmaceutical companies. One very important group of synthetic antibiotics are the sulphonamides. Antibiotics have been very successful. Coupled with improved hygiene, sanitation and diet, they have reduced illness caused by bacteria enormously. Unfortunately it's not the same story in every country around the world. Infectious diseases still kill many people in developing countries.

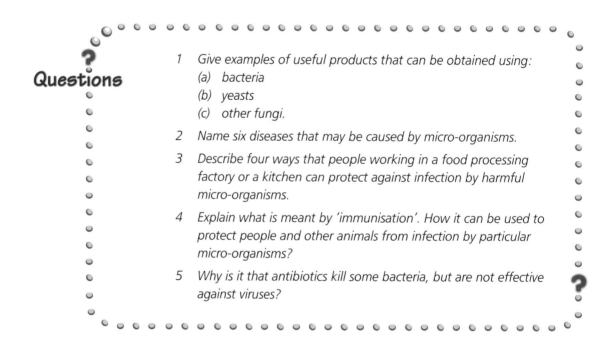

Questions

1   Give examples of useful products that can be obtained using:
    (a)   bacteria
    (b)   yeasts
    (c)   other fungi.

2   Name six diseases that may be caused by micro-organisms.

3   Describe four ways that people working in a food processing factory or a kitchen can protect against infection by harmful micro-organisms.

4   Explain what is meant by 'immunisation'. How it can be used to protect people and other animals from infection by particular micro-organisms?

5   Why is it that antibiotics kill some bacteria, but are not effective against viruses?

The human body

You need to know:

- *the structure of the human circulatory system, including the function of the heart, and the composition and functions of the blood*

- *how the structure of the thorax enables ventilation of the lungs*

- *that respiration may be aerobic or anaerobic depending on the availability of oxygen, and that 'oxygen debt' may occur in muscles during vigorous exercise*

- *how humans maintain a constant body temperature (by sweating and changing the diameter of capillaries)*

- *how the blood glucose levels are controlled by the hormone insulin.*

The circulatory system

Blood is pumped round your body by the heart. Together, the parts of the body it flows through are called the **circulatory system**. Blood vessels are tubes that carry blood. There are two types:

- **arteries** carry blood away from the heart to various organs
- **veins** carry blood back from the organs to the heart.

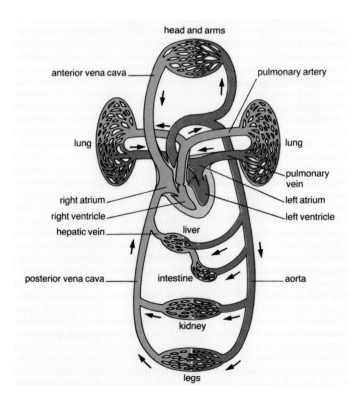

Within each organ the arteries and veins are connected by numerous much narrower blood vessels called **capillaries**. Every organ contains thousands of capillaries. As blood passes through the capillaries blood operates a 'delivery and disposal' service to each organ. Necessary chemicals diffuse into cells, others diffuse out.

Look at the picture below. You will see that there are two distinct parts to the circulatory system. Blood collects oxygen from the lung. It is **oxygenated**. The oxygen is bound to haemoglobin in the blood and carried to those parts of the body where it's needed. By the time the blood has passed through the rest of the body the oxygen has been removed. The **deoxygenated** blood is pumped by the heart back to the lungs to become oxygenated again. Blood passes through the heart twice on every circuit of the body.

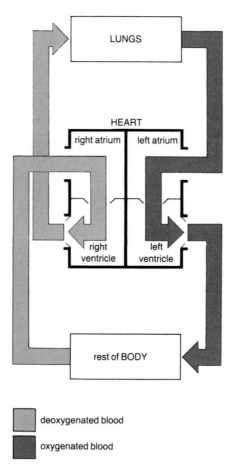

This is a simple 'picture' of how the blood passes around the body. Red is oxygenated blood. Blue is deoxygenated blood. You might find the left and right sides of the heart confusing. However, it's the usual way to show it in anatomy. Just imagine you are looking in a mirror. Your right side is the left side of your image. In the diagram (the image), the left side of the heart is actually on your right side.

The heart

The **heart** is the pump that beats about 70 times a minute. You can check a person's heart beat by taking their **pulse**. Nurse, doctors and sports trainers do this regularly. The heart has four chambers:

- left atrium   oxygenated blood arrives
- left ventricle   oxygenated blood leaves
- right atrium   deoxygenated blood arrives
- right ventricle   deoxygenated blood leaves

Blood always enters through an **atrium** chamber and leaves through a **ventricle** chamber. The two chambers are connected by a **valve,** which only allows the blood to pass in one direction. Oxygenated blood flows through the left side chambers. Deoxygenated blood flows through the right side chambers.

Taking a pulse

Find the artery on your wrist. Put your finger on the skin above the artery and press gently. You should be able to feel a slight but regular throb. This is your pulse (or heart rate). Count the number of throbs for 15 seconds, multiply by 4 and this is your pulse in beats per minute.

TRY IT YOURSELF

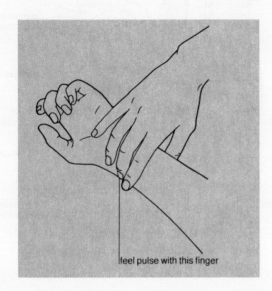

feel pulse with this finger

Your **resting heart rate** is the number of beats per minute when you are completely relaxed, rested and sitting down. Measure your pulse under these conditions and then stand for one minute. Take your pulse again. This is called the **standing pulse rate**. What is the difference?

Different things can cause the heart to beat more quickly. One is exercise. The other is nervousness and stress. You may want to investigate these in Unit 3.

The heart muscle contracts and relaxes, rather like clenching your fist and then opening it. As the muscle contracts, the heart pumps blood into arteries. When it relaxes, blood is pumped into veins. To keep contracting the heart needs oxygen. It gets it from a network of coronary arteries (remember it's arteries that carry oxygenated blood) that branch out over the heart wall. A heart attack occurs when one of these gets blocked.

Blood

Your heart pumps blood around your body through the network of arteries, veins and capillaries. Blood consists of a fluid (plasma) with red blood cells and white blood cells in it. Blood does several important jobs:

- red blood cells carry oxygen
- plasma carries substances such as food, excretory products and hormones, around the body
- white blood cells help fight diseases

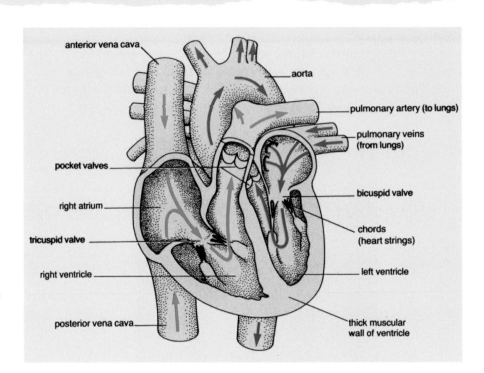

This is a more detailed 'picture' of where the blood passes when it circulates around the body. Red is oxygenated blood. Blue is deoxygenated blood.

- it makes sure that cells have the right conditions to work
- it transfers heat energy from metabolic reactions evenly around the body.

You should know what to do if somebody cuts himself or herself and bleeds. If you can't remember, check again on page 14.

An average sized person has about 5 dm^3 of blood. Find a 5 dm^3 beaker in the laboratory and you will see just how much this is. If somebody loses more than 2 dm^3, that person's life is in serious danger. Their blood pressure falls, slowing down the rate of flow of blood around the body. There are less red blood cells to carry oxygen around the body. The main outcome is that not enough blood gets to the brain. The person becomes unconscious and may die. Blood transfusions are used to replenish blood levels in the body.

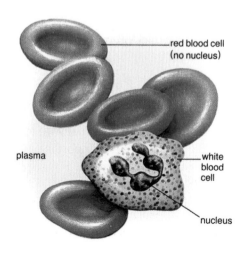

Blood consists of plasma, red blood cells and white blood cells. The two types of cells look very different. A red blood cell does not have a nucleus. It looks a bit like a doughnut that has been squashed from the middle on both sides. A white blood cell does have a nucleus and has a different shape. Red blood cells can be seen if a sample of blood is viewed through a microscope. The sample must be stained to show up the white blood cells.

Examining blood

You should not normally work with blood in the laboratory. However, if your teacher can obtain a supply of blood that's safe to use, try this experiment:

1   Put one drop of blood at the end of a microscope slide. Use another slide to spread it evenly and leave the smear to dry.

2   Use a light microscope (the technique is given on page 68) to look for red blood cells.

3   Now cover the smear with Leishman's stain. After a few minutes wash the slide under running tap water.

4   Let the slide dry again and then use the light microscope to look for white blood cells (their nuclei will appear blue).

TRY IT YOURSELF

The thorax

You have seen how important oxygen is and that blood is pumped around the lungs to get oxygen (become oxygenated). Air is drawn through the **nose**, via the throat (**pharynx**) and into the windpipe (**trachea**). The windpipe splits into two short tubes called **bronchi** and these divide into smaller tubes called **bronchioles**. It's rather like the branches of a tree. At the end of each bronchiole is a bunch of tiny air sacks called **alveoli**. This is where the blood obtains oxygen and gets rid of carbon dioxide.

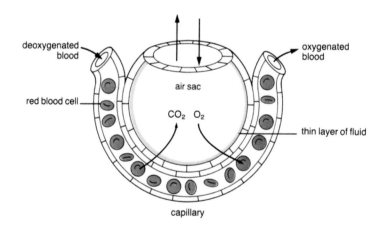

Deoxygenated blood passes around air sacs in the lungs. Carbon dioxide carried by red blood cells diffuses into the air sac. When you breathe out the carbon dioxide is exhaled. Oxygen diffuses from the air sacs into the red blood cells, oxygenating them. It's then transported to those parts of the body where it's needed.

When you breathe in (**inhale**) air is drawn into your lungs. The two lungs in your chest (the **thorax**) are protected by a cage of bones (**ribs**) between which are rib muscles. A dome-shaped structure, called the diaphragm, separates the lungs from the abdomen. When the rib muscles contract, the ribs move upwards and outwards. Your chest expands. The volume of the lungs increases, the pressure inside decreases and so air is drawn in (**inhaling**). Breathing out (**exhaling**) is the reverse. The rib muscles relax, the volume of the lungs gets smaller and the pressure inside becomes greater. Air is pushed out.

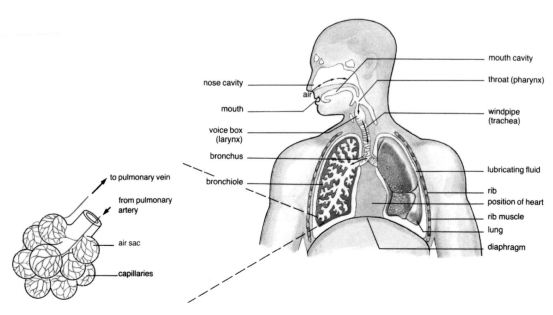

A simplified diagram of the breathing system.

Measuring lung capacity

Use a spirometer to measure vital capacity and tidal volume. The experiment must be carried out under the supervision of your teacher.

1   **Vital capacity**. Take a deep breath, as deep as you can, and exhale into the spirometer. This is the maximum volume of air that you can take into your lungs. Get others to try it, perhaps other students and some teachers. What kind of variations can you see?

2   **Tidal volume**. Now breathe normally and exhale a single normal breath into the spirometer. How does this volume compare with the vital capacity? Calculate what percentage the tidal volume is of the vital capacity using the formula:

$$\frac{\text{tidal volume}}{\text{vital capacity}} \times 100\%$$

Is the same percentage for everybody that did the test? What conclusions can you draw?

Respiration

Aerobic respiration

Inside the cells in your body, glucose reacts with oxygen to make carbon dioxide and water. Energy is also given out (it's an exothermic reaction).

glucose + oxygen → carbon dioxide + water + energy
$C_6H_{12}O_6$ $6O_2$ $6CO_2$ $6H_2O$

This is how you get energy from food. The process is called **aerobic respiration**. Glucose is the fuel and oxygen is essential for the fuel to be 'burnt' and produce energy.

All organisms, including you, need energy to stay alive. It's needed for growth, cell division and transporting chemicals. You also need energy to make muscles contract, send messages along nerves and keep the body warm.

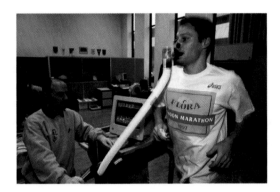

A respirometer can be used to measure how quickly a person uses up oxygen.

Breathing: oxygen in, carbon dioxide out

1 Set up the apparatus shown.

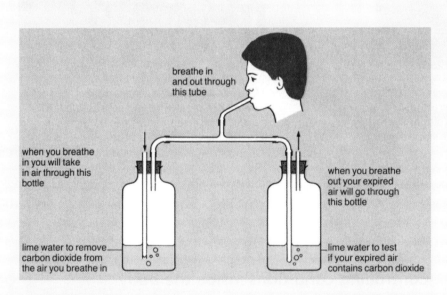

breathe in and out through this tube

when you breathe in you will take in air through this bottle

when you breathe out your expired air will go through this bottle

lime water to remove carbon dioxide from the air you breathe in

lime water to test if your expired air contains carbon dioxide

2 Breathe in. Air is drawn through limewater in the left test tube. This removes any carbon dioxide.

3 Breathe out. The expired air is blown through the limewater in the right test tube.

4 Continue to breathe in and out for a while. Check the contents of the two test tubes.

5 Limewater turns milky if carbon dioxide is bubbled through it (see page 93). What does this tell you about respiration?

Anaerobic respiration

Sometimes the body works so hard that it can't get enough oxygen for aerobic respiration. It turns to **anaerobic respiration**, but at a price. In this process your body turns glucose into lactic acid, releasing energy. No oxygen is needed.

glucose → lactic acid + energy

$C_6H_{12}O_6$ $2C_3H_6O_3$

Unfortunately lactic acid is a mild poison. It makes the muscles ache. The body can get rid of it once if it has enough oxygen (it gets 'burnt' up in the same way as glucose). The oxygen needed is called the **oxygen debt**. Anaerobic respiration produces far less energy than aerobic respiration, and it can't go on for long. But it's invaluable.

(a) A sprinter depends on energy from anaerobic respiration. There simply isn't time to get all the oxygen needed for aerobic respiration. The reason we all pant after running fast is that the body is desperately trying to get enough oxygen to burn off the lactic acid.

(b) Distance runners have a different problem. Their bodies learn to adjust and there comes a point in the race when the lactic acid is destroyed while the athlete is still running. It's called getting a second wind.

The training regimes for these athletes differ. Each is designed to prepare the athlete's body for the type of respiration it will rely on during the race.

Controlling conditions inside the body

It's important that the conditions inside our bodies don't change very much. If they did the cells would not work properly. The body does this by using **feedback systems**. It's just like a central heating thermostat. An electronic thermometer measures the room temperature. If the temperature falls below a pre-set value the information is fed back to the heating system. In response to the electronic message, the heating comes on and the room warms up. If the room gets too hot, the electronic thermometer feeds back the information and the heating is switched off.

We will look at two examples here: controlling body temperature and controlling glucose levels.

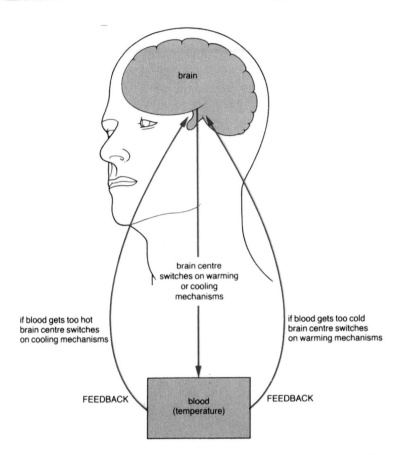

The brain is the nerve centre of the operation. It picks up signals from the body that something is not quite right and sends signals back to the appropriate places so that the body can correct matters. For example, if the body gets too hot, the brain switches on cooling mechanisms. If it gets too cold, heating mechanisms are switched on.

Maintaining body temperature

You have receptor cells whose job it is to sense temperature changes in the body. These cells are in a special control centre in the brain. The control centre then sends out messages along the nerves, which trigger different mechanisms in the body. Some of the mechanisms used are:

- Hairs on your skin trap air and help to insulate your body, keeping it warm. In cold weather the hairs stand up and trap a lot of air. In hot weather they lie flat with little or no air trapped between them.
- When blood flows close to surface of your skin heat energy is transferred to the surroundings. In cold weather the blood vessels near the surface become narrower and so less blood flows close to the skin. There is less heat loss. In hot weather, the blood vessels widen, more blood passes near the surface and there is greater heat loss.
- We sweat in hot weather. When the sweat evaporates it cools the skin's surface and the blood flowing just beneath it.

Maintaining glucose levels

It's important to have the right amount of glucose in your blood. If you eat food containing a lot of carbohydrate and sugars, the glucose level in your blood will rise. When the control centre in your brain receives messages that the glucose level is too high it tells cells in the pancreas to release the hormone insulin. This is carried around the bloodstream and converts glucose into glycogen. This in turn is stored safely in cells, especially in the liver and muscles.

Questions

1   Describe the passage of blood around the human circulatory system. Make sure you explain:

(a) what the heart does, and
(b) what blood consists of and its function in the body.

2   Describe the process of breathing, including the structure of the thorax. Your description should include the words:

- Nose
- Pharynx
- Trachea
- Bronchi
- Inhaling
- Exhaling

3   Explain the difference between aerobic and anaerobic respiration.

4   What is 'oxygen-debt'?

5   Describe two ways in which humans keep the temperature of their bodies constant.

6   Explain why it is important to control glucose levels in blood and describe how this is done.

2.2 Obtaining useful chemicals

Elements, compounds and mixtures

You need to be able to:

- *classify materials as elements (metals and non-metals), compounds or mixtures, using information provided or obtained by experiment*

- *give examples of substances used straight from the ground (gold, sulphur, limestone, marble)*

- *describe how some substances are separated before use (salt from rock salt, fractional distillation of crude oil)*

- *describe how a metal may be made from its oxide by reduction using carbon (iron from iron oxide and lead from lead oxide)*

- *know the chemical symbols for 20 common elements (see page 169).*

Some substances can be used straight from the ground, for example sand or sulfur. But usually they must be separated (or 'cleaned up') first. Salt from rock salt and useful substances from crude oil are examples. These substances are often the starting point for making other more useful substances. We call them **raw materials**. As well as rocks and minerals in the Earth, the air and sea are valuable sources of raw materials. From the air we get oxygen and nitrogen – really important gases. From seawater we get a number of chemicals and, of course, water.

Chemicals are all around you. Supermarket shelves are stocked with chemicals. Your body is a really complex mixture of chemicals. Chemicals are everywhere.

And you shouldn't forget the raw materials we get from living things, like cotton and wool from plants, wood from trees, leather from animals and so on. The world we live in really is an Aladdin's cave of raw materials offering endless possibilities fro making things that can benefit us all.

Extraction, quarrying, farming, fishing and forestry are important industries. They supply scientists with raw materials. Scientists make best use of these materials while doing all they can to protect the natural environment.

To make best use of chemicals you need to know more about them. Chemicals can be either elements or compounds. You will find the word 'substance' useful. You can use it to describe something that is an element, compound or mixture of one or more of these.

You may be told about some of the properties of a substance. You might find them by experiment. Either way, you need to be able use the information to say whether a substance is an element (metals and non-metals), compound or mixture.

Elements

Elements are the simplest substances. No matter what is done to an element it cannot be broken down into a simpler chemical substance. There are about 100 elements and each has its own unique:

- name and chemical symbol
- physical properties, e.g. density, electrical conductivity, melting point and boiling point
- chemical properties, e.g. reactions with water, oxygen, acids and other chemicals.

These physical and chemical properties do not change and can be used to recognise an element.

Elements can be metals or non-metals.

Metals are malleable, which means they can be beaten into sheets.

Metals conduct electricity, conduct heat and can be beaten into sheets or drawn into wire. There are more metals than non-metals.

Non-metals do not conduct electricity or heat (with the exception of carbon in the form of graphite) and are brittle.

Here are some important examples. You need to learn the names and their chemical symbols.

Metals Element	Chemical symbol	Non-Metals Element	Chemical symbol
Aluminium	Al	Bromine	Br
Barium	Ba	Carbon	C
Calcium	Ca	Chlorine	Cl
Iron	Fe	Fluorine	F
Lead	Pb	Hydrogen	H
Magnesium	Mg	Nitrogen	N
Potassium	K	Oxygen	O
Silver	Ag	Phosphorus	P
Sodium	Na	Silicon	Si
Zinc	Zn	Sulphur	S

REMEMBER

Elements are the simplest substances known. They cannot be broken down into anything simpler. Elements combine chemically to form compounds.

Silver is a metal. Like all metals, it conducts electricity and can be beaten into sheets or drawn into wire. Sulfur does not conduct electricity and is very brittle.

Set up this electrical circuit to test whether or not an element is a metal or a non-metal.

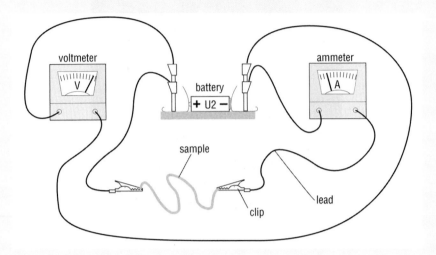

Try it with some samples given to you by your teacher.

Compounds

Elements combine by chemical reaction to form **compounds**. Simply mixing elements together does not make a compound. The elements that make up a compound are always present in the same ratios. This is why we are able to write chemical formulae for compounds. For example:

Compound	Chemical formula	Ratio of atoms in compound
Copper oxide	CuO	1 copper : 1 oxygen
Methane	CH_4	1 carbon : 4 hydrogens
Sulfuric acid	H_2SO_4	2 hydrogens : 1 sulfur : 4 oxygens

A compound has its own unique physical and chemical properties. Compounds can be identified from their properties. For example, the temperatures at which they melt and boil, and the chemical reactions they undergo (see qualitative analysis on page 85).

Atoms are held together in compounds by **chemical bonds**. These are either ionic bonds or covalent bonds. You can read about this on pages 187–190.

Mixtures

If you mix iron filings and sulfur powder, no matter in what proportions, we simply call it a mixture of iron and sulfur. It doesn't matter how much iron and how much sulfur is present. We still call it a mixture. It's quite straightforward to separate the iron and the sulfur. You just need a magnet to attract the iron filings and leave behind the sulfur. The mixture shows the combined chemical properties of iron and sulfur.

However, if you heat the mixture a reaction takes place and iron sulphide forms. This is a compound. Like any compound, the elements are present in fixed amounts. The formula FeS tells you that there are equal numbers of iron atoms and sulfur atoms. It has its own properties, quite different to those of iron and sulfur.

Obtaining raw materials

Raw materials are the starting point for manufacturing industries. They start life as part of the environment we live in – the Earth's crust, the water or the air. It costs money to extract them from the environment. It also costs money to purify them and more money to change them into useful substances. Why? Because every stage needs people, machines, buildings and energy – and all of these cost money. The cost of a substance depends on:

- how common the raw material is
- how easy it is to get the raw material
- how complicated the process is to change the raw material into the substance wanted
- how 'pure' the product is.

Substances from the ground

Some substances can be mined, quarried or extracted from the ground in some other way – and used just as they are. **Rock salt** is mined, crushed and put on roads to help melt ice in winter. **Limestone** is quarried and used as a building material in many parts of the country. **Marble** is also quarried and used for building. **Coal** is burnt in power stations to generate electricity. **Potassium chloride** is mined and put on the ground as a fertiliser.

A magnet can be used to separate iron from sulfur in a mixture. It will not separate the iron and sulfur in the compound iron sulphide however.

REMEMBER

The characteristic properties of a mixture are:

- there is no fixed proportion for the substances present
- its properties are the same as those of the substances that make it up
- the substances that make it up can be separated by physical means, for example, filtration, evaporation and chromatography.

Limestone is mainly calcium carbonate. In some parts of the country it is used as a building material. The yellow colour of the building blocks is due to 'rust' (iron oxide) in the limestone. Calcium carbonate and iron oxide are compounds. Yellow-coloured limestone is a mixture.

Making changes

Materials straight from the ground are useful. But mostly they are the raw materials from which many other substances are made. This involves changing them in some way.

There are two types of changes. You probably know about these already. **Physical changes** are things like melting a solid to make it liquid, and heating a liquid until it boils and becomes a gas. These are changes of state. The three **states of matter** are **solid**, **liquid** and **gas**. Importantly it is still the same chemical no matter what the state. Ice, water and steam are all the same chemical, water (H_2O). Physical changes are easily reversible. For example, ice melts to form water, and if you put it in a freezer it becomes ice again.

Chemical changes are just what the words say – changes that turn one chemical substance into a different substance. Unlike physical reactions, they are often difficult to reverse.

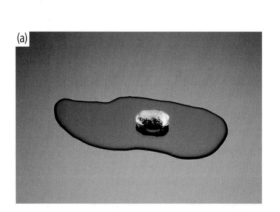

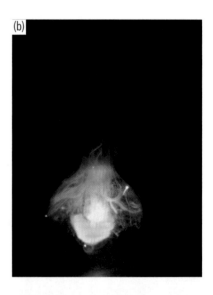

(a) A physical change. Ice melts to form water. The state changes from solid to liquid. But there is no chemical change. Ice and water are both H_2O.
(b) A chemical change. Sodium is a bright, silvery metal that reacts with chlorine (a yellow gas) to form a new substance – sodium chloride, a white solid. Sodium chorine is chemically very different to the substances it's made from.

Substances that are separated before use

Raw materials are mixtures. Usually substances must be separated from mixtures before they can be used. The raw material undergoes a physical change. Dissolving, filtration and evaporation are important techniques. You can read more about these techniques on pages 85–87 and 273–275.

Rock salt is mined. It's a mixture of sodium chloride and other substances. To extract the sodium chloride, the rock salt is washed with water. The sodium chloride **dissolves** to form a solution, leaving the unwanted rock. The mixture is filtered. The solution that passes through the filter paper is called the **filtrate** and the material left on the filter paper is the **insoluble residue**. Sodium chloride is obtained by **evaporating** the filtrate. This is called **evaporation**.

In some countries in the Persian Gulf pure water is obtained by **distilling** seawater. This is called **simple distillation**. Distillation is also used to get ethanol from a mixture of ethanol and water. This is the key process in whiskey distilleries all over Scotland.

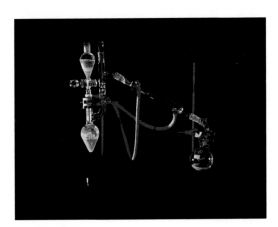

A liquid can be obtained from a mixture by distillation. Any dissolved solid remains in the distillation flask. If you want to obtain a sample of the dissolved solid, stop the distillation while there is still some solution in the flask. Dismantle the apparatus and pour the solution into an evaporating basin. Then evaporate in the usual way. The advantage of this method is that you can obtain samples of the solvent and the solute.

Crude oil comes from deep beneath the ground. It is an amazing cocktail of organic chemicals called hydrocarbons (meaning they are made of hydrogen and carbon only) and is very valuable. It's no coincidence that oil-producing countries are amongst the richest in the world. Crude oil can be separated by **fractional distillation**. Fractional distillation is used to separate mixtures of two or more liquids.

REMEMBER

- A **solute** dissolves in a **solvent** to give a **solution**.

- Soluble solids can be obtained from their solutions by evaporation.

- Solids can be separated from liquids by **filtration**. When filtering a mixture, the liquid passing through the filter is called the **filtrate** and the solid remaining on the filter is called the **insoluble residue**.

- A liquid can be obtained from a solution by **distillation**.

- Two or more liquids can be separated from one another by **fractional distillation**.

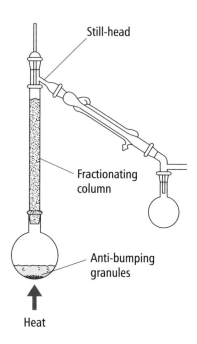

Still-head

Fractionating column

Anti-bumping granules

Heat

Fractional distillation is used to separate mixtures of two or more liquids. The length of the fractioning column and the surface area inside it determines the effectiveness of the separation.

The temperature at which the liquid distils over (its boiling point) can also be sued to identify it (see qualitative analysis on page 85). For example, the boiling point of water is 100 °C and of ethanol is 79 °C.

Metals from their ores

Ores contain a mineral of the metal mixed with waste material. Metals may be obtained from their ores by **reduction** (you can read more about this on pages 00–00). In **chemical reduction** carbon is often used. It is called a reducing agent. When the metal is found as an oxide the carbon reacts, removing the oxygen to form carbon dioxide and leave the metal.

For example:

iron oxide + carbon = **iron** + carbon dioxide
$2Fe_2O_3 + 3C \rightarrow 4Fe + 3CO_2$

lead oxide + carbon = **lead** + carbon dioxide
$2PbO + C \rightarrow 2Pb + CO_2$

Metals must usually be purified. How much depends on what they are to be used for, and affects the cost of the metal.

Aluminium is found in the ground as aluminium oxide. However, carbon cannot be used to reduce aluminium oxide. Aluminium is a reactive metal and carbon does not remove oxygen. Instead, aluminium is obtained by **electrolytic reduction**. The aluminium oxide is melted and electricity passed through the liquid oxide. Aluminium forms at the negative electrode and oxygen is given off at the positive electrode.

aluminium oxide = **aluminium** and **oxygen**

$2Al_2O_3 \rightarrow 4Al + 3O_2$

Other metals occur as salts such as chlorides, sulfates and nitrates. Various methods are used to get the metals, but use either chemical or electrolytic reduction.

REMEMBER

Metal ores are naturally occurring rocks containing the metal chemically combined with other elements (often oxygen). Metals can be obtained from their ores by a reduction reaction.

Questions

1   Classify each of the following materials as elements (metals and non-metals), compounds or mixtures using the information given:

   (a)   a silvery solid that conducts electricity and cannot be broken down into anything simpler

   (b)   a colourless liquid that boils at a fixed temperature and leaves no solid when it evaporates

   (c)   a blue liquid that that boils at a fixed temperature and leaves a blue solid when it evaporates

   (d)   a yellow solid that breaks very easily (it's brittle) and cannot be broken down into anything simpler

   (e)   a white solid that melts when heated strongly and decomposes when electricity is passed through the melt.

2   Describe tests you could use to tell if an element was a metal or a non-metal.

3   Classify each of the following materials as elements (metals and non-metals), compounds or mixtures:

   • river water
   • iron
   • chocolate
   • vegetable soup
   • salt
   • sugar
   • carbon
   • bread
   • water
   • air

4   Name three substances that can be used straight from the ground as raw materials for making useful chemicals.

5   Write a method for separating sodium chloride from seawater. Explain why the product is likely to contain small amounts of other chemicals.

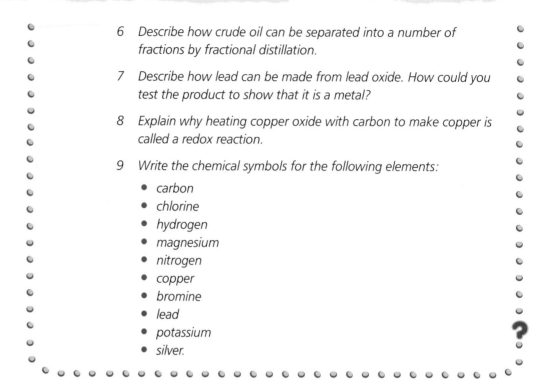

6   Describe how crude oil can be separated into a number of fractions by fractional distillation.

7   Describe how lead can be made from lead oxide. How could you test the product to show that it is a metal?

8   Explain why heating copper oxide with carbon to make copper is called a redox reaction.

9   Write the chemical symbols for the following elements:

  • carbon
  • chlorine
  • hydrogen
  • magnesium
  • nitrogen
  • copper
  • bromine
  • lead
  • potassium
  • silver.

Types of chemicals

You need to be able to:

  • *classify chemical compounds as inorganic or organic, given their formulae*

  • *identify examples of bulk chemicals (ammonia, sulfuric acid and polyethene) and of fine/speciality chemicals (medicines, dyes, pigments)*

  • *name some simple compounds, given their formulae, and state the formula, given the name of the compound (see below).*

Inorganic or organic?

The raw materials for making i**norganic compounds** are mainly non-living things such as rocks and minerals or the air. They are made of elements other than carbon (there are a lot to choose from – over a hundred). Some important examples are metals, glass, ceramics, fertilisers, sulfuric acid, nitric acid and ammonia. But the list goes on . . . and on.

Carbon may be only one of a hundred or so elements, but it forms over 10 million compounds, and the number is still rising. **Organic compounds** mainly come from living things and they all contain carbon. Examples are petroleum products, pharmaceuticals and polymers.

The rocks and sand are inorganic substances. The seaweed in the rock pools is made of organic substances. The children are made of both organic and inorganic substances!

You can spot whether a chemical is inorganic or organic from its chemical formula. If there are no carbon atoms (**C**), it's inorganic. If it has carbon atoms, it's organic. However, as with most things in life, it isn't quite this simple! Carbon dioxide, carbonates and hydrogen carbonates all contain carbon, but they are categorised as inorganic. You will see examples of these in the list of inorganic chemicals given below.

You need to learn the names and chemical formulae of the following examples of inorganic compounds.

Compound	Formula	Compound	Formula
Ammonia	NH_3	Barium chloride	$BaCl_2$
Carbon dioxide	CO_2	Sodium chloride	$NaCl$
Water	H_2O	Calcium carbonate	$CaCO_3$
Hydrochloric acid	HCl	Copper carbonate	$CuCO_3$
Sulfuric acid	H_2SO_4	Sodium carbonate	Na_2CO_3
Calcium oxide	CaO	Potassium nitrate	KNO_3
Iron oxide	Fe_2O_3	Silver nitrate	$AgNO_3$
Lead oxide	PbO	Barium sulfate	$BaSO_4$
Sodium hydroxide	$NaOH$	Copper sulfate	$CuSO_4$
		Sodium sulfate	Na_2SO_4

Here are some examples of organic compounds. Try to learn their names and chemical formulae. By the way, in industry many of these are still called by 'old names' and so these are given in *italics*.

Compound	Formula	Compound	Formula
Methane	CH_4	Benzene	C_6H_6
Ethane	C_2H_6	Ethanol (*ethyl alcohol*)	C_2H_5OH
Propane	C_3H_8	Ethanoic acid (*acetic acid*)	CH_3COOH
Butane	C_4H_{10}	Propanone (*acetone*)	CH_3COCH_3
Ethene (*ethylene*)	C_2H_4	Methanal (*formaldehyde*)	$HCHO$
Propene (*propylene*)	C_3H_6	Carbamide (*urea*)	$(NH_2)_2CO$

REMEMBER

You can tell from the chemical formula of a compound whether it is inorganic or organic. Organic compounds always contain the element carbon, and so you will see C in the formula. Inorganic compounds (apart from carbonates) do not.

Bulk and fine (speciality) chemicals

Bulk chemicals are ones that are made in very large quantities. They are the starting point for making other chemicals. Fine (or speciality) chemicals are made on a smaller scale and are usually more expensive. The primary chemical industries are petrochemical, chloralkali, sulfur, nitrogen and phosphorus.

This primary industry chemicals	. . . uses these raw materials	. . . to manufacture these bulk	. . . and supply secondary industries that make other bulk chemicals and fine/ speciality chemicals, e.g.
Petrochemical	Crude oil	Simple unsaturated hydrocarbons, like ethene and propene	Polymers Pharmaceuticals Dyes Agrochemicals
Chloralkali	Rock salt (sodium chloride) Limestone (calcium carbonate)	Chlorine Sodium hydroxide Sodium carbonate	Organic chemicals containing chlorine Hydrochloric acid Bleaches and disinfectants Detergents Glass and paper Solvents Other inorganic and organic chemicals
Sulfur	Sulfur Air	Sulfuric acid	Fertilisers Paints Pigments Detergents Fibres Plastics
Nitrogen	Nitrogen	Ammonia Nitric acid Carbamide	Fertilisers (mainly) Explosives Dyes Textiles Food Pharmaceuticals
Phosphorus	Phosphate rock	Phosphoric acid Salts of phosphoric acid	Fertilisers (mainly) Detergents Food Lubricants

Products made by the secondary industries may be bulk or fine/ speciality chemicals. Here are some examples of bulk and fine chemicals.

Bulk

- Some chemicals, such as hydrochloric acid
- Polymers like polyethene ('polythene')
- Fertilisers like ammonium nitrate
- Detergents

Fine

- Pharmaceuticals – chemicals used in medicines, such as anti-cancer drugs and drugs for heart disease
- Dyes
- Agrochemicals – chemicals used in pesticides, herbicides and fungicides

However, there is no clear distinction, as you can probably imagine.

REMEMBER

Bulk chemicals are produced in huge quantities. Fine or speciality chemicals are made on a much smaller scale.

Questions

1 Classify the following chemical compounds as inorganic or organic from their formulae:
  (a) magnesium oxide, MgO
  (b) sodium sulfate, Na_2SO_4
  (c) methane, CH_4
  (d) lead chloride, $PbCl_2$
  (e) ethanol, C_2H_5OH
  (f) propanone, CH_3COCH_3
  (g) ammonia, NH_3
  (h) hydrochloric acid, HCl.

2 State whether the following chemicals are bulk chemicals or fine/speciality chemicals:
  (a) ammonia
  (b) ethanol
  (c) food dyes
  (d) paracetamol
  (e) sulfuric acid
  (f) polyethene
  (g) indigestion tablets
  (h) pigments used in artists' paints.

3 Copy and complete the table below.

Name of compound	Chemical formula
Copper oxide	
Calcium hydroxide	
	CO_2
Zinc chloride	
	Na_2CO_3
	$AgNO_3$
Potassium sulfate	
	Fe_2O_3

Mixtures and formulations

You need to be able to:

- *explain the composition of a solution, suspension, gel, emulsion, foam and aerosol*

- *give an example of each type of mixture and explain why each is useful.*

Everything we see, handle and smell is a **mixture**. Even chemicals that are labelled 'pure' are mixtures. For example 99.9% ammonium sulfate contains 0.1% of other chemicals. So, even though it is almost all ammonium sulfate, actually it is a mixture.

Separating mixtures is a major job for scientists, as you read in the previous sections. It takes time, energy and money. The harder the scientist strives to make something pure, the more it costs.

Yet nearly all the chemicals we buy are mixtures, made by combining chemicals that have been separated and purified. This combination is usually to a given recipe, called a **formulation**.

Paints are formulations. Medicines are formulations. Washing powders are formulations. And the list goes on.

One substance is **dispersed** in another. The substance dispersed may be solid, liquid or gas. The medium in which it is dispersed may also be solid, liquid or gas. So there are lots of possibilities, and scientists use them all to make useful products.

Mixtures of solids and liquids

Many solids dissolve in liquids to give a clear **solution**. You can read about this on page 85. Some solids mix with a liquid to form a **suspension**. The solid doesn't dissolve, but it doesn't settle out either. It stays suspended in the liquid. The difference between a suspension and a solution is clear. Or rather, it isn't. You can't see through a suspension! Some solids mix with a liquid to make a **gel**. Gels are a kind of suspension, but they 'set' and become thick, for example, hair gel. The solid forms a network that traps the water.

Solution	Transparent solution of a solid dispersed in a liquid	Tea without milk, sugar in water
Suspension	Cloudy mixture of a solid dispersed in a liquid	Milk of Magnesia, toothpaste
Gel	Jelly-like mixture of a solid dispersed in a liquid	Hair gel, jelly

Hair gel is a jelly-like mixture of a solid dispersed in a liquid.

Mixtures of liquids

When you mix two liquids there are two possibilities for what happens. Some dissolve when they are mixed. We say the liquids are **miscible**. Others do not dissolve and you can see two layers. We say they are **immiscible**. Alcohol and water are miscible. Oil and water are immiscible.

Sometimes immiscible liquids can form a kind of suspension called an **emulsion**. Just like a suspension it appears cloudy (or opaque). An emulsifier is often added to stop droplets joining together to form a separate layer again.

Emulsion	Cloudy mixture containing tiny droplets of one liquid dispersed in another liquid	Paint, milk, cream, mayonnaise, salad cream

Both mayonnaise and milk are examples of emulsions – cloudy mixtures where tiny droplets of one liquid are dispersed in another liquid. In both cases, oil or fat is dispersed in water.

Mixtures of gases and liquids

Some gases are soluble in liquids. For example, carbon dioxide is slightly soluble in water. Lemonade is a mixture of dissolved solids (e.g. sugar and flavourings) and a dissolved gas (carbon dioxide) in water. All fizzy drinks are solutions of carbon dioxide.

Sometimes bubbles of a gas are trapped in a liquid and make a **foam**. It can also happen the other way round. Tiny droplets of liquid are dispersed in a gas. This is called an **aerosol**.

Foam	Bubbles of gas dispersed in a liquid	Whipped cream, froth on a glass of beer, washing lather, shaving foam
Aerosol	Droplets of a liquid dispersed in a gas	Spray deodorant, hair spray

Spray deodorant is an example of an aerosol – a mixture of tiny droplets of a liquid dispersed in a gas.

Mixtures of gases and solids

We talked about foams above. But as well as having bubbles of gas dispersed in a liquid, a foam can also be formed with the gas dispersed in a solid.

Foam	Bubbles of a gas dispersed in a solid	Sponge cake, foam rubber, clay soil

REMEMBER

A mixture consists of one substance dispersed (finely spread out) in another.

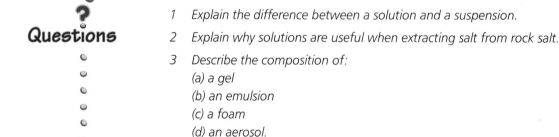

Questions

1 Explain the difference between a solution and a suspension.

2 Explain why solutions are useful when extracting salt from rock salt.

3 Describe the composition of:
   (a) a gel
   (b) an emulsion
   (c) a foam
   (d) an aerosol.
   Give an example of each type of mixture and what it is used for.

Knowing more about what you are working with

You need to:

- *describe the structure of the atom in terms of protons, neutrons and electrons*

- *have a basic understanding of ionic bonding as involving transfer of electrons (sodium chloride, magnesium oxide) and of covalent bonding as involving sharing of electrons (hydrogen chloride, water)*

- *know that energy is required to break chemical bonds and is given out when new bonds are formed*

- *know the meanings of the terms exothermic reaction and endothermic reaction*

- *be able to write symbol equations for the chemical reactions in this unit.*

How small can you go?

Try an experiment. Take a hammer to a stone and smash it (if you actually try this don't forget to wear safety glasses, and mind your fingers!). How small is the tiniest bit you get? There is a limit. You can see the bits, even if you need a microscope. But now try what scientists call a 'thought experiment'. Imagine being able to break up even the smallest bits. Could you go on forever or is there a limit? Well, the answer is that the smallest 'bit' would be an **atom**. This is unimaginably small – really tiny.

_____

Let's try to get an idea of just how small atoms are. Pencil 'lead' is actually carbon. If you draw a pencil line 3 cm long (the same length as the line drawn here) there will be about a hundred million atoms from end to end and about a million atoms across it.

Atomic particles

Atoms are made up of smaller particles – **protons**, **neutrons** and **electrons**. The atoms of any particular element have the same number of protons and electrons. You need to know about the structure of the atom. This table summarises what you need to know.

Sub-atomic particle	. . . is found	. . . with a charge	. . . and relative mass
Proton	in the nucleus	Positive (+1)	1
Neutron	in the nucleus	No charge (0)	1
Electron	moving in space around the nucleus	Negative (-1)	1 / 1850

...re the protons and neutrons are found. It is
...e electrons move in a fixed way around
...ces between the electrons and the protons

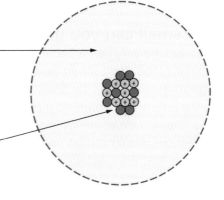

...........d the atom to a sports stadium, the nucleus would be the size of a table tennis ball and the electrons could be anywhere in the stadium.

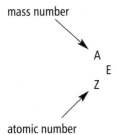

REMEMBER

A word of warning. We have described a **model** for the atom. A model is used by scientists to help them explain things they see. It is not a **fact**. If you go further in science you will find that models are being modified all the time to try to explain more and more facts.

region in which eight electrons are found

nucleus: consisting of protons and neutrons

This picture represents an oxygen atom. It consists of a nucleus and a region outside it where the electrons can be found.

Atoms and elements

The atoms of an element are the same as one another – almost! Every atom of a particular element has the same number of protons and electrons. The number of protons in an atom is called the **atomic number** (given the symbol Z). As atoms have no overall charge, the number of protons and electrons must be the same.

So the difference between the mass number and the atomic number tells you the number of neutrons:

mass number

$$^A_Z E$$

atomic number

A = number of protons + number of neutrons

Z = number of protons (and number of electrons)

$A - Z$ = number of neutrons

Isotopes

The number of neutrons can differ from atom to atom of the same element, but only within a very small range. For example, carbon can exist as carbon-12 and carbon-14. The atomic number of carbon is 6. All carbon atoms have 6 protons in the nucleus. In carbon-12 atoms there are 6 neutrons, but in carbon-14 atoms there are 8 neutrons. There is no difference in chemical reactivity, just in mass.

Atoms of the same element with different numbers of neutrons are called **isotopes**. The chemical properties of an element do not depend on what isotopes it's made up from.

Look at the following examples:

$$^{12}_{6}C \quad \text{carbon-12}$$

$$^{14}_{6}C \quad \text{carbon-14}$$

Representing isotopes of carbon.

This element	. . . has the atomic number	. . . which means each of its atoms has	Its atoms can have
hydrogen	1	1 proton and 1 electron	1 (most often), 2 or 3 neutrons
Carbon	6	6 protons and 6 electrons	6 (most often) or 7 neutrons
Sodium	11	11 protons and 11 electrons	12 (most often) or 13 neutrons
Chlorine	19	19 protons and 19 electrons	14 or 15 neutrons

The periodic table

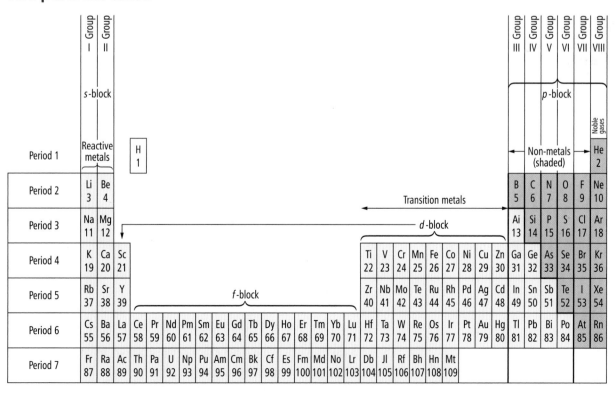

The **periodic table** is a clever way of arranging the elements. If they are put in order of atomic number it turns out that elements with similar properties occur at regular intervals. Look at the periodic table above. Elements in any one column have properties that are similar to one another. These columns are called **groups**. The rows are called **periods** and from left to right the elements in a period change from metals to non-metals.

The periodic table is one of science's great success stories. It summarises patterns and relationships of the elements in a simple form.

Electrons in atoms

The reactions of an element depend on how its electrons are arranged in its atoms. This is a very important idea.

To understand how atoms join together you need to know how their electrons are arranged. Modern theories are very sophisticated, but we will use an early simpler model. It is fine for helping you understand what's going on.

Electrons are found in shells around the nucleus. Try to imagine a ball. This represents a shell and the electrons move around the surface of the ball. Now imagine there are several balls of different sizes, each one enclosing a smaller one. Look at the diagram below.

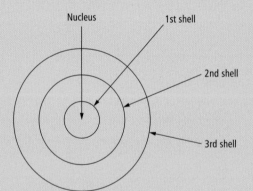

A representation of electron shells

Each shell can have only a certain number of electrons in it:

1st shell	2 electrons
2nd shell	8 electrons
3rd shell	18 electrons
4th shell	32 electrons

But again not everything is quite that straightforward (this is why the theory has been refined). The 3rd shell is filled until there are 8 electrons there. Then the next 2 go into the 4th shell. After this, the next 10 fill the 3rd shell again. You just have to learn the rule.

It is quite easy to work out where the electrons are in an atom of a particular element. First you need to know the atomic number of the

Extension Work

element. This tells you how many electrons there are altogether in the atom. Then start filling the shells:

Element	Atomic number	Number of electrons in				Shorthand
		1st shell	2nd shell	3rd shell	4th shell	
H	1	1				1
He	2	2				2
Li	3	2	1			2, 1
Be	4	2	2			2, 2
B	5	2	3			2, 3
C	6	2	4			2, 4
N	7	2	5			2, 5
O	8	2	6			2, 6
F	9	2	7			2, 7
Ne	10	2	8			2, 8
Na	11	2	8	1		2, 8, 1
Mg	12	2	8	2		2, 8, 2
Al	13	2	8	3		2, 8, 3
Si	14	2	8	4		2, 8, 4
P	15	2	8	5		2, 8, 5
S	16	2	8	6		2, 8, 6
Cl	17	2	8	7		2, 8, 7
Ar	18	2	8	8		2, 8, 8
K	19	2	8	8	1	2, 8, 8, 1
Ca	20	2	8	8	2	2, 8, 8, 2

How the electrons are arranged in an atom determines what types of bonds, and how many, that atom can form with other atoms.

You will see that helium (He), neon (Ne) and argon (Ar) have filled shells. This helps to explain why they do not usually form bonds with other atoms. In fact, the old name for these elements was the inert gases.

Chemical bonding
Elements combine to form compounds. Electrons are rearranged between the atoms of the elements in a way that chemical bonds form between atoms of different elements. The type of bonding helps us to explain the properties of compounds.

Ionic bonding
Ionic bonding involves transfer of electrons between atoms. This leaves one group of atoms with fewer electrons than protons. These are positive ions, called cations. The transfer means that each atom in another group has more electrons than protons. These are negative ions, called anions. Generally, metal atoms lose electrons to form cations and non-metal atoms gain electrons to form anions. The ionic bond is the attraction between the oppositely charged ions

Sodium chloride forms when sodium and chlorine react. Sodium atoms lose electrons and chlorine atoms gain them. We can represent this with dot-and-cross diagrams:

Sodium chloride, NaCl

Particle	Symbol	Arrangement of electrons
Sodium atom	Na	2,8,1
Sodium ion	Na^+	2,8
Chlorine atom	Cl	2,8,7
Chloride ion	Cl^-	2,8,8

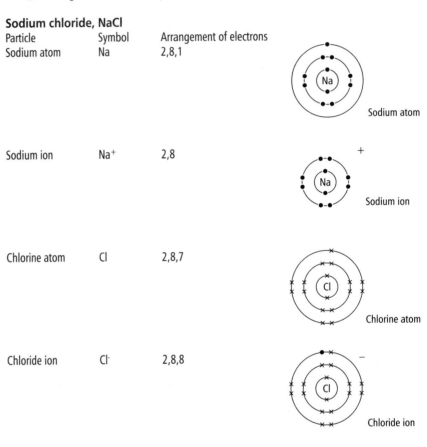

Sodium atom

Sodium ion

Chlorine atom

Chloride ion

Magnesium oxide forms when magnesium and oxygen react. Magnesium atoms lose electrons and oxygen atoms gain them. We can represent this with dot-and-cross diagrams:

Magnesium oxide, MgO

Particle	Symbol	Arrangement of electrons
Magnesium atom	Mg	2,8,2
Magnesium ion	Mg^{2+}	2,8
Oxygen atom	O	2,6
Oxide ion	O^{2-}	2,8

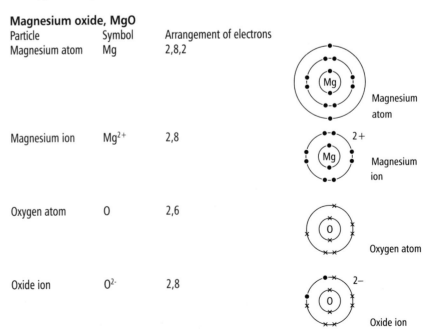

Magnesium atom

Magnesium ion

Oxygen atom

Oxide ion

Calcium chloride forms when sodium and chlorine react. Ca...
chlorine atoms gain them. We can represent this with dot-a...

Calcium chloride, CaCl$_2$

Particle	Symbol	Arrangement of electr...
Calcium atom	Ca	2,8,8,2
Calcium ion	Ca^{2+}	2,8,8
Chlorine atom	Cl	2,8,7
Chloride ion	Cl$^-$	2,8,8

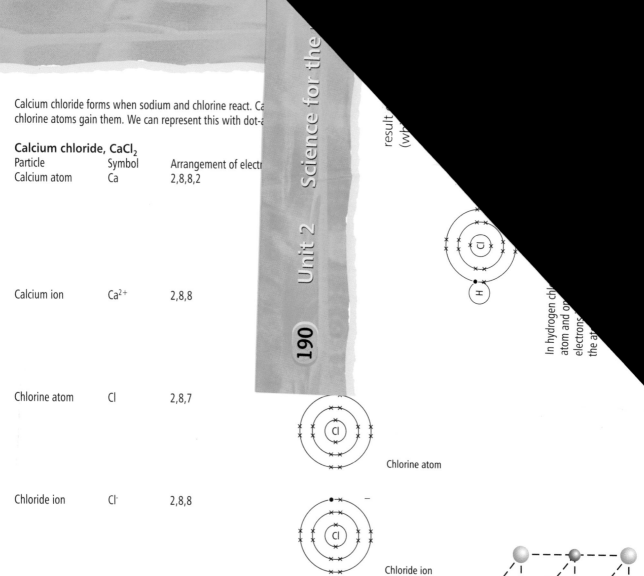

Chlorine atom

Chloride ion

result
(wh...

In hydrogen chl...
atom and o...
electrons...
the a...

Look carefully at the dot-and-cross diagrams. You will see that in each case the ions have filled shells of electrons. You will also see that the charges on cations and anions must balance one another as the compound does not have a charge.

Compounds with ionic bonding:

- have giant structures
- are solids with high melting points
- conduct electricity when they are melted
- are often soluble in water and insoluble in organic liquids (though there are exceptions to both these generalisations).

Covalent bonding

Covalent bonding involves sharing of electrons. Each atom shares one or more of its electrons with another atom. The covalent bond is the

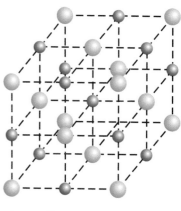

● Na$^+$ ○ Cl

The sodium ions and chloride ions in sodium chloride are arranged in a giant structure. The bonding between the oppositely charged ions is equally strong throughout the structure. This is why sodium chloride, like all compounds with ionic bonding, has a high melting point. It takes a lot of energy to break the bonds and enable the ions to move freely.

of both nuclei (which are positive) attracting the shared electrons which are negative). Some examples are given in the diagrams below.

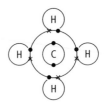

...ride, HCl, one hydrogen ...e chlorine atom share two ...in the covalent bond that holds ...oms together.

In water, H_2O, each hydrogen atom shares two electrons with the oxygen atom.

In methane, CH_4, each hydrogen atom shares two electrons with the carbon atom.

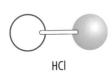

HCl

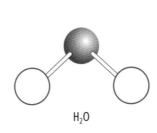

H_2O

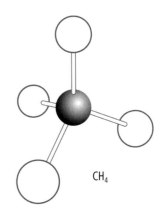

CH_4

Hydrogen chloride, water and methane have molecular structures. The bonding between atoms in a molecule is strong, but between one molecule and another is weak. This is why compounds with molecular structures have relatively low melting and boiling points. Not much energy is needed to break the bonds between one molecule and another. Molecules also have definite shapes. These can affect how they behave. For example, the effectiveness of therapeutic drugs owes much to the shapes of their molecules.

REMEMBER

The properties of a compound depend on:

- the type of bonding between its atoms
- the strength of the bonds between its atoms
- how its particles are arranged: giant structure or molecular structure.

Compounds with covalent bonding:

- have either molecular structures or giant structures
- are gases, liquids or solids
- do not conduct electricity
- are often insoluble in water and soluble in organic liquids (though there are exceptions to both these generalisations).

Energy changes during chemical reactions
All chemical reactions involve the transfer of energy, often in the form of heat energy.

Breaking and making chemical bonds
Whenever you try to pull two things apart that are attracted to one another you have to use your energy. Pick up some paper clips with a magnet and then take them off. It takes energy. So, not surprisingly perhaps, it takes energy to break chemical bonds. If it takes energy to break bonds you might expect that energy would be given out when bonds form. And that's just what happens.

Scientists can measure the strength of chemical bonds. They usually give the strength in terms of the energy needed to break one mole of bonds. The units are kJ mol^{-1} (which means kilojoules per mole of bonds). Here are some examples:

Bond	Energy (in kJ) to break one mole of bonds
C-H	435
Cl-Cl	243
H-Cl	432
C-Cl	346

Let's look at the reaction between methane and chlorine. In sunlight they react to form chloromethane, CH_3Cl, and hydrogen chloride, HCl.

$$CH_4 + Cl_2 \rightarrow CH_3Cl + HCl$$

We can calculate the energy change when this reaction takes place:

	CH_4 +	Cl_2	$\rightarrow$	CH_3Cl +	HCl
Bonds broken	C-H	Cl-Cl			
Energy required	435	243			
	Total	678			
Bonds formed				C-Cl	H-Cl
Energy given out				346	432
				Total	778

You can see that more energy is given out than was used to break the bonds in the reactants. The net change is a release of 100 kJ. Because the energy is given out, we show this using a minus sign, in other words we write -100 kJ.

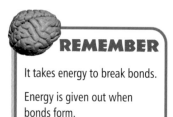

REMEMBER

It takes energy to break bonds.

Energy is given out when bonds form.

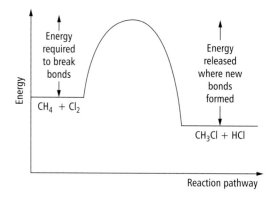

Representing the energy changes for the reaction $CH_4 + Cl_2 \rightarrow CH_3Cl + HCl$

It's the same idea with ionic bonds. For example, it takes 771 kJ to pull apart one mole of sodium ions, Na^+, and one mole of chloride ions, Cl^-, in sodium chloride. In magnesium oxide, it takes 3889 kJ to pull apart one mole of magnesium ions, Mg^{2+}, and one mole of oxide ions, O^{2-}.

Exothermic and endothermic reactions

You will probably carry out chemical reactions in the laboratory and find that some reaction mixtures get hot and others get cold. This is all to do with the breaking and forming of bonds. When a chemical reaction takes place bonds in the reactants must be broken. As the product forms new bonds are made.

Try these experiments to investigate the energy changes when chemical reactions take place. You should wear protective clothing and eye protection when trying these experiments. A risk assessment must have been carried out first.

Procedure
Ammonium chloride and water

1   Put about 4 cm depth of distilled water in a boiling tube. Record the temperature of the water with a thermometer.
2   Add a spatula measure of ammonium chloride to the water and stir it with the thermometer (take care, thermometers are fragile and can break easily).
3   Look at the thermometer and write down the temperature of the mixture.

Ammonium chloride   HARMFUL

Copper sulfate and zinc

1   Put about 4 cm depth of 1 mol dm^{-3} copper sulfate solution in a boiling tube. Record the temperature with a thermometer.
2   Add a spatula measure of zinc powder to the copper sulfate solution and stir with the thermometer (take care, thermometers are fragile and can break easily). Note: zinc powder is flammable so make sure there are no naked flames nearby.
3   Look at the thermometer and write down the temperature of the mixture.

Copper sulfate   HARMFUL

Zinc powder   FLAMMABLE

Hydrochloric acid and sodium hydroxide

1   Put about 3 cm depth of 2 mol dm^{-3} sodium hydroxide solution in a boiling tube. Record the temperature with a thermometer.
2   Add an equal volume of 2 mol dm^{-3} hydrochloric acid to the sodium hydroxide solution and stir with the thermometer (take care, thermometers are fragile and can break easily).
3   Look at the thermometer and write down the temperature of the mixture.

Hydrochloric acid   IRRITANT

Sodium hydroxide solution   CORROSIVE

Your teacher may suggest other experiments you can try.

In each case decide whether the reaction was exothermic or endothermic.

In the example you looked at above, we calculated that energy would be given out in the reaction:

$$CH_4 + Cl_2 \rightarrow CH_3Cl + HCl$$

But what happens to that energy? Well, it simply heats up the surroundings. The container in which the reaction takes place gets hotter, as does the air around it.

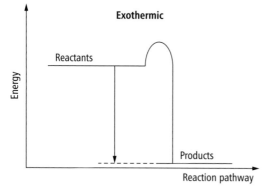

When less energy is needed to break bonds than is given out when new bonds form the reaction is said to be exothermic; the extra energy is usually given out in the form of heat energy. The surroundings get warmer.

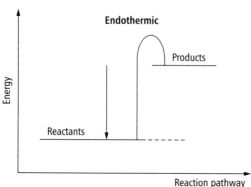

When more energy is needed to break bonds than is given out when new bonds form the reaction is said to be endothermic; the extra energy is transferred from the surroundings in the form of heat energy. The surroundings get cooler.

REMEMBER

Exothermic reactions give out heat energy and the surroundings get warmer.

Endothermic reactions absorb heat energy from the surroundings and the surroundings get cooler.

The temperature of an exothermic reaction can be maintained by cooling while the temperature of an endothermic reaction can be maintained by heating.

Questions

1 Describe the structure of the atom in terms of protons, neutrons and electrons. Make sure you write down their charges, relative sizes and whereabouts in the atom.

2 Explain in terms of electrons:
(a) ionic bonding   (b) covalent bonding.

3 Draw dot-and-cross diagrams to represent the bonding in:
(a) sodium chloride   (b) magnesium oxide
(c) hydrogen chloride   (d) water
In each case state whether the bonding is ionic or covalent.

4 Copy and complete the following:
It needs . . . . . . to break chemical bonds. When new bonds form . . . . . is . . . . You can recognise an exothermic reaction because the temperature of the reaction mixture . . . . You can recognise an endothermic reaction because the temperature of the reaction mixture . . . .

2.3 Materials for making things

Types of materials

You need to be able to:

- *classify materials as metals, polymers, ceramics and composites*

- *describe the uses of these materials and their advantages and disadvantages over naturally occurring materials*

- *use sources of data (tables, graphs, CD-ROMs, databases, the Internet) to find the physical properties of materials.*

Classifying materials

You might well find the terms element, compound, mixture, substance and material confusing. You looked at elements, compounds and mixtures on pages 168–171 and should know about the differences.

Scientists use the word substance to describe anything that is an element, compound or mixture. Some substances are processed into **materials** that can be used to make useful things. For example, buildings, clothing, trainers, mobile phones, surfboards, household goods and leisure products are constructed from materials.

The things you can see in this kitchen have been made for a purpose. The materials used for each must have the right properties.

There are four important types of manufactured material:

- metals
- polymers
- ceramics
- composites.

They are all solids. It's vital that scientists know about the properties of these materials. When searching for a material for a particular purpose, scientists will try to match the properties to the use.

Metals, ceramics, polymers and composites each have a different set of properties. The uses of materials depend on these physical properties. Here are some important properties that you need to know about. You can read about how to determine some of these on pages 115–123.

Density

The density of a material is the mass of 1 m^3 of that material. Density is an important property. Keeping the mass of something as small as possible is often important, for example, in aircraft. Materials with low densities are needed. However, these materials must also meet other requirements such as being tough and strong.

The first flight in a plane with an engine was in 1903. The Wright brothers designed, built and flew it. They understood the importance of low density materials! Nowadays engineers still use lightweight materials to make aircraft. However, nowadays the materials are much stronger and tougher than those used by the Wright brothers.

Electrical conduction

An electric current in a solid is a flow of electrons. When a solid is connected to a battery, the electrons at the negative terminal have more electrical energy than those at the positive terminal. If they are free to move in the solid, electrons will drift down the sample, converting some of the electrical energy into heat energy. In many applications a material that conducts electricity well is needed. At other times a good insulator (poor conductor) is needed.

An electric plug is a good example of an object with parts that conduct electricity and other parts that are electrical insulators. The prongs and terminals must be good conductors, but it would cause electric shocks if the casing also conducted electricity.

Thermal conduction

When a solid is given extra heat energy, its particles vibrate more. If each particle is firmly bound to its neighbours, it cannot vibrate without moving its neighbours. So heat energy injected at one end of a solid must inevitably be shared amongst more and more particles as time goes on. Heat energy is conducted along all solids; it flows from the hot end to the cold end. Just as with electrical conduction, for some uses materials with good thermal conduction are required (for example, heat exchangers), but at other times good thermal insulators are needed (for example, winter clothing, duvets and house insulation).

This cooking pot is made from metal. Metal is a good conductor of heat (it has a high thermal conductivity). However, the handle must be made of a material that is a poor conductor of heat (in other words, an insulator) otherwise the cook would find it difficult to remove the pot from the stove! It also helps if the pot is made from low-density materials so that it's light and can be lifted easily when full.

Strength, stiffness and hardness

Strength is important. Climbers need to know if a rope is strong enough to support their weight. Car manufacturers need to know if a car frame is strong enough to protect the driver and passengers in an accident. **Tensile strength** can be determined by adding weights to something until it stops stretching and breaks. The units used to measure it are Pascals (Pa). A strong material has strong bonds holding all of its particles in place. A large force is needed to move the particles away from each other. Some materials have weak bonds between their particles. When these materials are stretched, the weak bonds give way relatively easily, allowing the sample to break.

A thin wooden shelf is not particularly stiff and bends when heavy books are put on it. However, a thick wooden shelf is very stiff. There are several materials from which shelves can be made. First, you should choose one with a high tensile strength. Then you should make sure it is thick enough for the weight it has to support. Other things might influence your choice, such as cost and appearance.

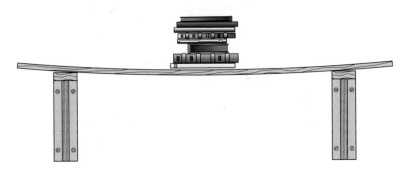

Materials with high tensile strength are usually stiff. The **stiffness** of a material tells you how easily it stretches or bends. For some uses materials need to be stiff. For others they need to be flexible or bendy. Bike frames must be stiff; fishing rods must be flexible. However, unlike tensile strength, stiffness depends on the material used *and* the shape and size of the object. So a thin wooden shelf will bend more easily under the weight of heavy books than a thick one made of the same material. A narrow piece of metal tubing will bend more easily than a tube with a wide diameter.

The **hardness** of a material is one of its most important properties. It tells you how resistant the material is to dents and scratches. Hardness is determined by the size of a dent made in a material by an object. Relative hardness is a comparison of the hardness of materials. For example, you can decide which is the harder of two materials by seeing which one will scratch or dent the other. Just like strength, the hardness of a material depends upon how strong the bonds between its particles are.

Drills made for drilling wood or bricks (masonry) are made of different materials. Masonry drills must have much harder tips than wood drills. If you visit a DIY store, look at the packaging and try to find out what very hard material is used on the tips of masonry drills.

Toughness

In a tough material the particles can change their position when enough force is applied. The material is said to be **plastic**. This might be confusing because plastic is also used to describe a number of things made from polymers (like a plastic ruler). In **brittle** materials the particles cannot change their position without allowing the sample to break into pieces. We also use the terms malleable (how easily a material can be flattened into a sheet) and **ductile** (how easily a material can be pulled into a filament or wire).

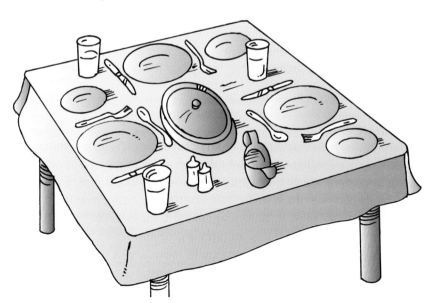

Getting the right material for the job is important when eating. Plates are usually ceramic. They are very hard and will not be scratched by knifes and forks. They are not affected by hot things. However, they do break very easily because ceramics are brittle. Picnic plates are usually made of a polymer. They are plastic rather than brittle and so don't break. However, they do scratch easily. Knifes and forks are usually metal (sometimes with a polymer handle). This is because they are strong yet malleable, allowing them to be manufactured into the right shape. What materials are used to hold drinks, and why?

Summarising the properties of materials

The table below summarises the differences in these properties. However, you should be aware that there are many exceptions. Scientists, technologists and engineers are always working to find ways of making materials with particular properties. **Cost** is not included in the list. But it is an essential consideration!

Property	Type of material			
	Metals	**Polymers**	**Ceramics**	**Composites**
Density	High	Low	Medium	Medium
Electrical resistance	Low	High	High	High
Thermal conduction	High	Low	Low	Low
Strength	High	Low	High	Low
Stiffness	High	Low	High	High
Hardness	Medium	Low	High	High
Toughness	High	High	Low	High

The properties of materials differ because of the different ways their atoms are arranged (the **structure**), the type of bonding and the strength of the bonding. The structure of each class of material gives it its unique mixture of properties. You will read about this later (pages 202–209).

The uses of metals, polymers, ceramics and composites

Materials are used to make things. You came across some examples in the previous section. The list, however, is almost endless. Just look around you and ask yourself what things are made of – and then ask why.

Construction

Technologists and engineers make **structures**. Structures are things we make to support other things. A bridges, is an example of a structure. Tables and chairs are also structures. Picture a bridge. It must be able to hold up its own weight as well as that of traffic passing over it. Structures usually need to be strong yet light, for example, planes, cars and boats. The reason for the strength is probably obvious. The reason for lightness is because it takes energy to move any of these. The lighter something is, the less energy is needed to move it. Less energy means less fuel, and less fuel means lower costs.

Metals and polymers are used to make structures. Ceramics are rarely used because of their brittleness. Glass is an exception where its transparency is an essential property. Composites such as reinforced steel and reinforced glass fibre are also used in construction.

The most effective use of materials comes from their properties together with clever ways of designing the structures. For example, a sheet of paper has little resistance to bending, but roll it into a tube and it becomes stiff. In the picture, the bridge has been designed for maximum strength with the minimum quantities of materials.

Wood is a naturally occurring material and is still used in construction. For example, many modern houses are built on timber frames. Joists and rafters are invariably made of wood. However, wood burns quite easily and is not easy to shape. Hardwoods, such as oak and teak, are the strongest and most long-lasting. Softwoods, such as pine, are less good but are still used. A major problem is that hardwood trees grow very slowly. It takes a lot of time and careful planning to make sure we do not use up the natural reserves before they can be replaced. Softwood grows relatively quickly and so this is less of a problem (but it still needs to be managed).

Clothing

Clothing is usually made from fibres. These can be knitted or woven into fabric. Naturally occurring materials such as cotton and wool or from synthetic fibres such as polyester and nylon are used. All of these materials are polymers.

Synthetic fibres are polymers made from crude oil. They have many advantages over naturally occurring materials. They can be made stronger, more hard-wearing, waterproof (if necessary), easier to wash and dry – and they can be made in huge quantities. However, crude oil is a finite resource, in other words it will not last forever. So this is a problem. Making polymers has the same problems of any manufacturing process, for example, possible effects on the environment. It's not easy to recycle most polymers. However, this is a problem that scientists know about and are working on and already some biodegradable polymers have been made.

Naturally occurring materials have the advantage that they are renewable. For example, cotton seed can be sown each year.

Equipment

The word equipment covers a vast range of things such as tools, cooking utensils, containers, sports equipment, machinery, musical instruments and so on. Often they are made from a variety of materials, each chosen for a specific purpose.

The clothing worn by this climber has been designed to protect him from the cold. It's made of polymer fibres woven to ensure that air is trapped between them (air is a poor conductor of heat). To be used in such conditions the fibres must also be hard wearing. The rope is also made of polymer fibres.

An electrician's screwdriver uses two types of material. The handle must be an electrical insulator. It could be made from ceramics, but these would be too brittle and break easily. So a polymer is used. The shaft must be stiff and strong. It's made out of metal.

Think about the properties of materials used to make tennis rackets, mobile phones, guitars, furniture and cars. Try to list them.

Finding out about the properties of materials

There are many databases available to find the physical properties of materials. They come in different forms, for example, CD-ROMs, data books and the Internet. Data may be presented in various forms such as tables and graphs. You need to be able to find data as and when you need it.

? Questions

1 Classify the following materials as metals, polymers, ceramics and composites:
   (a) aluminium foil   (f) bathroom tiles
   (b) clingfilm   (g) iron nails
   (c) pottery   (h) copper tubing
   (d) steel reinforced concrete (i) rubber tubing
   (e) nylon rope   (j) glass fibre reinforced plastic.

2 For each of the things listed below, state three important properties for the materials from which they could be made:
   (a) window   (f) light switch
   (b) table   (g) fire hose
   (c) shopping bag   (h) shirt
   (d) car jack   (i) cup and saucer.
   (e) ice cream container

3 Clothing can be made from natural materials or synthetics. Give two examples of each and gives reasons for choosing natural or synthetic.

4 Find resources where the properties of materials are given. Make a note of the resources and whether the data is given in the form of a table or graph. You could try data books, CD ROMS or the Internet. Ask your teacher for guidance.

5 Use the resources you identified in the last question to find values for (a) density, (b) thermal conductivity, (c) strength for two examples each of a
   • metal
   • ceramic
   • polymer
   • composite.

Explaining the properties of materials

You need to:

(a) *know the characteristic properties of metals (electrical conductivity, malleability and hardness) and be able to relate them to a simple model of metallic structure in terms of positive ions in a sea of electrons*

(b) *know the characteristic properties of polymers (flexibility, behaviour on heating, and hardness) and be able to relate them to a simple model of long chains entangled with one another, and sometimes cross-linked, and in terms of the side groups on the chains*

(c) *know the characteristic properties of ceramics and be able to relate them to simple models of giant structures to explain the effects of firing clay, and explain the properties of silicon oxide (sand) and aluminium oxide as giant molecular and ionic structures*

(d) *explain the properties of composites in terms of the properties of their components, including the effect of plasticisers on polymers*

(e) *explain the effect on the properties of a material of modifying it at a molecular level (cross-linking, side chains and chain length in polymers, and alloying in metals)*

(f) *be able to select materials for a particular product given a specification for the product.*

Structure, bonding and properties

Scientists have developed their ideas about how atoms combine with one another to form compounds. They have worked out why some chemical bonds are more difficult to break than others and they have worked out how the bonded atoms are arranged in three-dimensions. These ideas can be used to explain the properties of materials. They can also be used by scientists to work out how materials can be modified to make them more useful.

A quick reminder

All materials are made out of atoms. As we saw on page 170, atoms can bond with each other to form chemical compounds. These compounds can have molecular or giant structures.

- In molecular structures, the smallest particles present are molecules. The bonding between atoms in a molecule is strong (covalent bonding) but between one molecule and another it's weak.

- In giant structures, the smallest particles may be atoms or ions. There are three types of giant structure:
  - metals: ions held together by lose electrons by metallic bonds
  - ionic compounds: oppositely charged ions held together by ionic bonds in crystalline lattices
  - giant covalent compounds: atoms held together by covalent bonds in lattices (some are crystalline, others are amorphous).

Metals, ceramics and composites have giant structures. Polymers have molecular structures, but unlike chemical compounds with molecular structures, the molecules are very large.

Metals

Metals are:

- good conductors of electricity and heat
- tough (they are malleable and ductile)
- strong
- fairly hard (though this varies from metal to metal).

The properties of metals can be changed by making them into alloys. These are mixtures of more than one metal, usually made by heating and mixing the metals in the right proportions, melting them and letting them cool.

Structure and bonding

Metals have **giant structures.** When metal atoms are placed close to each other, they each lose one or more electrons. Each atom becomes a positive ion. Electrons float around in the space between the positive ions. The positive ions are 'glued together' by their attraction for the negative electrons. **Metallic bonding** is strong because the attractive forces are equally strong throughout the giant structure. We often describe metallic bonding as positive ions embedded in a sea of 'free' electrons. And what we mean by 'free' electrons are those that are not bound to one particular atom.

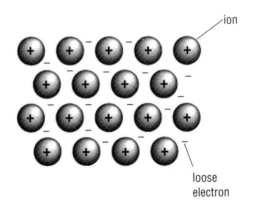

Cations embedded in a sea of 'free' electrons. This is a useful way of picturing the bonding in metals.

When an alloy is made from two ormore metals, the structure and bonding is changed slightly. The alloy has different properties to the metals from which it's made.

Electrical conduction

The electrons in a metal are free to move through the gaps between the ions. So when a metal is made part of an electric circuit its electrons move easily from one end to the other. This is why metals are good conductors of electricity.

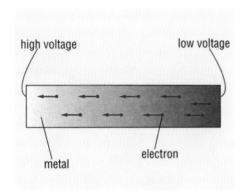

An electric current is a flow of electrons.

Thermal conduction

If one end of a solid is heated, the heat energy gets shared amongst more and more of its particles. The rest of the solid becomes hot. Bonds between particles transfer the heat energy from one particle to the next. Metals are different. Heat energy still flows from the heated end to the cold end, but it does so relatively quickly. The 'free' electrons carry it. So metals are good conductors of heat.

Toughness and malleability

Metals are tough and malleable. When large forces are applied to them, they change shape before they break. This is because the 'free' electrons can move. Layers of ions in the giant structure can slip past each other, taking the electrons with them. Importantly, when a metal changes shape, the forces holding its ions together stay the same. This means that metals can be squashed into sheets (**malleable**) or drawn out to make wire (**ductile**). The sheets and wires are still strong because the bonding between the atoms is just as strong even after the processing.

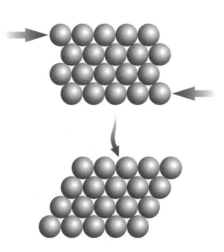

Metals are tough because planes of atoms can slide past one another without breaking apart.

Density, strength and hardness

Metals are dense because the bonds between their ions are strong. The 'free' electrons pull the ions into regular structures known as **lattices**. Materials that have their particles arranged in regular arrays are crystalline. Each ion is pulled strongly towards its neighbours, locking it firmly into place on the lattice. The ions are packed closely together, giving a **high density**.

Metallic bonding is strong throughout a giant structure. It takes a lot of energy to pull the ions apart. Therefore metals are strong.

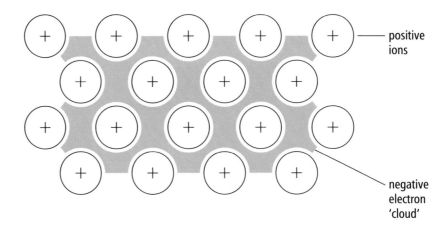

positive ions

negative electron 'cloud'

The giant structures of metals have the same arrangement of ions throughout, held in place by the cloud of 'free' electrons. The ions are packed closely together, making metals dense and strong.

Although metals are generally dense, this varies. For example:

Metal	Density/kg m^{-3}
Magnesium	1700
Aluminium	2700
Titanium	4500
Iron	7900
Lead	11,350

This explains why metals such as aluminium and titanium are used in the aerospace industry.

Similarly, the hardness of metals varies. Some are quite soft, others are much harder.

Polymers

You have probably heard of the Stone Age and the Iron Age. Well now we live in the 'polymer age'. People learned how to make useful things from stone and then iron. During the 20th century scientists and technologists learned how to exploit a new type of material – polymers.

The properties of polymers were summarised earlier (page 198) along with those of metals, ceramics and composites. Although there are exceptions, the polymers are mainly useful because they are flexible, tough and are good electrical insulators.

Nylon is a product of the polymer age. It has many uses, including clothing, rope, toothbrush bristles and mechanical components such as pulley wheels.

Structure and bonding

Polymers have **molecular structures.** They consist of molecules that contain a large number of atoms. These are made from simple molecules that have been joined together by chemical reaction into long chains. The atoms are held together by covalent bonds. These bonds are strong. The bonding between one molecule and another is relatively weak, but still strong enough to hold the molecules in place. As well as the weak bonds between molecules, the chains are often tangled, making it difficult to pull them apart.

Polythene	PVC	Polystyrene

Many polymers are based on carbon. In these, each polymer has a central chain of carbon atoms, surrounded by other atoms (in many cases hydrogen). This picture shows the arrangement of carbon and hydrogen atoms in poly(ethene) (more commonly called **polythene**). The properties can change dramatically when hydrogen atoms are replaced by other atoms or groups of atoms, for example, **PVC** (where there are chlorine atoms rather than hydrogen atoms) and **polystyrene** (where one hydrogen atom on every other carbon atoms has been replaced by a phenyl group, C_6H_5-).

The properties of a polymer chain can be modified by:

* changing the **chain length**
* changing the atoms attached to the central chain of atoms (these are often called **side groups**)
* **joining chains** together by chemical reaction
* adding a substance called a **plasticiser** (which, as the name suggests, makes the polymer more plastic, in other words makes it more flexible).

The longer a polymer chain is, the stronger the bonding is between one molecule and another (though it is still weak compared to a covalent bond). Sometimes chains are linked to one another by covalent bonds. This makes it far more difficult to pull the molecules apart, meaning that the polymer is stronger.

Effect of temperature

Polymers usually have low softening temperatures. Each polymer molecule needs only a small amount of heat energy to break free from its neighbours. However, the effect of heat is different on two types of polymers. **Thermoplastic** polymers soften and return to their original state on cooling. **Thermosetting** polymers soften but then become much stiffer on cooling. This is because cross-links have been formed between the chains. A chemical reaction took place during the heating.

Stiffness, strength and toughness

Polymers are not stiff. Their molecules slide past each other without much difficulty when they are pulled. So when a polymer is stretched, it gets longer. Polymers are not very strong either. Although it is difficult to break the covalent bonds within each molecule, it is not difficult to separate the molecules from each other.

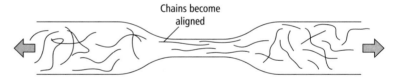
Chains become aligned

If a polymer is pulled in one direction the weak bonds between molecules are broken and the material stretches. The molecules become less tangled and line up in the direction of the pulling force. You already know that breaking bonds releases energy. Try this simple experiment. Take a piece of BluTac and stretch it, compress it, stretch it and so on several times. You will see that it gets warmer.

If the force used to pull a polymer is large enough, the polymer will not return to its original shape when the force is removed. This means that polymers, like metals, are **plastic**. Plastic materials are tough; they change shape rather than snap when subjected to sudden shocks.

Thermal and electrical conduction

There are no loose electrons in a polymer, so polymers can't conduct electricity. They are insulators. Polymers are also poor conductors of heat. Heat energy is conducted very slowly along a length of polymer. When heated, each molecule vibrates more. This vibration (and therefore heat energy) is passed from one molecule to another through the weak bonds that connect them.

Ceramics

Ceramics are very useful materials.
are good electrical insulators. How
They are very brittle.

Structure and bonding

Ceramics have giant structures. U
than one type of atom. Two type
the type of atoms involved. You
and covalent bonding (see page

Ionic bonding: one type of at
gains electrons. This leaves son
negatively charged. Strong ele
structures called lattices. Mate

Unit 2 Science for the need

Strength, st
The strong
stiff and
neighb

208

Covalent bonding: electrons from one atom are shared by another
atom. This gives a strong bond between the atoms. As you will have
seen, the atoms in molecules are held together by covalent bonds, but
the bonding between one molecule and another is relatively weak.
Sometimes the covalent bonds link atoms in a giant structure with a
regular repeating pattern. We call this a crystalline lattice.

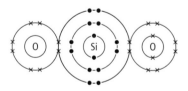

Silicon dioxide is another example of
a ceramic material. In its giant
structure, silicon atoms, Si, and
oxygen atoms, O, are held together
by covalent bonds. The arrangement
of atoms is the same throughout the
material.

Potters 'fire' clay pots and ornaments. This means heating them at a high temperature in an oven.
During the process the clay dries out and the atoms bond together to form the giant structure of
a ceramic.

...iffness and hardness

...onding between particles in ceramics makes them strong, ...ard. You need a large force to pull one particle away from its ...ours.

...oughness

Ceramics are **brittle** because, unlike metals, their atoms cannot slip past each other without completely disrupting the lattice. As you force one plane of atoms apart from another, the arrangement becomes unstable and the solid suddenly falls apart.

Melting point

The melting point of all ceramics is very high. A great deal of heat energy is required to break the strong bonds between their atoms.

Electrical and thermal conduction

There are no loose electrons in a ceramic, so it can't conduct electricity. Ceramics are good electrical insulators. Heat energy put in at one end of a ceramic is conducted slowly to the other end. As each atom vibrates more, the vibration (and therefore heat energy) is passed to its neighbours. Many ceramics contain small gaps in their structure (pores) and these contain air. This makes them very good thermal insulators.

Composites

Composites are combinations of two or more different types of materials. They aim to get the best of both worlds, and more. For example, ceramics have one major defect. They are brittle. Were it not for this, ceramics would be ideal for many purposes because they are so stiff, hard and strong. However, a composite consisting of a ceramic mixed with a tough material such as a metal or a polymer has the best properties of both materials. It can be stiff, hard, strong and tough.

Reinforced concrete

Concrete is very strong when it's compressed. A concrete slab can take very heavy loads before it breaks. However, concrete is very weak when stretched or if you try to bend it. It cracks suddenly. In other words, it's a typical ceramic.

So beams and joists in structures cannot be made with pure concrete. If they didn't crack under their own weight, they certainly would when the rest of the structure was placed on top of them. The answer is to combine the concrete with steel. In other words, to make a composite material – reinforced concrete. Steel rods or mesh are arranged in the concrete before it sets. The result is a composite material that combines the hardness of a ceramic with the toughness of a metal.

Reinforced concrete is widely used in large structures such as buildings, roads and bridges. Like all ceramics, it is too hard to be shaped easily, so it has to be cast in moulds. Its combination of strength, hardness and cheapness is unrivalled.

Encasing steel rods and mesh in concrete gives the builder a material that has both high compressive strength and high tensile strength.

Glass reinforced plastic (GRP) is a composite. It has the toughness of a polymer with the hardness and stiffness of a ceramic. It's particularly good for making stiff sheets. GRP is therefore widely used for making small boats and car panels.

Glass reinforced plastic

Polymers lack hardness and stiffness. This limits their use. However, by reinforcing a polymer with ceramic fibres (for example, glass or carbon) the material has the toughness of a polymer with the hardness and stiffness of a ceramic.

Selecting materials for a product given its specification

The final task for the materials scientist is to match the material to its purpose. The steps are straightforward.

You need to look at the specifications for the product. List the properties that the material must have. Now make some educated guesses about the best types of material to use. Once you have done this you can begin to refine your search. Use databases to find the data you need.

Finally you must consider costs!

Questions

1   List the properties of:
   (a) metals
   (b) ceramics
   (c) polymers
   (d) composites
   which make them useful for different applications.

2   For each of the things listed below, state three important properties for the materials from which they could be made:
   (a) window
   (b) table
   (c) shopping bag
   (d) car jack
   (e) ice cream container
   (f) light switch
   (g) fire hose.

3   For each of the properties below, give the names of types of materials which have that property:
    (a) transparency
    (b) high strength
    (c) high melting point
    (d) low electrical resistance
    (e) high density

4   Name the type of material that is most likely to have this set of properties:
    (a) tough, high density, good electrical and thermal conduction
    (b) poor thermal conduction, stiff, low density and hard
    (c) tough, low density, low melting point and transparent
    (d) tough, hard, stiff and strong.

5   Think about the following materials: metals, ceramics, polymers and composites. Which have strong bonds between the atoms present and which have weak bonds between molecules?

    Fill the gaps in these sentences:

    (a) Materials are made out of . . . .
    (b) All atoms have a . . . . at their centre, surrounded by shells of . . . .
    (c) Atoms bond together to form either . . . . or . . . .
    (d) An electric current is a flow of . . . .
    (e) Atoms which share electrons with one another have . . . . bonds.
    (f) Atoms which give or receive electrons from each other have . . . . bonds.
    (g) Metallic bonds are formed when each atom loses one or more . . . .
    (h) A material with long chain molecules is a . . . .
    (i) A material which is a mixture of a ceramic and a metal has a . . . . structure.

6   Describe the characteristics of a composite and explain its advantages over other materials for certain applications.

7   Explain how the properties of a metal can be changed by making an alloy.

8   How can the properties of a polymer be changed?

2.4 The importance of energy

Energy

Are you energetic?

Who do you know who is energetic? People with lots of energy are usually very active – playing and working hard. In science, energy has a similar meaning. Energy is the capacity to do work. The more energy something has, the more work it can do. For example, the more energy there is stored in a battery the longer it will power a torch.

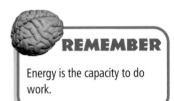

REMEMBER

Energy is the capacity to do work.

We know energy when we see it. Or do we? What we actually see, feel or hear each day is the result of energy changes. It's quite hard to say just what energy is. It's easier to say what it can do. When energy changes from one form to another it can make things move or it can make things get hotter. It can make light and sound. Movement, heat, light and sound are all forms of energy.

The wound mainspring in a clockwork toy has energy stored in it. When released the spring makes the toy work. The rubber band in a model aeroplane is turned many times before being released. The rubber band is stretched by the turning and has stored energy in it. When released it turns the propeller and moves the plane. In both cases the energy is in the form of **potential energy**. You can't see it, but it is there!

This model aeroplane is powered by a rubber band. To make it work the rubber band is turned many times until it's twisted and tight. As the rubber band unwinds its potential energy gets less. When it's released some of the potential energy changes into kinetic energy. A force is exerted on the propeller, it turns and the plane flies. Like anything that is moving, the flying plane has kinetic energy.

REMEMBER

Potential energy: the energy something has because of its position.

Kinetic energy: the energy something has because it is moving.

Chemical energy: the total of the potential energies and kinetic energies of the particles that make up the chemical.

The water in the stream has more potential energy when it is at the top of the mountain than when it reaches the bottom. As it falls some of its potential energy is changed into kinetic energy. This is the basis of hydroelectric power (see page 000).

REMEMBER

Forms of energy:

Potential

Kinetic

Heat

Light

Sound

Electrical energy

Nuclear

Chemical

Potential energy is the energy stored due to position. The stretched rubber band has more potential energy (and, therefore, it can do more work) than when it's not stretched. It has more potential energy because of its different position. The same is true for the wound and unwound spring.

Anything that moves has **kinetic energy**. However, something will only move if a force acts upon it. A tennis ball moves if it is dropped. Gravity provides the force and the ball is pulled to the ground. The ball also moves if it is hit with a tennis racket. The moving tennis racket provides the force. How you hold the racket provides the direction, hopefully!

Energy resources

You need to:

- *know that fossil fuels (natural gas, oil, coal) are useful energy resources*

- *appreciate the problems of using fossil fuels (global warming, limited deposits)*

- *know that nuclear fuels and renewable energy resources (wind, solar, hydroelectric, wave and tidal power) may be used as alternatives to fossil fuels*

- *appreciate the problems of using nuclear fuels (problems of radioactive emissions, disposal of waste) and of using renewable sources (unreliability and possible effects on the environment).*

It starts with the Sun

We need energy to make things work, including ourselves. The source of energy for our bodies is the food we eat. The source of energy to power a car is petrol. The source of energy to cook with is usually gas or electricity. But where does all this energy come from in the first place? Well, by far and away the major source is the Sun.

In the Sun nuclear fusion (atoms combining) changes mass to energy. The Sun sends out this energy in the form of radiation. Some of this energy, though only a very little, reaches the Earth. But it's enough for us to feel warm, because of the infrared (IR) radiation, and even get sunburned, because of the ultraviolet (UV) radiation.

Only a small amount of the Sun's radiation reaches us. However, even a tiny amount of UV radiation can harm the skin – causing sunburn or even melanomas (skin cancers). You should always take care on bright sunny days.

Plants use some of the visible light that reaches Earth to make more complicated chemical compounds (sugar and starch) and plant tissues from simple compounds (carbon dioxide and water). They do this by photosynthesis. The process of photosynthesis converts carbon dioxide and water into sugar and oxygen.

$$\text{carbon dioxide + water} \xrightarrow{\text{light and chlorophyll}} \text{sugar + oxygen}$$

The substance that gives leaves their green colour is called chlorophyll. This works with the light to make the chemical change happen. Some of the sugar is converted into starch for storage. You can read more about photosynthesis on page 137.

However, most of the sunlight that reaches a leaf bounces back (it's reflected) or passes through without any effect (it's transmitted). Only 5% is used to make sugar and starch – and only then if the growing conditions are ideal. Animals eat plants. But again, the conversion of energy from the sugar and starch is low. For example, only 4% of the energy stored in the plant is transferred to a cow's tissues.

You have probably heard of Einstein's famous equation, $E = mc^2$. The importance was that Einstein recognized that matter and energy could be changed into one another and found a mathematical formula to describe it. This is what Einstein looked like at the time of his great breakthrough – far from the usual image we see of him.

Humans get energy from eating plants. They are a 'fuel' for us to burn inside and give us energy to do things. However, humans are omnivores – they eat animal products as well as plants. On simple energy conversion grounds eating animal products is very inefficient. But it isn't that simple. Our food must provide more than just energy. For a healthy life we also need vitamins and minerals.

The major sources of energy are:

	In the UK	In the world
Oil	35%	39%
Coal	35%	30%
Gas	24%	19%
Nuclear	5%	4%
Hydroelectric	1%	6%
Other	0%	2%

Other sources of energy, which have not yet been fully exploited, are solar, wind, tidal and wave energy.

Fossil fuels

Where they come from

The coal, oil and natural gas we use began life as living things. Millions of years ago prehistoric forests and organisms living in the sea died and began to decay. Layer upon layer decayed and were compressed under increasingly high pressures. They ended up as coal, oil and natural gas – what we call **fossil fuels**. Fossil fuels are examples of primary energy resources. They are concentrated sources of energy. This energy is released when they are burnt.

So you can see that even the fossil fuels upon which we depend so much are a result of solar power!

Fossil fuels are extracted from the Earth for our use.

- Coal can be mined from the surface (open cast mining). This is relatively cheap and simple. However, as these deposits run out more complicated mining techniques are being used to get coal from deep beneath the ground and beneath the sea. This mining is very costly.

- Oil is a valuable commodity and rightly earned the nickname 'black gold'. In the UK we get oil from wells under the bed of the North Sea. In other parts of the world oil wells are drilled on dry land. Oil exploration is big business.

- Gas is drilled for like oil. In the UK gas reserves were discovered under the bed of the North Sea. The gas is piped directly into homes and factories. It provides us with a valuable source of energy.

But no matter how clever scientists are at finding new sources of fossil fuels and ways of getting them out of the ground the simple fact remains that supplies will not last forever. They are finite.

REMEMBER

The energy stored in fossil fuels is chemical energy. It is a combination of the stored potential and kinetic energy of the molecules that make up the chemicals present in these fuels.

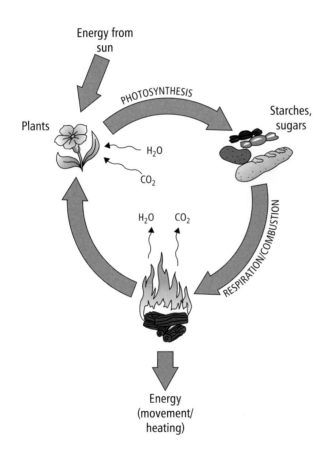

Everything that comes around goes around!

Heat and electricity

Fossil fuels may be burned directly to give heat. Your school or college may have gas or oil-fired central heating. Some houses still have open coal fires. Burning fossil fuels needs oxygen and something to get the process started. What then happens is almost the reverse of photosynthesis. Complicated compounds react with oxygen to make the simple compounds carbon dioxide and water. Carbon monoxide, a poisonous gas, and carbon (in the form of smoke) can be produced if there is not enough oxygen.

fossil fuel + oxygen → carbon dioxide and water

Most coal is used to make electricity for the National Grid. The coal is burned and the heat produced is used to boil water. Steam from the boilers turns giant turbines and these produce electricity. Oil and gas can also used as the fuel in power stations, though the technology is a bit different and so each power station can only use one type of fossil fuel.

Oil and gas have one big advantage over coal. They are easier to move around! They can be pumped through pipelines to the places where they are needed. These distribution pipes for North Sea gas are part of a network that allows buildings in cities and towns to have gas 'on tap'.

Perhaps surprisingly wood is the main source of energy for heating and cooking for most people in the world. They live in Africa and much of Asia. It is a renewable energy source provided new trees are planted. Unfortunately this is not always the case. Such a source of energy would never meet the demands of the so-called 'developed' energy-hungry countries.

But there are problems . . .

Limited supplies

How long do you think fossil fuel reserves will last? It has been estimated that the world's coal supplies will run out in 300 years, oil in 60 years and gas in 50 years. Of course, these figures are only approximate. Much depends on how sensibly we use the fossil fuels.

You can read about efficiency on pages 227–34.

At the moment we waste a lot of the energy we get from fossil fuels. Good 'house-keeping' will extend the use of fossil fuels and make reserves last a bit longer. But they will run out eventually.

Global warming

Most scientists agree there the Earth is becoming a warmer place to live. There are mixed views about how much warmer it is getting, the causes and what can or should be done about it.

It's believed that some gases trap heat that radiates from the surface of the Earth. It's important that some is trapped otherwise the Earth would be a very cold place to live. But too much being trapped leads to global warming and this can affect the environment. This is called the greenhouse effect. Getting the balance right is important.

These palm trees grow in some sheltered spots in southwest England where the climate is mild. It may be that we will see them growing further and further north as a result of temperature changes from global warming.

As you read earlier, all fossil fuels produce carbon dioxide when they burn. And carbon dioxide is a very good or bad (depending on how you look at it!) greenhouse gas. Some scientists have estimated that doubling the amount of carbon dioxide in the atmosphere would cause a 3 °C rise in temperature.

Impurities cause problems

Fossil fuels consist of complex organic compounds, mainly consisting of just carbon and hydrogen. The only products of combustion are carbon dioxide and water. However, impurities containing sulfur are usually found in the fossil fuels. These produce sulfur dioxide, which dissolves in rain and makes it slightly acidic. This 'acid rain' can be extremely damaging, both to living organisms and to buildings made from limestone. Scientists have found ways to control sulfur dioxide emissions.

What should happen to the waste?

Mining for coal underground creates large heaps of soil and rock that were dug from the ground in order to get at the coal. These 'spoil heaps' are not good to look at. In 1968 one of them collapsed in the Welsh mining village of Aberfan and killed many children in the school. Many spoil heaps are now landscaped to improve their appearance.

Car exhausts produce poisonous gases such as carbon monoxide and oxides of nitrogen.

Other uses for fossil fuels

There is another problem. While the main use of fossil fuels is to provide us with energy, they are also vital starting material for the production of plastics, pesticides, pharmaceuticals and many other useful products. You can read more abut this on page 000.

Alternatives to fossil fuels

Fossil fuels are non-renewable. Once they are burned that's it! Well, strictly speaking they are renewable but it takes a very long time for a dead tree to become coal! Scientists have been trying to make effective use of other energy supplies. They have investigated and started to make use of solar energy, hydroelectric power, wind, tidal and wave energy. These are all renewable energy sources. So, unlike fossil fuels, they won't run out.

It might seem that renewable energy sources such as solar energy, wind, tidal and wave energy are ideal – non-polluting and limitless. However, there are two problems:

- Reliability – the sun doesn't always shine and the wind doesn't always blow
- Effect of the environment – what difference might it make to an area if rivers were dammed for hydroelectric power stations?

Scientists need to tackle these problems if these sources are to become major suppliers of energy.

Solar energy

You may have a calculator that doesn't need a battery. But it only works in bright light. This is because it is powered by a solar cell. A solar cell can convert solar energy directly into electricity. The best ones can convert 30% of the solar energy that falls upon them. Unfortunately they are expensive. As the technology improves prices may fall.

If only we could use the Sun's energy directly! Scientists have calculated that 1,000,000,000,000,000,000 (1 million million million) joules of energy reach the Earth from the Sun every second! This is more than enough to supply the most energy-hungry people across the world. But at the moment we haven't found the technology to harness this solar energy.

Solar cells are expensive. However, for specialist uses such as providing power for this satellite, they are really useful.

The Sun can be used to heat water and houses directly. You may have seen some houses with **solar heating panels** on their roofs. The solar panels collect energy from the Sun. Water trickles through narrow pipes in the panels and is heated. This water then has to be heated further in the usual way, but it certainly reduces the amount of energy needed from fossil fuels. It's been calculated that even in the UK on a cloudy day a 3 m by 3 m solar panel (9 m^2) could collect almost 250 W of solar energy. You can imagine that in some parts of the world solar panels could make a really significant contribution to energy demands. However, this energy cannot be stored.

Hydroelectric power

When streams and rivers tumble down mountainsides the water loses potential energy. This can be captured and changed into electricity. The rivers are dammed and the water is channelled through huge turbines. Norway is an example of a country with suitable locations for hydroelectric power stations. It is that country's major energy source. Not all parts of the UK have suitable places, but the Scottish Highlands and Snowdonia (North Wales) are suitable locations. However, before building such power stations the possible impact on the environment must be worked out.

Wind

Windmills have been around for centuries, since about 600 AD in fact. The kinetic energy of wind is used to do work. Once windmills used wind power to turn grindstones, for example, to grind wheat. Recently they have been used to generate electricity. In suitable areas it's been calculated that they can make a significant contribution to energy needs. Unfortunately the wind isn't reliable. It can't be trusted to blow every day! Also, for many people, the sight of a wind farm on top of a hill is not pleasing to the eye.

Large wind 'farms' are being built, for example, in Cornwall. Modern windmills don't look much like the old-style windmills!

Wave

Sea waves are a possible source of energy. However, there are a number of technological and environmental problems to overcome. Like wind, the waves are unreliable. Also, the devices to trap the energy would need to withstand extreme weather conditions. Maintenance may be a problem, as well as the possibility of the equipment getting in the way of shipping.

Tidal

The rise and fall of the tide can be used to turn turbines and generate electricity. The most well-known tidal power station is at the Rance Estuary in Brittany, France. There have been a number of concerns about the effect of these schemes on wildlife and the environment.

The radioactive decay of uranium can be controlled. These control rods are used to slow down the process. The more deeply they are immersed, the slower the reaction. To speed up the reaction they are slowly withdrawn.

Nuclear energy

Uranium is a fuel. It is used in nuclear power stations. One kilogram of uranium can give the same amount of energy as 1,000,000 kg of coal. But it isn't burned liked fossil fuels to get energy. The energy comes from radioactive decay of unstable uranium atoms. Each atom splits into two almost equal parts (the process is called nuclear fission), releasing energy. If the splitting is not controlled the result is a nuclear explosion. However, scientists can control the splitting and this is the process used in nuclear reactors.

Nuclear power stations don't have the same drawbacks as coal-fired power stations. There are no harmful emissions, for example, no carbon dioxide (greenhouse effect) or sulfur dioxide (acid rain) is given off. The process is, in this sense, 'clean'. Radioactive emissions from nuclear reactors are rare. Safety is high priority and every precaution is taken. But accidents do happen and you may have heard about:

- Windscale, now called Sellafield, in 1957
- Three Mile Island in the USA, in 1979
- Chernobyl in the former USSR, in 1986.

Find out more about these if you are interested.

Nuclear reactors do produce radioactive waste, however, which must be stored where it can do no harm. It takes thousands of years for the waste to become harmless.

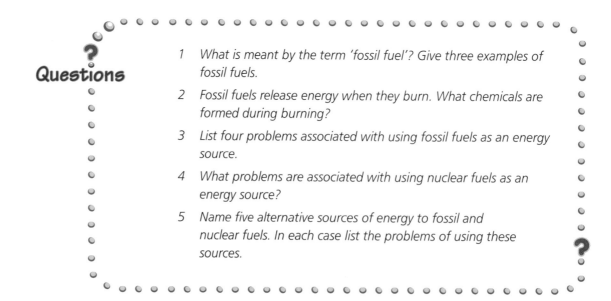

?
Questions

1   What is meant by the term 'fossil fuel'? Give three examples of fossil fuels.

2   Fossil fuels release energy when they burn. What chemicals are formed during burning?

3   List four problems associated with using fossil fuels as an energy source.

4   What problems are associated with using nuclear fuels as an energy source?

5   Name five alternative sources of energy to fossil and nuclear fuels. In each case list the problems of using these sources.

Transferring energy

You need to be able to:

- *describe how, in processes of energy transfer, energy is conserved but tends to spread out and become less useful.*

Energy comes in many forms: potential, kinetic, heat, light, sound, electrical, nuclear and chemical. But it's only 'useful' when it is being used to heat something or make something work. This always involves changing energy from one form to another. In practice it's never this simple. Two or more forms of energy are produced.

Have you ever got close to an electric light bulb? The idea is to convert electrical energy (electricity) into light energy. But you will notice that the bulb gets very hot. The electrical energy is converted into light, but also into heat. So only some of the electrical energy is 'useful', in other words does what you want it to (make light). What does the heat do? It makes particles such as atoms and molecules move a bit faster. In other words, their kinetic energy increases.

Using a battery powered electric motor to lift a weight.

Step one
In the battery, chemical energy is converted to electrical energy. But the wires resist the flow of electricity and get warm. So
    chemical energy → electrical energy + heat energy

Step two
The battery pushes current through the motor. Electrical energy is converted into kinetic energy and turns a winch. But the bearings get hot because of friction. So
    electrical energy → kinetic energy + heat energy

Step three
Kinetic energy is converted into potential energy as the winch lifts the weight. Air molecules resist the movement of the weight. It's a type of friction. The effect is small, but nonetheless a very small amount of kinetic energy is converted into heat. So
    kinetic energy → potential energy + heat energy

If we look at the whole process, we can see that each energy conversion is 'inefficient' in that only some of the energy transferred at each step does what we want it to. At each step some is 'wasted' in the form of heat.

REMEMBER

The first law of thermodynamics:

Energy cannot be created or lost.

(But it can be wasted!)

REMEMBER

The second law of thermodynamics:

When energy is used (work is done) some 'escapes' and spreads itself out, usually in the form of heat. Not all the energy does the work you wanted it to; it becomes less useful.

REMEMBER

When chemical energy is changed into electrical energy some of it is wasted as heat energy. We can summarise this in an 'energy equation' such as:

chemical energy → electrical energy (useful energy) + heat energy (wasted energy)

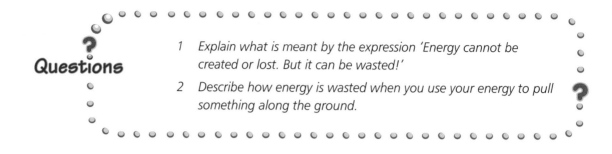

Questions

1   Explain what is meant by the expression 'Energy cannot be created or lost. But it can be wasted!'

2   Describe how energy is wasted when you use your energy to pull something along the ground.

Obtaining useful energy

You need to:

- *know how electricity is generated from the burning of fossil fuels*

- *be aware of the relative costs of various energy resources (natural gas, mains electricity, batteries)*

- *explain why an appropriate source of energy is selected for a particular task (natural gas for general heating in the laboratory, electrical heating for flammable liquids, batteries when working in the field).*

Generating electricity

Like most of us you probably take electricity for granted. It is always there. It's just about impossible to list all the things that work because of electricity! But where does it come from? How does it reach our homes and the places where we work and where we enjoy our leisure time? The answer to the first question is **power stations**. The answer to the second question is the **National Grid**.

Fossil fuels and nuclear fuels are primary sources of energy. But the energy locked up in them must be released. When it is we get heat (by burning fossil fuels or by nuclear decay). In power stations this heat is used to boil water. Not to make a cup of tea (at least not directly), but

This is a coal-fired power station. Electricity generated here is fed into the National Grid and distributed around the country to even very remote areas. We take the electricity that 'comes out of the wall' for granted. But it is a complicated process that turns coal into light and heat in your home, not to mention running all the other electrical appliances and gadgets. A large power station might produce 1,000,000,000 joules of energy every second – about the same as every person in the UK working flat out!

to produce steam. The steam is heated so that it gets very hot and is at a very high pressure. Huge steam turbines are driven by this steam and spin around at high speeds.

The turbines connect to the coils of large electricity generators. The coils carry current and act as big electromagnets. As they spin they induce a high voltage in fixed coils that surround them. They act like giant dynamos – a kind of electric motor in reverse. A current flows and this is fed into the National Grid.

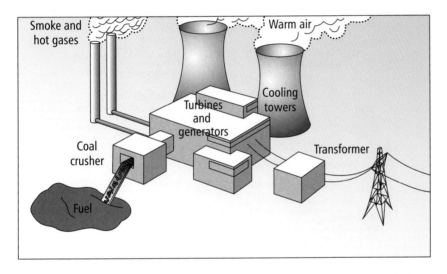

Coal is mined and brought to the power station. It's crushed and fed into large furnaces. The heat when it burns produces steam that drives turbines. These are linked to generators and produce electricity.

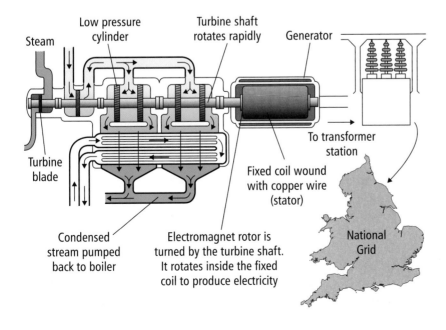

How a large generator works.

The current from a power station's generators is fed into the National Grid and distributed around the country. This map shows the main power lines. There are many other smaller lines that distribute the electricity to homes, offices and factories.

Energy costs

Energy doesn't come cheap. Mining or drilling for fossil fuels is expensive. Transporting them to where they are needed costs money. The food we eat (our 'fuel') is expensive to produce, not to mention the cost of cooking it.

And if we want electricity, the cost goes up. Power stations are not very efficient. About two-thirds of the energy available from the fossil fuels (the primary source) used is wasted. The major loss is as heat energy in the cooling towers. There are heat losses because of friction in the various moving parts. In the transformers energy is wasted through heat and sound. It all adds up, and so electricity is expensive.

In a typical home we use energy for heating (66%), hot water (20%), cooking (7%) and lighting (7%). Some fuels are used directly in fires, stoves, room heaters and central heating systems. Others are used to produce electricity, as you saw in the previous section. Electricity is used in fires, convection heaters and storage heaters, as well as for the many appliances and gadgets that surround us.

Mains electricity and gas

Your house, school or college undoubtedly uses mains electricity and may well also have a natural gas supply. These two energy sources have advantages and disadvantages. You are charged per kilowatt hour (kWh) that you use. Typical charges are:

Gas   1.198 p per kWh plus a service charge of between 10 and 11 p per day

Electricity   6.50 p per kWh plus a service charge of between 10 and 11 p per day

So you can see that electricity seems a more expensive option than gas. But there are other considerations, such as the cost of equipment, servicing and repair.

How much electricity is used is measured on the electricity meter in your school or home. 1 unit of electricity is 1 kilowatt hour. It isn't easy to say just how much electricity costs because there are various 'deals', for example Economy 7 night-time electricity, available.

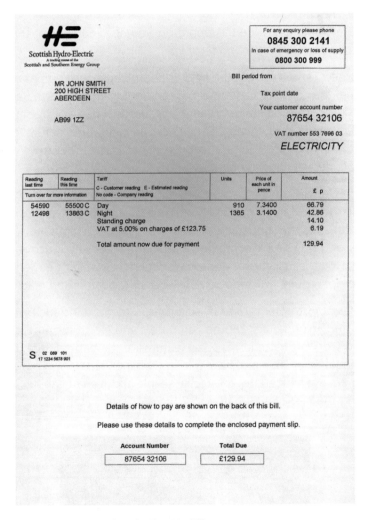

The cost of electricity is itemised on the electricity bill.

It's cheaper to run this laptop from mains electricity than from batteries. However, there are some circumstances where mains electricity just isn't available!

Electricity from batteries is far more expensive than mains electricity. But it's convenient and it would be impossible to power many devices using mains electricity. The price of batteries depends on the type of battery. Long-life batteries cost more than normal ones, and rechargeable batteries are much more expensive.

Scientists need energy

You need energy to be a scientist. For example, when you work in the laboratory you will need to heat things, stir mixtures and use electronic measuring instruments. How do you choose the most appropriate tool for the job?

In the laboratory

There are several ways to heat things in the laboratory. You can read about this on page 27. Other devices in the laboratory also need energy to make them work, such as stirrers, pumps, measuring instruments, calculators and computers.

In the field

If you are working outside the laboratory you need equipment that is easily transported, robust and reliable.

Gas burners can be used in the field to heat things. They do not use methane, the gas we call 'natural gas' and get from the North Sea. Instead they use propane or butane. This 'bottled' gas is also used by plumbers and in the kitchen. For people who cannot get natural gas piped to their homes, Calor gas cookers are available. They run from large cylinders of liquefied butane.

Electrical devices cannot be plugged into the wall when you are working in a field, up a mountain or beside a stream. Instead you must use batteries as the source of electrical energy. The voltages are small (usually only up to 12 V compared with mains electricity which is 240 V). However, electronic devices work perfectly well off batteries as they do not require much power, unlike electric heaters and machinery.

Examples of instruments used by scientists in the field include pH meters and colorimeters. Laptop computers and electronic notepads can also work off batteries. The key features of the batteries are that they should be reliable and have a long working life. Many types of battery are available, both non-rechargeable and rechargeable. Selecting the best type of battery for the purpose is vital.

Scientists can use 'bottled gas' when working in the field. They can cook food and provide themselves with the energy to work. They can use it in experiments to heat substances. The gas being burned is not methane ('natural gas'). It is either propane or butane.

Scientists can take their computers with them wherever they work. But the life expectancy of the batteries is probably only around 2 hours. So it's important not to leave them on when they aren't being used. Most automatically go into 'sleep' mode to save energy.

Questions

1   Describe how fossil fuels are used to generate electricity.

2   This question is about comparing the costs of electricity and gas.
   (a) Find out the costs of using electricity or gas in your home or school. You will need to find some recent bills.
   (b) What exactly does the user have to pay for?
   (c) What are the 'hidden' costs of using electrical or gas equipment and appliances?
   (d) Which seems to giver better value for money – electricity or gas?

3   What determines how much it costs to buy a battery?

4   Which is the cheapest way to run a CD player – using a battery or mains electricity?

5   Suppose you were in a desert, a long distance from the nearest laboratory. You want to carry out some simple experiments. You need to heat things, work in the dark and be able to record data on your laptop computer. What sources of power would you use in each case and why?

6   Why should you use an electric heater rather than a Bunsen burner to heat flammable liquids such as petrol and ethanol?

Energy efficiency

You need to:

- *understand the meaning of the term efficiency when applied to simple energy transfers in mechanical and electrical appliances*

- *understand the advantages to the user, and to society, of making and using devices with high efficiency, by considering the benefits of low energy lamps compared to filament lamps*

- *know how heat losses by conduction, convection and radiation may be minimised*

- *explain the use of heat exchangers to enable waste energy to be captured and recycled*

- *compare the relative merits of water and anti-freeze in terms of their heat capacities and appreciate why both have a role to play as coolants.*

Efficiency

Scientists are interested in how energy is stored and how it can be changed from one form to another. Energy is expensive and so it's important not to waste it, whether in the home, the office or an industrial plant.

Efficiency is the measure of how much useful energy we get out when we put energy into a machine. Scientists try to design machines that give as much energy out we put in. This would be 100% efficiency. Unfortunately it never happens! No machine is 100% efficient. Some energy is always wasted.

$$\text{efficiency} = \frac{\text{useful energy}}{\text{input energy}} \times 100\%$$

Worked example

A car is a complicated machine. Most cars run on petrol. The petrol is the fuel that provides the energy for the engine. From experiments scientists can measure the input energy and useful energy. The difference is 'wasted' energy. For example, using petrol the following values were found:

Input energy	Useful energy	Wasted energy
300 J	90 J	210 J

The efficiency of the petrol driven car $= \dfrac{90}{300} \times 100 = 30\%$

The 'wasted' energy is lost heating up the car and the air outside. It can never be used to power the car.

Mechanical machines

We depend on machines to make work easier for us. Manufacturing and service industries depend on machines. Levers, pulleys and gears are simple machines. More complicated machines consist of a number of these simple ones.

(a)    (b)

(a) Many machines are force multipliers. They increase the force you apply. This hoist enables the mechanic to lift a weight he would not be able to lift alone. (b) Other machines change the direction of a force. The screwdriver is being turned in one direction and the screw moves forward in another direction. This is because of the thread on the screw. The screwdriver and screw form a simple machine.

A machine needs an **effort** to move a **load**. In a machine that's a force multiplier, the effort moves further than the load. You can measure the load and effort, and the distances moved by each.

$$\text{efficiency} = \frac{\text{load} \times \text{distance moved by load}}{\text{effort} \times \text{distance moved by effort}} \times 100\%$$

Imagine you are lifting something with a hoist. The load is 100 N and it takes an effort of 20 N to move it. To lift the load by 50 cm, the effort has to move 270 cm.

$$\text{So the efficiency of the hoist} = \frac{100 \times 50 \times 100}{20 \times 270} = 92.6\%$$

The reason it isn't 100% is because some of the energy put in was needed to overcome the friction between the rope and the pulleys and between the pulleys and their axles. This was 'wasted' energy.

Electrical appliances

Electrical appliances are used for many things. However, their efficiencies are less than 100%. Wires carrying an electric current heat up. The greater the electrical resistance of a metal, the more it will heat up. As resistance depends on size and shape (see page 000) thin, long wires heat up more than thick, short ones made of the same metal. Some of the electrical energy is converted into heat and this is wasted energy.

A filament light bulb is very inefficient. It works because light is emitted when the filament gets hot (just as the bars of electric fires glow when they are turned on). About 90% of the electrical energy is used to heat up the filament and only about 10% is converted to light.

Low energy lamps are more efficient than filament lamps. They don't get as hot as filament bulbs because more electrical energy is changed to light and less to heat energy. And in terms of a light bulb, heat energy is wasted energy.

High efficiency devices

The benefits of high efficiency devices are clear. There is not as much wasted energy. Efficiency can be increased by careful design and choice of materials to make the moving parts in machines and appliances. For example:

- keeping the number of moving parts as few as possible
- using lubricants such as oil or graphite to reduce friction
- using materials whose surfaces are smooth so that friction is reduced
- size and shape of conducting parts in electrical appliances.

Reducing heat losses

Heat energy moves from one place together in one or more of three ways:

- conduction
- convection
- radiation.

Heat energy passes through a material (solid, liquid or gas) by **conduction**. Heating one part of the material makes the particles move more. In turn they bump into neighbouring particles, causing them to move more. In gases and liquids the particles move around more quickly. In solids, the particles vibrate more rapidly.

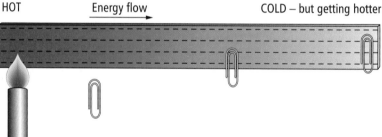

Heat energy is conducted along a metal rod when one end is heated. One by one the paper clips drop off because the Vaseline holding them to the bar becomes runnier as it gets hotter.

In gases and liquids, the particles move more and spread out when they are heated. This means the gas or liquid becomes less dense (it's 'lighter'). This part rises (because it's lighter) and is replaced by cold gas or liquid. This is now heated and also rises. The gas or liquid that had already risen begins to cool, become denser and sinks. It's the old story of 'hot air rising'. This movement of heat energy is called **convection**.

The heater makes air particles move more and spread out. So this part of the air in a room becomes lighter and rises. Fresh colder air gets nearer to the heater and this in turn gets hotter and rises. Hot air cools slowly and sinks. The movement of air results in convection currents.

All objects radiate energy, mainly infrared energy. Heat energy transferred by **radiation** does not need a material to travel through. Heat energy can pass through empty space (a vacuum) by radiation.

The most common way of losing energy is by conduction. You can reduce heat lost in this way by good insulation. This is the reason many people have double-glazed windows, loft insulation and perhaps cavity filled walls.

Pipes are used to carry hot gases and liquids in industrial plants. To reduce heat loss they are wrapped in an insulating material.

You can compare the effectiveness of different types of insulating material using a simple experiment.

TRY IT YOURSELF

Procedure
It's best to use a copper can if the school has one. Otherwise you can use a glass beaker.

1   Place the copper can on a heatproof mat away from the edge of the bench.

2   Boil some water in a kettle and half fill the can with boiling water (TAKE CARE not to splash yourself or somebody near; boiling water scalds the skin).

3   Time how long it takes for the water to cool to:
    (a) 60 °C and (b) 30 °C.

4   Pour the water out and let the can cool down. Wrap some woolen material around it and repeat the experiment.

5   Repeat the experiment several times using different types of material. Try to find out what are the most effective insulators.

You could also compare the effectiveness of different drinks containers that are sold as flasks for keeping hot drinks hot and cold drinks cold.

Recycling energy

Steam is used to drive turbines in electricity generators. It takes energy to convert water to steam. Much of this energy is used to turn the turbines. The steam cools down. However, the steam is still hot (just not as hot) and if it's simply vented to the outside, energy is lost. This steam could be used to heat the buildings, to heat water or for other purposes. In this way less energy is lost as much of it is captured and recycled.

There are many examples of energy being released in the form of heat. **Heat exchangers** can be used to capture this heat energy and recycle it. In a heat exchanger a liquid passes through tubing. The tubing is put wherever the temperature needs to be increased or decreased, for example in a hot gas or a hot liquid. Heat energy is conducted through the tubing.

This solar panel is a heat exchanger. Energy from the Sun heats water that is pumped through tubing in the panel.

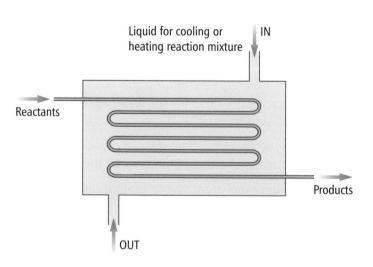

In many industrial chemical plants the reaction temperature must be controlled. Sometimes reaction mixtures need to be heated up; at other times they must be cooled. Heat exchangers are used to do this. The material that separates the hot from the cold areas must be a good thermal conductor.

You could try this simple experiment to show how heat exchangers work.

Procedure

1 Set up a 400 cm³ beaker so that it is wrapped in some insulating material and has a copper coil resting in it. Using rubber tubing, connect one end of the coil to a tap and put the other end in a sink. Do not turn the tap on.

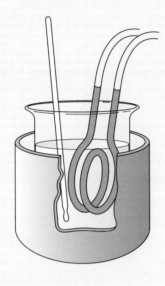

2 Boil a kettle of water and pour in enough water to cover the copper coil.
3 Record the temperature of the water every minute until it reaches about 30 °C.
4 Empty the beaker and turn on the tap so that water is passing through the copper coil.
5 Again, boil a kettle of water and pour in enough water to cover the copper coil.
6 Record the temperature of the water every minute until it reaches about 30 °C.

Compare the results of the two experiments.

Water is used to cool car engines. However, in the winter antifreeze is added to prevent the water from freezing. Antifreeze is ethylene glycol (its correct chemical name is ethan-1,2-diol).

Ethylene glycol is a better conductor of heat than water. It has a lower specific heat capacity:

Water	Antifreeze (ethylene glycol)
It takes 4.18 joules to heat 1 g of water by 1 °C (the specific heat capacity of water = 4.18 J g⁻¹ °C⁻¹)	It takes 2.42 joules to heat 1 g of antifreeze by 1 °C (the specific heat capacity of antifreeze = 2.42 J g⁻¹ °C⁻¹)

So antifreeze is a more effective coolant than water. However, it is also much more expensive than water! In practice motorists add just enough antifreeze to stop the water in the car radiator from freezing. The ideal mixture is 50:50 water and ethylene glycol.

Questions

1   Explain 'efficiency' when it's used to describe simple energy transfers in mechanical and electrical appliances.

2   Here are data for the car described on page 228 using a battery and gas as the sources of energy:

Source of energy	Input energy	Useful energy	Wasted energy
Battery	100 J	80 J	— J
Gas	200 J	— J	110 J

Copy the data and fill in the gaps in the results.
Calculate the efficiency of using: (a) a battery, (b) gas.
Which is the most efficient source of energy: petrol, battery or gas?

3   Describe the advantages of low energy lamps over filament lamps. Try to find out how much each type costs and how long they last for.

4   Describe how heat is lost from a building such as your school or home. How can these heat losses be kept as low as possible?

5   In a central heating system hot water is pumped around pipes to radiators. Describe how heat energy in the water is transferred to the air in a room and warms it up.

6   Draw a diagram to show how a heat exchanger can be used to cool down hot gases produced in an industrial process. Explain how this 'captured' energy can be recycled.

7   Why is antifreeze added to car radiators in the winter?

Heating systems at work

You need to:

• be able to recall and use the formula power = (voltage × current) to calculate the power of an electric circuit

• carry out simple calculations using the formula power = energy/time to calculate power in watts (W) and to calculate the energy usage in kilowatt-hours (kWh) for electrical appliances

• compare the costs of using different electrical appliances.

Electrical power

Everything that uses electricity needs **power**. If you look at different pieces of electrical equipment, at home or in the laboratory, you will see that they each have a power rating, given in watts (W) or kilowatts (kW).

The power ratings of some electrical equipment powered by mains electricity (240 volts)

Piece of equipment	Current/A	Resistance/Ω	Power rating/kW
Three bar electric fire	12.5	19	3
Kettle	8.7	27	2
Hair dryer	4.2	58	1
Microwave oven	2.7	89	0.65
Drill	1.25	192	0.3
Refrigerator	0.5	480	0.12
Lamp	0.3	800	0.06

Power = voltage × current

You can calculate the power of an electric circuit using the formula:

power = voltage × current

The electric plate requires much more power than does the light in the microscope.

Worked examples

1   A music system runs off a mains voltage of 240 volts and a current of 0.05 amps.

   Therefore, the power needed to make it work properly = 240 × 0.05 = 12 watts

   To change this to kilowatts, divide by 1000

   The power needed by the music system = 12/1000 = 0.012 kilowatts

REMEMBER

1 watt = 1 joule of energy per second

1 kilowatt = 1000 watts = 1000 joule of energy per second

2   A calculator uses a 6 volt battery. A current of 0.08 amps passes through it.

Therefore, the power used by the calculator =
$6 \times 0.08 = 0.48$ watts

To change this to kilowatts, divide by 1000

The power needed by the calculator =
0.48/1000 = 0.00048 kilowatts

Power = energy/time

You can also calculate power from the energy needed by using the formula:

power = energy/time

If an electrical appliance uses 1000 joules of energy for 100 seconds, its power rating is given by:

power = 1000/100 = 10 joules per second = 10 watts =
10/1000 = 0.1 kilowatts

Energy = power × time

Provided you know the power rating of an electrical appliance it's straightforward to work out how much energy it uses, using the formula:

energy = power × time

Worked example

Calculate the energy used when:

(a) an electric cooker (power rating 14 kilowatts)

(b) a refrigerator (power rating 0.1 kilowatts)

are each run for 4 hours.

Energy used by cooker = power rating × time = 14×4 =
56 kilowatt hours

Energy used by refrigerator = power rating × time = 0.1×4 =
0.4 kilowatt hours

It costs 140 times as much to run the cooker for the same time as the refrigerator. Fortunately, unlike the refrigerator, the cooker doesn't have to be on all the time!

The refrigerator uses less energy and, therefore, costs less to run for the same time as an electric cooker.

You will use a number of electrical devices in the laboratory. Industry makes use of many electrical appliances. It's useful to be able to compare the cost of running them. You can do this by calculating the energy used and then multiplying by the cost of one unit of electricity (one kilowatt hour).

Suppose a unit of electricity costs 6.5 p.

Then in the example above it costs:

    56 × 6.5 p to run the electric cooker for 4 hours
    = 365 p = £3.65

and

    0.4 × 6.5 p to run the refrigerator for 4 hours
    = 2.6 p

Extension Work

Work and power: some formulae to remember and be able to use

Scientists often use formulae with symbols to represent different quantities. Some important formulae to do with work and power are given here.

Work is done when a force moves something. And this takes energy. Try to remember:

work done = energy used
= force × distance moved in the same direction as the force

In scientific shorthand you would write

$$E = F \times d$$

where E = energy used in joules (J)
        F = force in newtons (N)
        d = distance moved in the same direction as the force in metres (m).

Power is the rate at which work is done and, therefore, the rate at which energy is used.

$$\text{Power} = \frac{\text{work done}}{\text{time taken}} = \frac{\text{energy used}}{\text{time taken}}$$

In scientific shorthand you would write:

$$P = \frac{E}{t}$$

where P = power in watts (W)
        E = energy used in joules (J)
        t = time taken in seconds (s).

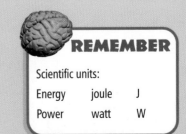

REMEMBER

Scientific units:

Energy	joule	J
Power	watt	W

How much energy?
Often it is quite easy to measure energy changes.

Work done
You have already seen one example of this (on page 000). When work is done the energy change equals the force used times the distance the object moves in the direction of the force:

$$E = F \times d$$

where E = energy change when work is done in joules(J)
       F = force in newtons (N)
       d = distance moved in the direction of the force in metres (m).

Potential energy
First you need to use the formula:

$$F = m \times a$$

where F = force in newtons (N)
       m = mass of object in kilograms (kg)
       a = acceleration of object in metres per second squared (m s^{-2}).

When something is dropped, the acceleration due to gravity is g. If an object has a mass of m, it has a gravity force of mg. This is its weight.

Now imagine lifting the object. If it's lifted through a height of h, it would gain mgh of potential energy since $E = F \times d$. In this case, the distance moved (d) is the height it was lifted through (h).

$$E = F \times h = mg \times h$$

where E = energy used in joules (J)
       F = force in newtons (N)
       m = mass of object in kilograms (kg)
       a = acceleration of object in metres per second (m s^{-1})
       g = acceleration due to gravity
       h = height it was lifted through in metres (m).

Kinetic energy
You need to use the formula:

$$E = \tfrac{1}{2} mv^2$$

where E = kinetic energy of the moving object in joules (J)
       m = mass of object in kilograms (kg)
       v = speed of object in metres per second (m s^{-1}).

Heat energy
You need to use the formula:

$$E = msT$$

where E = energy gained by an object when it is heated in joules (J)
       m = mass of material being heated in kilograms (kg)
       s = the heat needed to raise the temperature of 1 kg of the material by 1 °C (this is called the specific heat capacity) in J kg^{-1} °C^{-1}
       T = temperature change in degrees Celsius (°C).

Extension

So you need to measure the mass of material being heated and the temperature change. You would need to look up the specific heat capacity of the material, for example, using a database.

Electrical energy
You need to use the formula:

$$E = VIt$$

where E = electrical energy, or work done by an electric current on a
         device (like a light bulb or an electric motor) in joules (J)
     V = voltage in volts (V)
     I = current in amps (A)
     t = time in seconds (s).

So you need to measure the voltage and current, and the time for which the circuit was switched on.

Questions

1   Write down the formula for power in terms of current and voltage.
    Use the formula to calculate the power of these electric circuits:
    (a) a two-bar electric fire using 240 volts and a current of 8 amps
    (b) an electric drill using 240 volts and a current of 1.5 amps
    (c) a torch using a 3 volt battery and a current of 0.1 amps
    (d) a laptop computer using 240 volts and 0.25 amps.

2   Use the formula power = energy/time to calculate the power in
    watts (W) of the following:
    (a) an electrical appliance that uses 1000 joules of energy in 10 seconds
    (b) an electrical appliance that uses 600 joules of energy in 1 minute
    (c) an electrical appliance that uses 12 000 joules of energy in
         10 minutes
    (d) an electrical appliance that uses 3600 joules of energy in 1 hour

3   Calculate the energy usage in kilowatt-hours (kWh) for the following:
    (a) a two-bar electric fire using 240 volts and a current of 8 amps
         left on for 6 hours
    (b) an electric drill using 240 volts and a current of 1.5 amps used
         for 3 hours
    (c) a torch using a 3 volt battery and a current of 0.1 amps used for
         15 minutes
    (d) a laptop computer using 240 volts and 0.25 amps used for 4 hours.

4   Put the following electrical appliances in order of increasing costs to
    use for the same time as one another:
    (a) a two-bar electric fire using 240 volts and a current of 8 amps
    (b) an electrical appliance that uses 1000 joules of energy in 10 seconds
    (c) an electric drill using 240 volts and a current of 1.5 amps
    (d) a torch using a 3 volt battery and a current of 0.1 amps
    (e) a laptop computer using 240 volts and 0.25 amps used for 4 hours
    (f) an electrical appliance that uses 12000 joules of energy in 10 minutes.

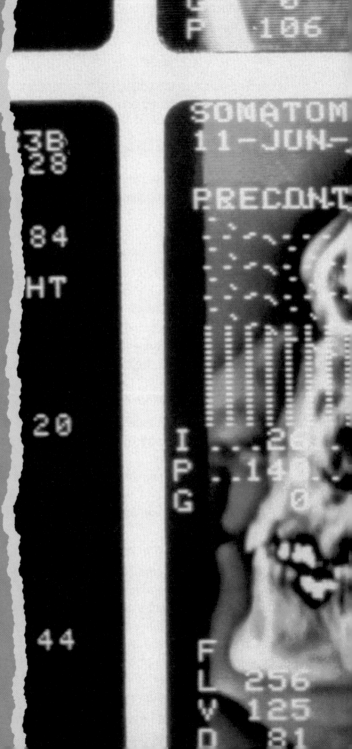

This unit will help you to:

Understand how scientifc skills and knowledge are applied in the world of work. Scientists are employed in a wide range of activities. For some people it's the central part of their job. For others, it isn't, but it helps them to be more effective in what they do. Scientists use skills and knowledge they have learned to tackle problems, from straightforward routine work to more complex and challenging problems. Scientists make, test and control. Their areas of work include:

- making useful products using chemical reactions and checking their quality

- making and testing instruments (in particular electrical and elecronic devices) and machines

- monitoring living organisms – plants, animals (including humans) and micro-organisms.

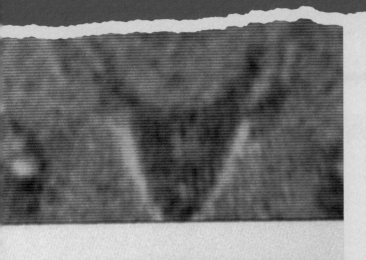

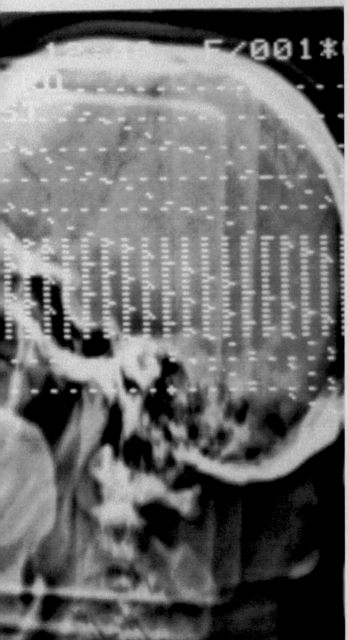

Science at work

In this unit you will learn about:

Science in the workplace   242

Making useful products   254

Instruments and machines   286

Monitoring living organisms   312

3.1 Science in the workplace

The ways science is used

Scientists have many different job titles and roles. Scientific work includes research, development, production, analysis and education. Before you go any further, read about some of this work.

You need to:

- *identify local, national and international businesses and service providers that use science*

- *put their employees into one of three classes: major, significant and small users of science*

- *find out where the organisations are located and why*

- *identify the types of scientific activity that are carried out and the job titles and qualifications of the people who perform them*

- *find out what skills scientists need in addition to their qualifications*

- *find out what careers are available in science and science-related areas.*

Scientific research

Research is at the heart of many science-based organisations. Finding new ways of growing and cultivating crops, new pharmaceuticals and other health products, new ways of communicating . . . the list is endless.

Research scientists discover new information. It's their job. They use a range of practical techniques together with their know-how to solve problems. They devise and carry out experiments to test their ideas. These experiments may lead to new ideas and new materials or processes. They may also lead to old ones being rejected. Scientific ideas are accepted for as long as they seem to work. When they don't work, for example, some new information is found that the ideas do not explain, new ideas replace them.

Research leads to innovation. Mobile phones have come a long way since they were first introduced. Nowadays it's possible to send pictures as well as a voice messages.

Geneticists carry out important scientific research. Cross breeding different varieties of animals and plants makes it possible to combine their best qualities. Selective breeding of sheep, choosing the best animals for breeding, has allowed modern varieties to have higher yields of wool or meat.

Scientific development

Scientific research leads to ideas, materials and products that may have the potential to benefit society. However, these discoveries must be **developed**. Many industrial science-based businesses have Research and Development (R & D) sections. For example, research leading to the discovery of a new therapeutic drug is followed by years of painstaking development before it can be used to treat medical conditions.

New knowledge is not much good until it's put to use. The laser was invented before anyone could think of a use for it. It was 'a solution looking for a problem'. Lasers now have many uses, including in the telecommunications industry, where they can transmit light pulses along optical fibre cables. These lightweight cables can carry signals for long distances without needing boosters and without distortion, unlike the coaxial cables that they are replacing. Capacity is also enormously increased, with tens of thousands of signals being transmitted simultaneously. There are many other examples of 'solutions looking for a problem'.

Some scientific problems are theoretical and are solved through thought and not practical work. For example, Einstein developed his theories of relativity without using experiments.

Production

After research and development, a new material or product can be manufactured for sale. This might be a new strain of wheat, a cosmetic product, an electronic gadget . . . once again the list is endless.

Scientific manufacturing constantly strives to be 'greener'. This means understanding the manufacturing process and doing everything possible to reduce waste materials and waste energy, and being sensitive to the environment. There have been significant advances recently in the area of 'green science'.

Kevlar is a polymer. After its discovery and years of development work it finally went into production. Kevlar is used to make helmets for Formula 1 drivers and bulletproof vests. No doubt on-going research and development will find other uses for this remarkable material.

Analysis

In all areas of scientific activity, **analysis** has a key role. Analysis is about taking something and breaking it down into its parts. You can identify the parts and work out how they fit together. Analysis involves characterising and, if possible, identifying:

- Characterising: finding the properties of a material
- Identifying: recognising a material by comparing its properties with those of known materials.

Scientists characterise and identify materials using practical techniques such as environmental monitoring, strength measurements and chemical tests. You can read more about this on pages 28–48.

In the science-based services, analytical scientists have many jobs to do. For example, forensic scientists collect and analyse all kinds of substances from the scene of a crime. In hospital pathology laboratories, they analyse samples of such things as blood and urine to diagnose diseases and to monitor the progress of treatments.

In industry, analytical scientists have to check the quality of manufactured products. The analysis may need to be very careful and detailed, for example, to ensure safety in the food and drugs industries, and accuracy in the engineering of machine parts.

DNA fingerprinting is a powerful way of identifying a person. In this forensic laboratory, much of the testing is automated. However, the analytical scientist must programme the robot to carry out the correct tests and must also be able to interpret the data correctly.

Analysis usually involves measurement and the collection of numerical data. Analytical scientists must know about accuracy, precision, uncertainty and so on. You can read about this on pages 28–48.

Education through science

People's health and quality of life has improved greatly because of the National Health Service. But it's not just about treating illness using drugs or surgery. The trick is to educate people to try and prevent disease in the first place. It's also cheaper this way.

Over the years scientific research has provided us with vast amounts of information about smoking. Once it was considered to be beneficial. It seemed obvious. Smoking relaxed you, made you feel better, and so it must be good. Tobacco smoke was not recognised as a hazard. Now the risks of smoking are well known.

Politicians need facts and figures to make decisions. For example, the decision to spend money on public works to provide clean drinking water and safe sewage disposal did much to improve public health. Diseases like cholera and typhoid have been eradicated in the developed world. Polio has been significantly reduced in the UK.

Scientists have shown that tobacco smoke causes respiratory diseases like bronchitis, emphysema and lung cancer. They have also shown the harm caused by passive smoking. The evidence is strong enough for victims of passive smoking to have a good case for suing tobacco companies for damages in court.

Scientists have also shown that the respiratory system can recover to some extent when the smoker gives up, providing no real damage has already been done. But science can only support education. Many people still smoke – the addictive effects of tobacco are hard to suppress. Using scientific knowledge to the public good is not always easy!

Prevention is better than cure. However, if things do go wrong, we rely on medical scientists to:
- diagnose the problem
- provide an appropriate treatment or therapy (course of treatment) to aid recovery
- monitor the course of the condition, to check whether the treatment is working or needs changing and if the condition is getting better or worse.

Science businesses

Science-based companies

Businesses and service providers that use science vary in size. Some are small, with just a few employees. These are often called 'smes' (small and medium-sized enterprises). These are usually local. A number are very large organisations that operate nationally or internationally.

Here are some organisations that employ scientists:

biotechnology companies	breweries
chemical companies	clinics and hospitals
dental services	environmental health departments
Engineering companies	food and drink manufacturers
Forestry	manufacturing companies
pharmaceutical companies	research institutions
schools, colleges and universities	water authorities

Finding out which organisations use science

National and international science-based organisations are relatively easy to find out about. They are usually 'household' names and nearly always have a well established and informative website. Whenever you are in a shop or a supermarket just look for the name of the makers on the goods.

You will probably find it easy to identify the big businesses in the area where you live. They employ large numbers of people, occupy large buildings and often have big car parks. The local hospital might be an example. However, in some cases you may not find it so easy to find out what part science plays in their work.

Other organisations will be much smaller and may be harder to identify. Again, it may or may not be easy to tell how much big a part science plays in their work.

Service providers, such as hospitals, veterinary surgeries, environmental health laboratories, county analysts and public health departments are often centrally located in a town or somewhere that they can be reached easily.

This checklist might help you find out which organisations in your locality use science.

Manufacturing or processing	Service providers
Growing or raising plants and animals, e.g. farms, market gardens, horticulture and agriculture research centres	Promoting the health of individuals, e.g. hospitals, sports clinics, fitness centres
Products from plants, animals or micro-organisms, e.g. food, clothing, medicines, natural dyes	Communication, e.g. television and radio studios, telephone networks
Refining of materials used as energy resources, e.g. crude oil, natural gas, coal	Working with the environment, e.g. conservationists, environmentalists
Chemical products, e.g. medicines, paints, dyes, fertilisers, plastics, cosmetics	Animal welfare, e.g. vets
Materials, e.g. metals, alloys, plastics, ceramics, glass, composites, 'smart' materials	Education and training in science and technology, e.g. schools, colleges of further education, universities
Extraction of resources, e.g. water, gas, oil, gravel, clay, stone, minerals	Distribution and sales of food and other products, e.g. supermarkets, farm shops, transport businesses
Mechanical machines and electrical gadgets, e.g. household appliances, earth-moving equipment, industrial plant	Analysis of materials and substances, e.g. environmental health, pathology, forensic, quality control, materials testing laboratories
Processing and packaging of products, e.g. processed foods, food packaging	Distribution of energy resources, e.g. electricity, gas

Manufacturing or processing businesses make their money from selling the products. The success of a new product and the company that manufactures it depends on:

- the price of the product
- the cost of its production
- the level of investment in future developments.

Costs must be kept down, but safety and the necessary quality must not suffer. Prices must cover costs, but not be too high for the product to sell. Investment in initial outlay must pay for people as well as equipment. Profits must cover and pay off this investment and then provide for investment for expansion or the introduction of new improved methods.

Organisations that are service providers may be businesses or be funded directly or indirectly by government using some of the taxes collected by the Inland Revenue. Many research organisations get funding from research councils established to monitor and support research in the UK.

Where you might look

It will probably be easy to identify large businesses or places of work such as hospitals. Finding out about smaller businesses may be more challenging. Similarly, some organisations will have a very clear science aspect to their work while for others the 'science' may be less obvious. Here are some ideas for finding information.

- **People**

Ask your family and friends. There is every chance that some of them work in science-based organisations or know somebody that does.

- **Paper-based resources**

You could, for example, look in books and magazines (try to find *The Directory of Small Businesses* in your local library), ask at the careers service and look in *The Yellow Pages*. Also, local councils publish annual reports in which you might find useful information. The *Directory of Independent Hospitals* and the *IHSM Health and Social Services Year Book* might be helpful. Past issues of local and national papers (usually available on CD-ROM) often contain interesting articles about the successes and failures of local businesses.

- **The Internet**

You could try an Internet search. Use a search engine to help you find information.

- **Organisations**

The local Chamber of Commerce (which publishes business directories with contact details and brief descriptions of what each company does) may be able to help. Science, Engineering and Technology (SET) Points and education/business partnerships may also have useful information.

? Questions

1   *What do you think the terms local, national and international mean when used to describe science-based businesses and service providers?*

2   *Find out the names of local businesses and service providers that use science, and describe briefly what they do.*

3   *Find out the names of four national and four international businesses and service providers that use science. Describe briefly what they do.*

Science-based jobs

You may well have an image of a scientist – wearing a white lab coat and working logically using carefully planned experiments. Well, not all scientists wear white coats and for many imagination and luck play a significant part. There are many examples of discoveries where luck played its part. However, most people agree about what science is and so you can often tell if a job is science-based or not.

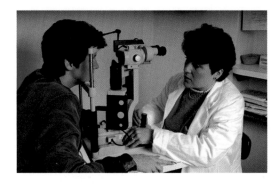

In some occupations, although people do not use science all the time, they need to use scientific ideas to be able to do their jobs properly. Many people are more effective if they are able to use scientific knowledge in their work.

Here are some people who use science in their work:

agricultural/horticultural/forestry/fishery workers	chemical/gas/petroleum workers
chiropodists	engineers (all types)
doctors, dentists, nurses and midwives	food processing workers
geologists	laboratory technicians
meteorologists	occupational therapists
opticians	pharmacists
physiologists	physiotherapists
radiographers	science teachers
speech therapists	beauticians and hairdressers

You don't just find scientists in laboratories. They may be working in a desert, by the side of a river, on the top of a mountain or deep beneath the sea. And they are working on everyday problems that affect all of us.

In some jobs, people do not use science as the major part of their work. However, they can often do their jobs better if they have some knowledge of science. Examples include photographers, hairdressers, chefs and gardeners.

Perhaps we don't think of chefs as scientists. They may not even think of themselves as scientists! However, they may be able to do better in their profession if they understand some scientific principles such as the chemical changes that happen to food when it's cooked and the ways in which to maintain high standards of hygiene.

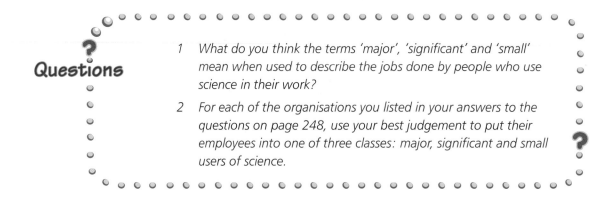

Questions

1   What do you think the terms 'major', 'significant' and 'small' mean when used to describe the jobs done by people who use science in their work?

2   For each of the organisations you listed in your answers to the questions on page 248, use your best judgement to put their employees into one of three classes: major, significant and small users of science.

Where you find science-based organisations

The location of a science-based organisation depends on many factors. Here are some of the major ones that need to be taken into consideration. They are in no particular order as a factor that is really important for one organisation may be less important for another.

The organisation must be located so that:

- raw materials for manufacturing processes can be obtained and transported to the factory
- the manufactured or processed products can be distributed
- samples for analysis can be brought to a laboratory providing a service such as analysis
- necessary services such as electricity, gas and water can be obtained
- waste disposal and effluent discharge can be managed
- energy supplies are available, especially when there are unusually high demands
- any impact on the environment is as small as possible
- the costs of buying or renting the site are not too high

This oil refinery is near the river so that crude oil can be delivered by ship for processing. The network of roads and railway lines also allows products to be distributed easily. Hospitals are often near a town centre, easily reachable by car, bus or train.

- transport to and from the organisation allows good access for employees and goods
- security can be maintained
- there is an adequate supply of people with the right experience and qualifications (from cleaners through to managers).

In discussions with your teacher and other students you may come up with other factors.

Look at the science-based organisations in the area where you live.
List the reasons for each organisation being located where it is.

Questions

More about science-based jobs

In Unit 1 you read about working safely in science, following standard procedures, handling scientific equipment and materials, and recording and analysing scientific data. This is what scientists do in their jobs. Their work could be grouped under three main headings:

- **Making**, e.g. growing plants, synthesising chemicals, constructing electronic equipment
- **Characterising**, e.g. identifying micro-organisms, analysing chemicals, determining the physical properties of materials
- **Controlling**, e.g. making things grow better, making sure chemical reactions go at a safe speed, using sensors to monitor change.

In all of these areas, scientists use their skills and scientific knowledge to tackle problems. The 'problem' might be a routine quality check on a product from a manufacturing process. On the other hand it might be non-routine, like working out what to do when a quality check suggests something has gone wrong in the manufacturing process. The problem might be quite straightforward and simple. It might be complicated, with many factors contributing to it.

All scientists need a broad understanding of scientific ideas and concepts. They need to be able to handle commonly used equipment and materials. But science is a huge area (as you are probably discovering). Nobody can know it all. These days scientists usually work in teams. Each scientist has specialist knowledge and skills. Between them, the members of the team should have all the necessary knowledge and skills. Getting the right team depends on good management and, hopefully, will lead to a successful project.

Scientists need other skills as well. They need to be able to:

- **Communicate** with others, e.g. in writing and verbally, with other scientists and with people with not much scientific knowledge.

Communication of data and ideas is central to the progress of science. Scientists 'publish' their work so that it can be tested by others. This is often done by writing a report for colleagues within their company or, if it's to be spread more widely, by writing an article for a scientific journal. Journals are often available electronically through the Internet.

- **Use information technology** effectively, e.g. to collect, manipulate and communicate data.

Within an organisation, communication has to be well organised to be effective. Paper systems are giving way to electronic mail. Computers linked by modems through the telephone system are giving rise to an 'information super-highway'.

- **Manage relationships** with other people, e.g. work in a team, supervise others, understand your own responsibilities within a team and that others depend upon your work

Experienced scientists often supervise the work of less experienced scientists. This means guiding their work and helping them to do their jobs properly. In this way inexperienced scientists increase their knowledge and skills (both scientific and professional).

- **Manage resources**, for example, work within time limits, work within the amount of money allocated to a project, work with finite supplies of materials (in other words, do not assume that once a sample for analysis is used up there is plenty more available if the analysis is not complete)
- **Manage time**, for example, be able to organise the work so that it gets done efficiently and effectively.

These are often called 'key skills'. However, they might be better called 'professional skills'. They are the skills scientists must add to their scientific knowledge and skills.

Science qualifications

After obtaining this qualification there are many routes open to you.

You could stay in full-time education (either in the sixth form or at a college of further education) and study for an advanced level science qualification. This could be:

- an AVCE in Science (Advanced Vocational Certificate in Education), 6- or 12-unit awards

or

- GCE AS and A levels in biology, chemistry or physics (there are also some other science-related GCEs that you might find interesting so talk with your science teachers or careers teacher).

You might be able to get a job in a science-based organisation and study further on day-release courses or evening courses.

Vocational qualifications, such as NVQs (National Vocational Qualifications) can be gained while working full-time. Some employees run Foundation and Advanced Modern Apprenticeships schemes. These are training schemes during which, among other things, you will work towards an NVQ.

Beyond advanced level there is an enormous range of science and science-related qualifications that can be studied at university. You will need to take as much advice as you can, read a lot, talk to people and, if possible, visit the universities that run the degree courses that you are interested in.

Careers in science

Advice is best sought from your careers teacher or careers office. Professional bodies such as the Institute of Biology, Institute of Physics, Royal Society of Chemistry and man others provide lots of useful leaflets and other guidance. Once again, the Internet will give you access to much of this.

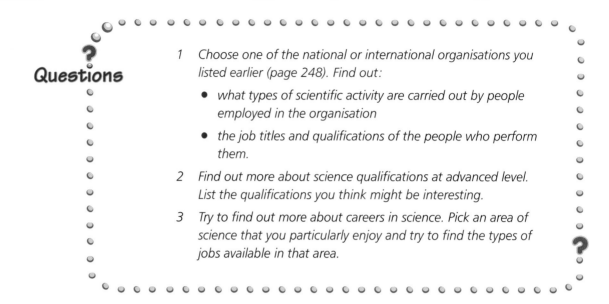

Questions

1   Choose one of the national or international organisations you listed earlier (page 248). Find out:

   • what types of scientific activity are carried out by people employed in the organisation

   • the job titles and qualifications of the people who perform them.

2   Find out more about science qualifications at advanced level. List the qualifications you think might be interesting.

3   Try to find out more about careers in science. Pick an area of science that you particularly enjoy and try to find the types of jobs available in that area.

3.2 Making useful products

From laboratory to industrial plant

You may have already read about how naturally occurring materials such as rocks, minerals and crude oil can be made into more useful products by chemical reaction. The chemical and pharmaceutical industries exist for this purpose. Like any businesses, they must be profitable and get the maximum amount of product of the required purity as cheaply and quickly as possible. The scientists must know about chemical changes. Their work must be quantitative. In other words, they need to be able to measure quantities of chemical products accurately and calculate the yield. You can read more in *Obtaining useful chemicals*, page 167.

Scientists who make chemicals in the laboratory are often called synthetic chemists. It's their job to find possible ways of making compounds. Methods that look promising are tried on a larger scale in pilot plants. It's here that most of the problems that come with scaling up (in other words, making much larger quantities) are sorted out. Chemical engineers have the job of making a big enough chemical plant for industrial production.

Getting products cheaply and quickly

You need to be able to:

- *describe the factors that affect how quickly a reaction occurs*

- *explain the terms: actual yield, theoretical yield, percentage yield*

- *explain that some processes are based on reversible reactions and that the conditions affect the yield of the products.*

Rates of chemical reactions

The need to control reaction rates

Manufacturers usually want to make products as quickly as possible. This generally means lower production costs. It isn't always the case, however. For example, some reactions get faster and faster until they are out of control – and the result can be disastrous. Scientists need to and can control the speed of chemical reactions. They do this to:

- control a production process – how quickly the product is made
- control energy transfer – to make sure a reaction mixture doesn't get too hot or too cold
- ensure safety – to make sure that reactions don't get out of hand.

Scientists and engineers work together to ensure that reaction rates in industrial and other processes are controlled.

In 1974 there was a major disaster in Flixborough. There was a uge explosion in a chemical plant manufacturing nylon. Cyclohexane escaped and exploded in an uncontrollable reaction with oxygen. Twenty eight people died. Understanding how to control chemical reactions is vital scientific work.

Rate of reaction

The rate of a chemical reaction is determined by measuring the changes in concentration of either reactants or products.

$$\text{Rate of reaction} = \frac{\text{change in concentration}}{\text{time taken for change}}$$

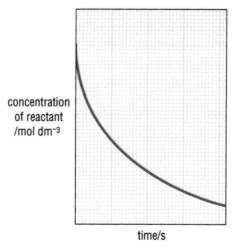

concentration
of reactant
/mol dm⁻³

time/s

This graph shows how the concentration of a reactant decreases as a chemical reaction takes place. Can you draw a graph to show the change in concentration of a product?

The concentration of reactants decreases in a reaction, while the concentration of products increases. Some reactions are almost instant, for example, the precipitation of an insoluble salt, while others are slow. In fact, some reactions are so slow that it is difficult to see that they are taking place at all by simply looking at them. For example, cars where the paintwork is scratched become rusty. This is a chemical reaction between oxygen and water vapour in the air and iron. You know rust when you see it, but you could watch a car all day and not notice a change.

Factors affecting rate

The rate of a chemical reaction is affected by:
- the concentration of reactants
- temperature

and may also be affected by:
- the surface area of a solid
- the presence of a catalyst.

Concentration of reactants

The rate of reaction increases with increasing concentration of reactants. It decreases with decreasing concentration of reactants. For example, magnesium reacts with hydrochloric acid:

magnesium + hydrochloric acid → magnesium chloride + hydrogen
$Mg(s)$ + $2HCl(aq)$ → $MgCl_2(aq)$ + $H_2(g)$

The rate of this reaction can be judged by how quickly the mixture effervesces (fizzes), giving off hydrogen. Effervescence is more vigorous with more concentrated samples of acid. You can show this in a simple experiment. Add separate lengths of magnesium ribbon to samples of hydrochloric acid of differing concentration. To make it a fair test, other factors that might affect the rate must be the same in each experiment, for example temperature, and the lengths that the ribbon is cut into.

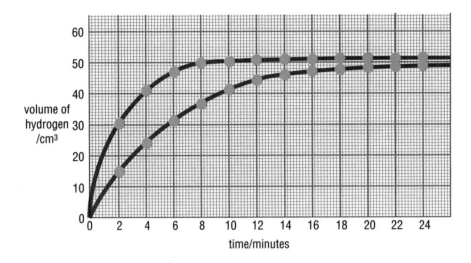

Zinc reacts more quickly with 2 mol dm^{-3} sulfuric acid than with 1 mol dm^{-3} sulfuric acid. These graphs show the results of two experiments. Can you draw the graph that you would get if 0.5 mol dm^{-3} sulfuric acid was used?

Reactions slow down as reactants become used up. This is because their concentrations are decreasing and, as we have said, rate depends on concentration.

The rate of reaction between two gases increases with increasing pressure. This is because higher pressures bring the reactants closer together. Therefore, the concentration increases, which increases the reaction rate.

Temperature
An increase in temperature increases the rate of a chemical reaction. For example, a 10 °C rise in temperature roughly doubles the rate of reaction at room temperature. Similarly, decreasing the temperature will cause a reaction to slow down.

Powdered magnesium (right-hand test tube) reacts more rapidly with hydrochloric acid than does magnesium ribbon. Why is this?

There are two ways to cook potatoes faster. You could fry them in oil (a higher temperature than if you boil them in water) or you could cut them into small pieces.

Surface area
The more finely divided a solid is, the more rapidly it reacts with a liquid or a gas. The surface area is the amount of surface that is

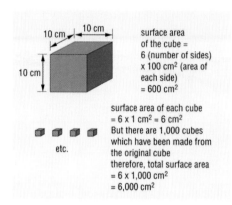

surface area
of the cube =
6 (number of sides)
x 100 cm² (area of
each side)
= 600 cm²

surface area of each cube
= 6 x 1 cm² = 6 cm²
But there are 1,000 cubes
which have been made from
the original cube
therefore, total surface area
= 6 x 1,000 cm²
= 6,000 cm²

Breaking a solid into smaller pieces increases its surface area.

exposed. A powdered solid has a higher surface area than the same mass of the solid in the form of lumps or granules.

Catalysts

Catalysts are substances that increase the rate of a chemical reaction. Importantly, they are not used up in the reaction. Catalysts can be recovered chemically unchanged at the end of the reaction. Catalysts are central to most industrial processes. Making a reaction go faster and using less energy saves money.

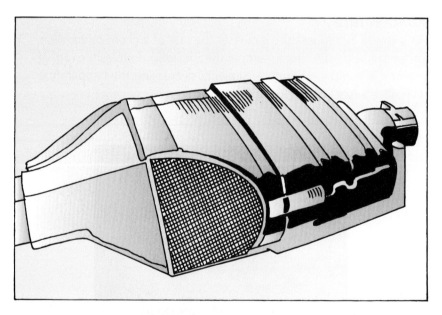

Cars often have catalytic converters to reduce the amounts of poisonous gas in the exhaust fumes. The catalysts used (platinum and iridium) are very expensive and so a very thin layer is spread on an unreactive cheaper material. You can see from the picture that a honeycomb structure is used. Can you explain why?

The rates of chemical reactions that occur in our bodies, and in the cells of other animals and plants, are also controlled by catalysts. These biological catalysts are called enzymes.

Here is a summary of the factors affecting how fast a chemical reaction takes place.

The rate of reaction could be increased by:
- increasing the concentration of reactants
- increasing the temperature
- increasing the surface area (if a solid is involved)
- using a suitable catalyst

The rate of reaction could be decreased by:
- decreasing the concentration of reactants
- decreasing the temperature
- decreasing the surface area (if a solid is involved).

Explaining rates of reaction

Gases consist of atoms or molecules moving about in a chaotic way. Similarly, in solution, ions or molecules move about randomly.

For a reaction to occur, particles (atoms, ions or molecules) of reactant must collide with one another. The more often particles collide, the faster the reaction. Not all collisions lead to reaction. Those that do are called effective collisions. Particles must have sufficient energy to undergo an effective collision. This means they must have sufficient energy for the chemical bonds to break. This energy is called the activation energy. This model of how chemicals react is called collision theory. Put simply, the lower the activation energy, the faster the reaction.

This model should help you understand how conditions affect the rate of a reaction.

SURFACE AREA
surface area of
calcium carbonate **low**

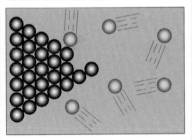

surface area
higher – more calcium carbonate
exposed to collisions

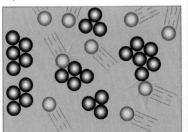

The effect of surface area, concentration and temperature on the rate of a chemical reaction can be explained by a simple model.

Extension Work

Concentration.
Concentration is the number of particles in a given volume. The more particles in the reaction mixture (the higher the concentration), the greater the number of collisions and, therefore, the faster the reaction. Both the total number of collisions and the number of effective collisions increases. The proportion of effective collisions is not changed.

CONCENTRATION
concentration of hydrochloric acid **low**

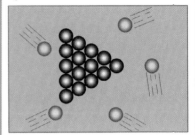

concentration
higher – more chance of particles colliding

TEMPERATURE
temperature **low**

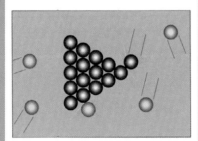

temperature
higher – particles collide with more energy

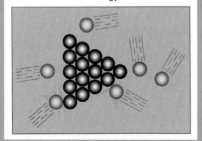

Temperature. Particles move more quickly at high temperatures than at low temperatures. Because of this, they have greater energy. This has two effects. At higher temperatures:

- particles collide with one another more frequently (because they are moving more rapidly)
- the number of effective collisions is higher (because a greater proportion of the particles have sufficient energy to overcome the activation energy).

Together, these effects mean that increasing the temperature of a reaction mixture increases the rate quite markedly. The total number of collisions increases and the proportion of collisions that are effective is higher.

Surface area. Increasing the surface area of a solid exposes more of it to other substances with which it might react. This allows more effective collisions to occur. The outcome is a faster rate of reaction.

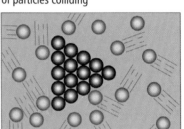

Yields

It's important to measure how much of a product you get from chemical reaction. All you need to do is weigh it. The mass obtained is called the **actual yield**.

But how much might you have expected to get? If you carried out the reaction and:

- all of the reactants were changed into the product you wanted
- you managed to isolate it without losing any (for example, leaving some behind on the filter paper if you had to filter it)

the quantity you would get is called the **theoretical yield**.

You will probably be given formulae to calculate the theoretical yields for compounds you make in the laboratory.

Worked examples

1   Copper can be made by reacting copper oxide with carbon.
    1.0 g of copper oxide can make 0.80 g of copper
    So if you started with 5.0 g of copper oxide the theoretical yield of copper would be
    5.0 × 0.80 g = 4.0 g

2   Magnesium sulfate crystals can be made by reacting magnesium oxide with sulfuric acid.
    1.0 g of magnesium oxide can give 6.2 g of magnesium sulfate crystals
    So if you started with 2.0 g of magnesium oxide the theoretical yield of magnesium sulfate crystals would be
    2 x 6.2 g = 12.4 g

REMEMBER

Read the **Extension work** if you want to understand how we know that '1.0 g of copper oxide can make 0.80 g of copper' and '1.0 g of magnesium oxide can give 6.2 g of magnesium sulfate crystals'.

The actual yield is nearly always less than the theoretical yield. There may be a number of reasons for this including:

- the reactants are not used up completely
- the reactants may give a mixture of products, and only one is what you want
- some reactants or products are lost when you are transferring them during the preparation.

The **percentage yield** tells you about the efficiency of the preparation.

$$\text{percentage yield} = \frac{\text{actual yield}}{\text{theoretical yield}} \times 100\%$$

Worked examples

1   3.2 g of copper was made from 5.0 g of copper oxide.
    Actual yield = 3.2 g
    Theoretical yield = 4.0 g (see calculation earlier)
    Therefore percentage yield = $\frac{3.2}{4.0} \times 100$ = 80%

2   8.3 g of magnesium sulfate crystals were made from 2.0 g of
magnesium oxide.
Actual yield = 8.3 g
Theoretical yield = 12.4 g (see calculation earlier)
Therefore percentage yield = $\frac{8.3}{12.4} \times 100 = 67\%$

Before you try this work make sure you understand the ideas in
Extension Work 'Quantities and amounts' on page 33. You need to
know about relative atomic mass and relative formula mass, and how
to convert quantities into amounts and back again.

Working out theoretical yields

You read above that '1.0 g of copper oxide can make 0.80 g of copper'
and '1.0 g of magnesium oxide can give 6.2 g of magnesium sulfate
crystals'. These are the theoretical yields. But how do we know?

There are three steps:

Step 1   Write down the balanced chemical equation.

Step 2   Find out the relative atomic masses of the atoms involved
and calculate the relative formula masses of reactants and
products.

Step 3   Use the chemical equation to work out how much product
can be made from the quantity of reactants being used.

When a compound is made in the laboratory, or in a large industrial
plant, often one of the reactants is present 'in excess'. This means that
there is more than enough of it for the reaction. In cases like this, the
yield of product depends on the reactant that is not present in excess.

Example 1

Calculate the theoretical yield of copper from 1 g of copper oxide.

Step 1

For the reaction between copper oxide and carbon to make copper the
equation is

$$2CuO \text{ (s)} + C \text{ (s)} \rightarrow 2Cu \text{ (s)} + CO_2 \text{ (g)}$$

Step 2

Relative atomic masses		Relative formula masses		
Cu	63.5	CuO	63.5 + 16	= 79.5
C	12	CO_2	12 + 16 + 16	= 44
O	16			

Step 3

2CuO (s)	C (s)	=	2Cu (s)	CO$_2$ (g)
2 × 79.5 g	12 g	=	2 × 63.5 g	44 g
159 g	12 g	=	127 g	44 g
1 g	$\frac{12}{159}$ g	=	$\frac{127}{159}$ g	$\frac{44}{159}$ g
1 g	0.075 g	=	0.80 g	0.28 g

So, 1 g of copper oxide can make 0.80 g of copper.

Note: You can also calculate that 0.075 g of carbon is needed and 0.28 g of carbon dioxide would also be produced. In practice, an excess of carbon is used. For example, 0.5 g may be used, which means that (0.5 − 0.075) g = 0.425 g remains unused.

Example 2
Calculate the theoretical yield of silver chloride from 3 g of silver nitrate.

Step 1
For the reaction between silver nitrate solution and sodium chloride solution to make silver chloride and sodium nitrate solution the equation is

$$AgNO_3 \text{ (aq)} + NaCl \text{ (aq)} \rightarrow AgCl \text{ (s)} + NaNO_3 \text{ (aq)}$$

An excess of sodium chloride solution is used and so only the quantities of silver nitrate and silver chloride need be calculated.

Step 2

Relative atomic masses		Relative formula masses		
Ag	108	AgNO$_3$	108 + 14 + (3 × 16)	= 170
N	14	AgCl	108 + 35.5	= 143.5
O	16			
Cl	35.5			

Step 3
As sodium chloride is in excess we only need worry about the quantities of silver nitrate and silver chloride.

AgNO$_3$ (aq)	NaCl (aq)	=	AgCl (s)	NaNO$_3$ (aq)
170 g		=	143.5 g	
1 g		=	$\frac{143.5}{170}$ g	
30 g		=	$\frac{143.5}{170} \times 30$ g	
30 g		=	25.3 g	

So, 30 g of silver nitrate can make 25.3 g of silver chloride.

Soluble salts

You need to be careful when calculating the theoretical yield of a soluble salt. This is because they usually crystallise with water of crystallisation. But the balanced equation doesn't show this.

For example

$$MgO \text{ (s)} + H_2SO_4 \text{ (aq)} \rightarrow MgSO_4 \text{ (aq)} + H_2O \text{ (l)}$$

But magnesium sulfate crystallises as $MgSO_4.7H_2O$ (s).

Relative atomic masses		Relative formula masses		
Mg	24	MgO	$24 + 16$	$= 40$
O	16	$MgSO_4.7H_2O$	$24 + 32 + (4 \times 16)$	
			$+ 7[(2 \times 1) + 16]$	$= 246$
H	1			
S	32			

Rather than write the equation, we summarise the reaction **and** the crystallisation.

MgO (s)	H_2SO_4 (aq)	=	$MgSO_4.7H_2O$ (s)
40 g		=	246 g
1 g		=	$\dfrac{246}{40}$ g
1 g		=	6.2 g

So, 1 g of magnesium oxide can make 6.2 g of magnesium sulfate-7-water.

Magnesium burns in air to form magnesium oxide. When heated strongly the magnesium flares up and in seconds is changed completely to magnesium oxide.

Reversible reactions

Many chemical reactions seem to change reactants to products until one of the reactants is used up. Then they stop.

However, many reactions do not 'go to completion'. The reactants are never used up completely. The reaction mixture always contains both products and unused reactants. This means that the actual yield of product is lower than the theoretical yield. In other words, the percentage yield is less than 100%. Chemists need to understand how they can control the composition of the reaction mixture, just as they know how to control the rate of a chemical reaction.

What happens is that reactants react to give products, but as soon as they are formed the products begin reacting to reform the original reactants. We call this a **reversible reaction**. The reaction conditions affect how much of product is in the reaction mixture. When the rate of the forward reaction is the same as the reverse reaction, we say that **equilibrium** has been reached.

We show that a reaction is reversible by using $\longleftrightarrow$ rather than $\rightarrow$ in the chemical equation, for example,

carbon monoxide + hydrogen $\longleftrightarrow$ methanol
CO (g)   + $2H_2$ (g) $\longleftrightarrow$ CH_3OH (g)

and

ethane + steam $\longleftrightarrow$ ethanol
C_2H_4 (g) + H_2O (g) $\longleftrightarrow$ C_2H_5OH (g)

(Both of these reactions are used in the petrochemical industry.)

The position of equilibrium tells us the proportions of reactants and products at equilibrium. To get a good yield of product, we need to make the position of equilibrium 'move to the right'. In other words, we need to increase the proportion of product in the reaction mixture.

The position of equilibrium, and therefore the yield of product, can be affected by changing:

- the concentrations of reactants and/or products; for example, removing products from the reaction mixture as they form
- the pressure of a gaseous reaction mixture; for example, high pressures will increase the yield of product where there are fewer product molecules than reactant molecules (and vice versa)
- the temperature of the reaction mixture; for example, if the reaction is exothermic, raising the temperature will decrease the yield of product, and if it is endothermic the yield of product will increase.

Catalysts do not affect the position of equilibrium.

The cost of making a chemical
You need to think about several factors when deciding how much it costs to make a chemical in the laboratory, as outlined below.

Raw materials
How much did the chemicals used (the reactants, also called 'raw materials') cost to buy? You can find this information by looking up prices in a chemical supplier's catalogue. You will need to know which chemical suppliers the chemical was bought from and in what quantity.

Worked examples
1. 5.0 g of magnesium oxide was used to make a magnesium salt. 500 g had been bought from a chemical supplier for £26
   Therefore the cost of 5.0 g was £ $\frac{26}{500} \times 5.0 = £0.26 = 26$ p

2. 100 cm³ of dilute sulfuric acid was used in a preparation. 2.5 dm³ had been bought from a chemical supplier for £16
   Therefore the cost of 100 cm³ was £ $\frac{16}{2500} \times 100 = £0.64 = 64p$

(Note that 2.5 dm³ had to be converted to 2500 cm³ to do the calculation.)

Solid chemicals are usually available in various sizes, for example, 50 g, 100 g, 250 g, 500g and 1000 g (1 kg). Liquids can often be bought in quantities of 100 cm³, 250 cm³, 500 cm³ and 1000 cm³ (1 dm³ or 1 litre). When you know the cost of the quantity bought, you can calculate the cost of the quantity you used.

Energy

You can read about using energy in the laboratory and how much it costs in Unit 2 (pages 224–225).

Equipment

You can find the costs in the same way as for a chemical, by looking in a scientific supplier's catalogue. Of course, unlike a chemical, the equipment can be used again (provided it isn't broken!).
Even so it's usual to build into the costs of the product you made something for depreciation of the equipment. This means something to reflect the decrease in value due to 'wear and tear'. All equipment will eventually wear out or break and have to be replaced. The amount you build in depends on how many times you think the equipment can be used and, perhaps, repair costs during its lifetime. As a rule of thumb you could take this to be about 1–2% of the purchase price.

Labour

Often the most expensive part of any production or service is people's time. Labour for making a chemical in the laboratory includes the time of the people making the chemical, technicians and other support staff and supervisors. To estimate these costs you will need to find out about typical wages and salaries.

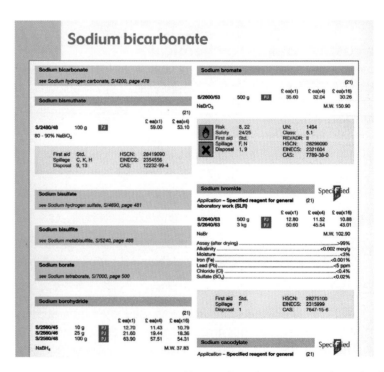

The cost of a chemical depends on its purity and how much you buy. The purer a chemical is, the more it costs (purification processes are not cheap). And, just like shopping in the supermarket, buying larger quantities can be better value for money.

Making chemicals in the laboratory

You need to:

- *prepare pure, dry products using three different types of chemical reaction*

- *explain the underlying chemistry involved in each type of reaction*

- *explain the industrial importance of each reaction.*

For each preparation you carry out, you need to:

- *know the type of reaction used*

- *measure the actual yield*

- *present the product in a suitable sample tube, with its name, date of preparation and relevant hazard warnings*

- *write balanced chemical equations to describe reactions, given the formulae of reactants and products*

- *calculate the mass of product that could be obtained from a specified amount of reactant (theoretical yield)*

- *calculate the percentage yield of a reaction from the theoretical yield and the actual mass of product obtained*

- *calculate the costs of making a given amount of product.*

Some important types of chemical reaction

Acid-base reactions

Acids are neutralised by **bases** to give solutions of salts. Water is the only other product of reaction:

acid + base → salt + water

Bases that dissolve in water give alkaline solutions, in other words with pH greater than 7. These solutions are called **alkalis**. Magnesium oxide is a base. Sodium hydroxide is a base that dissolves in water to make sodium hydroxide solution – an alkali. Here are two examples of acid-base reactions:

Acids are substances that dissolve in water to give acidic solutions, in other words with pH less than 7. Alkalis are bases that dissolve in water to give alkaline solutions, in other words with pH greater than 7. Distilled water has pH 7.

hydrochloric acid + magnesium oxide → magnesium chloride + water

$$2HCl\ (aq)\quad +\quad MgO\ (s)\quad \rightarrow \quad MgCl_2\ (aq)\quad +\ H_2O\ (l)$$

nitric acid + sodium hydroxide → sodium nitrate + water

$$HNO_3\ (aq)\ +\quad NaOH\ (aq)\quad \rightarrow \quad NaNO_3\ (aq)\quad +\ H_2O\ (l)$$

'Sulphate of ammonia' is a well-known fertiliser. Its correct chemical name is ammonium sulfate. It is made by an acid–base reaction between sulfuric acid and ammonia.

Acids also react with **carbonates** to give salts. However, unlike the reaction with bases, carbon dioxide is also produced.

acid + carbonate → salt + water + carbon dioxide

For example,

calcium carbonate + hydrochloric acid → calcium chloride + water
$$CaCO_3 \text{ (s)} \quad + \quad 2HCl \text{ (aq)} \quad \rightarrow \quad CaCl_2 \text{ (aq)} \quad + H_2O \text{ (l)}$$

\+ carbon dioxide
\+ CO_2 (g)

Precipitation

Soluble salts dissolve in water to give solutions of their ions. For example, magnesium sulphate ($MgSO_4$) dissolves in water to give a solution of magnesium ions, Mg^{2+}(aq), and sulfate ions, SO_4^{2-}(aq). An insoluble salt such as barium sulfate, $BaSO_4$, will precipitate if a solution containing barium ions is mixed with one containing sulfate ions.

'Chrome yellow' is used for painting yellow lines on the road. It's correct chemical name is lead chromate(VI). It's made by a precipitation reaction between potassium or sodium chromate(VI) and lead nitrate.

REMEMBER

We use (aq) in chemical equations to show that something is dissolved in water.

Precipitation and ionic equations

Silver chloride is insoluble in water. It can be prepared by mixing solutions of silver nitrate and sodium chloride.

silver nitrate + sodium chloride → silver chloride + sodium nitrate
$$AgNO_3\text{(aq)} + \quad NaCl\text{(aq)} \quad \rightarrow \quad AgCl\text{(s)} \quad + \quad NaNO_3\text{(aq)}$$

Now

- Silver nitrate, $AgNO_3$, dissolves in water to give a solution of silver ions, Ag^+(aq), and nitrate ions, NO_3^-(aq).
- Sodium chloride dissolves in water to give a solution of sodium ions, Na^+(aq), and chloride ions, Cl^-(aq).
- When these solutions are mixed, silver chloride precipitates, but the other ions remain in solution as sodium nitrate is soluble.

So the equation could be written:

$AgNO_3(aq) + NaCl(aq) \rightarrow AgCl(s) + NaNO_3(aq)$

$Ag^+(aq) + NO_3^-(aq) + Na^+(aq) + Cl^-(aq) \rightarrow AgCl(s) + Na^+(aq) + NO_3^-(aq)$

But you will see that some of the ions (shown in *italics*) are in solution both before and after the reaction. They don't take any part in the reaction. They are **spectator ions** (they just stand on and watch while the others react!). Leaving the spectator ions out the equation can be written:

$Ag^+(aq) + Cl^-(aq) \rightarrow AgCl(s)$

We call this an **ionic equation**.

Redox

In a **redox reaction**, **oxidation** and **reduction** reactions occur simultaneously. The term comes from **red**uction-**ox**idation.

Gain or loss of oxygen

Most metals react with oxygen to give the metal oxide. They are oxidised. An example is iron rusting:

iron	+	oxygen	$\rightarrow$	iron(III) oxide
$4Fe\,(s)$	+	$3O_2\,(g)$	$\rightarrow$	$2Fe_2O_3\,(s)$

The oxygen can be removed from metal oxides, leaving the metal. This is called reduction. The reactions can be used to obtain metals such as iron, lead or copper from their ores. For example,

copper(II) oxide	+	hydrogen	$\rightarrow$	copper	+	water
$CuO\,(s)$	+	$H_2\,(g)$	$\rightarrow$	$Cu\,(s)$	+	$H_2O\,(l)$

REMEMBER

There are two useful definitions of oxidation and reduction:

- in terms of gain and loss of oxygen:
  oxidation is the gain of oxygen; reduction is the loss of oxygen

- iin terms of gain and loss of electrons:
  oxidation is the gain of electrons; reduction is the loss of electrons

Iron is made in greater amounts than any other metal. It's obtained from its ores in a blast furnace. There are two redox reactions involved:

iron(III) oxide	+	carbon	$\rightarrow$	iron	+	carbon dioxide
$2Fe_2O_3\,(s)$	+	$3C\,(s)$	$\rightarrow$	$4Fe\,(s)$	+	$3CO_2\,(g)$
iron(III) oxide	+	carbon monoxide	$\rightarrow$	iron	+	carbon dioxide
$Fe_2O_3\,(s)$	+	$3CO\,(g)$	$\rightarrow$	$2Fe\,(s)$	+	$3CO_2\,(g)$

In each case, the metal oxide has been **reduced** (oxygen has been lost). The substance that brings this about is called a **reducing agent**. So, carbon, carbon monoxide and hydrogen are all acting as reducing agents. These substances gain oxygen. They have been **oxidised**.

Electron transfer

Redox reactions may be defined in terms of the transfer of electrons. A substance that loses electrons is **oxidised**. One that gains electrons is **reduced**.

An example is the displacement of a metal from a solution containing its ions. For example, when zinc is placed in an aqueous solution of copper(II) sulphate, it dissolves to give a solution of zinc sulphate, and copper forms.

$$\text{zinc} + \text{copper(II) sulfate} \rightarrow \text{zinc sulfate} + \text{copper}$$
$$Zn\,(s) + CuSO_4\,(aq) \rightarrow ZnSO_4\,(aq) + Cu\,(s)$$

Electrons are transferred from zinc atoms, Zn, to copper(II) ions, Cu^{2+}. The zinc atoms become zinc ions, Zn^{2+}, and the copper(II) ions become copper atoms, Cu.

Silver is displaced from a solution of its ions by copper. This is because copper is more reactive than silver (it's above copper in the electrochemical series).

The **electrochemical series** places metals in order of their reactivity:

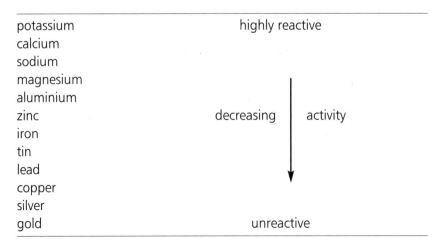

potassium	highly reactive
calcium	
sodium	
magnesium	
aluminium	
zinc	decreasing activity
iron	
tin	
lead	
copper	
silver	
gold	unreactive

REMEMBER

OILRIG:
Oxidation **i**s **l**oss of electrons and **r**eduction **i**s **g**ain of electrons.

A metal that is above another in the electrochemical series will displace it from a solution of its salts. However, the metals above zinc will not precipitate from solutions of their salts. This is because they are so reactive that they react with water.

Redox reactions and ionic equations

When salts dissolve in water they break up to give solutions containing their ions. Copper(II) sulfate dissolves to give a solution of copper(II) ions, $Cu^{2+}(aq)$, and sulfate ions, $SO_4^{2-}(aq)$. This means that we can write the equation rather differently:

$$Zn\ (s) + Cu^{2+}\ (aq) + SO_4^{2-}\ (aq) \rightarrow Zn^{2+}\ (aq) + Cu\ (s) + SO_4^{2-}\ (aq)$$

We see that the sulfate ions, $SO_4^{2-}(aq)$, are present in solution before and after the reaction. They are spectator ions. The ionic equation for the displacement reaction is:

$$Zn\ (s) + Cu^{2+}\ (aq) \rightarrow Zn^{2+}\ (aq) + Cu\ (s)$$

This type of equation is known as an ionic equation. Its use here has the advantage that it represents the displacement of copper from a solution of any of its soluble salts by *zinc*.

Electrons are transferred from zinc to copper(II) ions. This can be represented with two half-equations:

$Zn\ (s) \rightarrow Zn^{2+}\ (aq) + 2e^-$ zinc is being oxidised (loss of electrons)
$Cu^{2+}\ (aq) + 2e^- \rightarrow Cu(s)$ copper(II) ions are being reduced (gain of electrons)

The ionic equation for the reaction is obtained by 'adding' these two half reactions. The electrons (e⁻) cancel out.

$Zn\ (s)$	$\rightarrow$	$Zn^{2+}\ (aq) + 2\ e^-$
$Cu^{2+}\ (aq) + 2\ e^-$	$\rightarrow$	$Cu\ (s)$
$Zn\ (s) + Cu^{2+}$	$\rightarrow$	$Zn^{2+}\ (aq) + Cu\ (s)$

Some basic techniques

You should have practised and be confident about using the techniques for handling scientific equipment and glassware that were described in Unit 1. These include:

- transferring substances
- mixing, stirring and heating substances
- measuring, in particular using a balance and measuring volumes of liquids.

Some methods for making chemicals are given below. However, before you start you should read about ways of separating a product from a reaction mixture and how it may be purified. There are a number of important techniques that you need to know about: crystallisation, decantation, filtration and centrifuging, and distillation.

technique

CRYSTALLISATION

USE   A dissolved solid (for example, a soluble salt) can be obtained from **aqueous solution** by crystallisation.

EQUIPMENT AND MATERIALS
- Solution to be evaporated
- Evaporating basin
- Method of heating

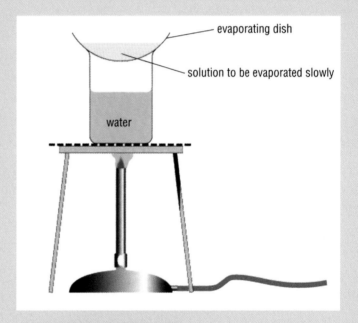

A solution can be evaporated slowly using this apparatus. The Bunsen burner flame should be adjusted so that the water in the beaker is just boiling gently. A hotplate or an electrically heated steam bath could be used in place of the Bunsen.

Blue copper sulfate crystals form as this solution of copper sulfate is evaporated.

METHOD
1 Pour the solution into an evaporating basin.

2 Put it on a source of heat (hot water bath, hotplate or electrical steam bath). (Note: if you are not in a hurry, the solution can be left to evaporate slowly at room temperature. The slower the rate of evaporation, the larger the crystals that form.)

3 Heat the solution gently to evaporate water.

4 When crystals begin to appear, stop heating. As the mixture cools, crystals will continue to form. (Note: this is because solid compounds are usually less soluble in cold water than in hot water.)

5 Separate the crystals by filtration.

Decantation

Sometimes a solid settles to the bottom of a reaction mixture. In this case, most of the liquid can be poured off. You must take care not to disturb the solid. This is called **decantation**. Alternatively, a dropping pipette can be used to remove the liquid from above the solid that has settled out. You need to be careful not to put the pipette in too far and disturb the solid.

Filtration and centrifuging

A solid (for example, a product that is precipitated from solution or unused solid reactant) can be separated from a reaction mixture by **filtration**. A filter funnel and filter paper are used.

FILTRATION

USE This technique can be used to separate a solid from a liquid. It can be used for all types of solutions. The method described below is for a mixture of a solid and an aqueous solution.

EQUIPMENT AND MATERIALS
- Mixture of solid and aqueous solution to be separated in a beaker
- Filter paper and filter funnel
- Beaker, or other suitable container, to collect the filtrate in

METHOD 1 Fold the filter paper as shown and place it in the funnel.

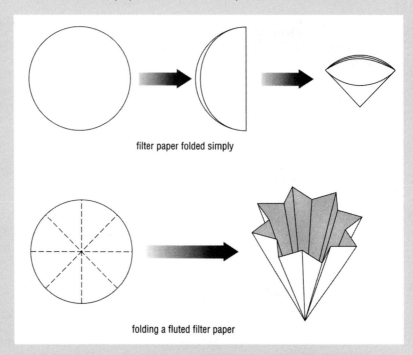

filter paper folded simply

folding a fluted filter paper

How to fold a filter paper. Liquids filter more quickly through a fluted filter paper than one that has been folded simply. Why do you think this is?

technique

technique

2 Pour the mixture into the folded filter paper.

Place the folded filter
paper in a funnel.

3 Make sure that all of the solid is transferred to the filter paper
by rinsing the beaker with distilled water and adding the
washings to the filter paper.

REMEMBER

The liquid that passes through a filter paper is called the filtrate. The solid that
remains on the filter paper is called the residue.

technique

SUCTION FILTRATION

USE Filtration of very finely divided solids can be very slow. Suction
filtration can be the answer. It can be used for all types of solutions.
The method described below is for a mixture of a solid and an
aqueous solution.

**EQUIPMENT AND
MATERIALS**
- Mixture of solid and aqueous solution to be separated in
a beaker

- Buchner or Hirsch funnel, with circle of filter paper to fit

- Filtration flask

- Vacuum water pump

METHOD 1 Connect the filtration flask to a water pump.

2 Decide whether to use a Buchner funnel or a Hirsch funnel.

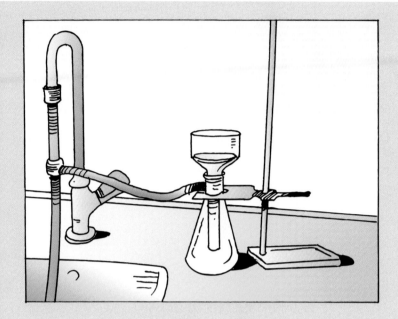

Setting up the suction filtration apparatus

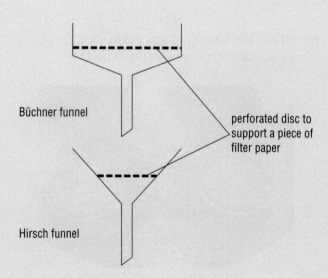

Büchner funnel

perforated disc to support a piece of filter paper

Hirsch funnel

The choice of Buchner or Hirsch funnel depends on the quantity of solid to be collected by filtration.

3   Place a piece of filter paper in the funnel. Wet it with a little distilled water to bed it down.

4   Turn the pump on to draw the liquid through the filter paper.

5   Make sure all of the solid is transferred to the filter paper by rinsing the beaker with distilled water and adding the washings to the filter paper.

technique

CENTRIFUGING

USE

This is a useful technique for separating very finely divided solids that tend to clog up filter paper.

EQUIPMENT AND MATERIALS

- Mixture of solid and aqueous solution to be separated
- Centrifuge with centrifuge tubes

METHOD

1 Put the mixture into a centrifuge tube.

The centrifuge tube has a tapered bottom so that very small amounts of solids can be recovered.

2 Place the tube in the centrifuge and put in another tube, containing a similar volume of water, as a balance.

A centrifuge. The speed at which the tubes inside spin round can be controlled.

3 Turn on the centrifuge, at a slow speed to begin and then gradually increase the speed. The tube spins round very fast, forcing the solid to the bottom of the tube.

4 Decant the liquid or remove it with a dropping pipette.

5 Wash the solid by adding a small amount of water, shaking the mixture and centrifuging again.

6 Repeat the washing process a few times.

Distillation

A liquid can be obtained from a reaction mixture by distillation. Aqueous solutions can be heated with a Bunsen burner to obtain water. However, a heating mantle or water bath should be used where flammable liquids are involved. The technique was described in 'Qualitative chemical analysis' (Unit 1, page 85).

Methods for making chemicals

Using acid–base and acid–carbonate reactions to make salts

Salts can be made from the reaction of acids with bases and with carbonates. The method depends on the solubility of reactants and products:

	Soluble	Insoluble
acids	all common acids	
bases	sodium hydroxide, potassium hydroxide, calcium hydroxide (slightly soluble), ammonia	all other metal oxides and hydroxides
salts	all nitrates all chlorides, except . . . all sulfates, except . . .	silver chloride, lead chloride barium sulfate, lead sulfate, calcium sulfate (slightly soluble)
carbonates	sodium carbonate, potassium carbonate	all other carbonates

MAKING SOLUBLE SALTS FROM AN ACID AND AN INSOLUBLE BASE OR CARBONATE

USE This technique can be used to make soluble salts from an acid and an insoluble base or an insoluble carbonate. The chemical reaction that takes place is an acid–base neutralisation.

EQUIPMENT AND MATERIALS
- Beaker
- Glass rod
- Tripod, gauze and Bunsen burner
- Evaporating basin
- Filtration apparatus (both normal and suction)
- Some possible reactants:

technique

technique

(The quantity of oxide used should be 10–20% more than quantity given below; this is to make sure there is a sufficient excess.)

Name of oxide	Mass of oxide	Name of acid	Quantity of acid
magnesium oxide	2.4 g	hydrochloric acid	50 cm^3
		nitric acid	50 cm^3
		sulfuric acid	25 cm^3
copper(II) oxide	7.95 g	hydrochloric acid	50 cm^3
		nitric acid	50 cm^3
		sulfuric acid	25 cm^3
zinc oxide	8.1 g	hydrochloric acid	50 cm^3
		nitric acid	50 cm^3
		sulfuric acid	25 cm^3

Name of carbonate	Mass of carbonate	Name of acid	Quantity of acid
calcium carbonate	10 g	hydrochloric acid	50 cm^3
		nitric acid	50 cm^3

Notes

In each case the concentration of the acid is 2 mol dm^{-3}.
Other quantities can be used provided they are in the same proportions.

METHOD

1 Place the dilute acid in a suitably sized beaker, together with a glass rod to prevent the solution from 'bumping' when it is heated.

2 Put the beaker on a wire gauze supported by a tripod. Heat gently with a Bunsen burner.

3 Add the insoluble base a little at a time, stirring between additions, until no more solid dissolves (you will be able to see the excess).

4 Filter the hot solution through a folded filter paper and collect the filtrate in an evaporating dish.

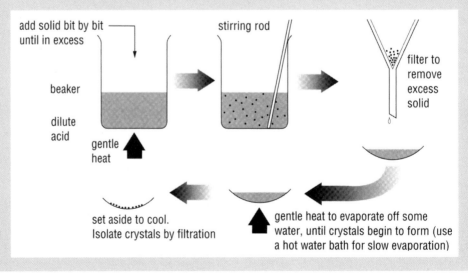

add solid bit by bit until in excess

stirring rod

filter to remove excess solid

beaker

dilute acid

gentle heat

set aside to cool. Isolate crystals by filtration

gentle heat to evaporate off some water, until crystals begin to form (use a hot water bath for slow evaporation)

5 Place the dish on a wire gauze supported on a tripod. Heat gently with a Bunsen burner until the crystals begin to appear. Put the dish to one side and allow it to cool. The salt will crystallise.

6 Separate the crystals by suction filtration and place in a desiccator for at least 24 hours to dry.

7 Determine the actual yield of the salt obtained by weighing the product.

8 The theoretical yield must be based on the acid used as the oxide or carbonate is present in excess.

9 Calculate the theoretical yield.

10 Estimate the cost of making the salt by finding the prices of reactants in a chemical supplier's catalogue.

MAKING SOLUBLE SALTS FROM AN ACID AND AN ALKALI

USE This technique can be used to make soluble salts from an acid and an alkali. The reaction that takes place is an acid-base neutralisation.

EQUIPMENT AND MATERIALS

- Conical flask
- Universal indicator paper
- Glass rod
- Burette and stand
- Tripod, gauze and Bunsen burner
- Evaporating basin
- Suction filtration apparatus
- Some possible reactants:

These volumes are based on 2 mol dm^{-3} acids and alkalis
Note 2 mol dm^{-3} hydrochloric acid is an IRRITANT
2 mol dm^{-3} ammonia is a LOW HAZARD
all other solutions used are CORROSIVE

---

10 cm^3 hydrochloric acid reacts with about:
10 cm^3 sodium hydroxide; 10 cm^3 potassium hydroxide; 10 cm^3 ammonia

10 cm^3 nitric acid reacts with about:
10 cm^3 sodium hydroxide; 10 cm^3 potassium hydroxide; 10 cm^3 ammonia

10 cm^3 sulfuric acid reacts with about:
20 cm^3 sodium hydroxide; 20 cm^3 potassium hydroxide; 20 cm^3 ammonia

Note: Other quantities can be used provided they are in the same proportions.

---

technique

technique

technique

HEALTH AND SAFETY   Wear eye protection (goggles for corrosive substances).

METHOD

1   Place the dilute acid in a burette and the alkali in a conical flask (use a safety filler if a pipette is used).

2   Add the acid a little at a time, mixing the contents of the flask thoroughly between additions. After each addition use the glass rod to put a drop of solution on a piece of Universal indicator paper. Initially the paper turns blue. When nearly enough acid has been added the paper will turn green. At this stage add the acid more slowly, a few drops at a time. Stop when the paper turns yellow.

3   Pour the solution from the conical flask into an evaporating dish. Place the dish on a wire gauze supported on a tripod. Heat gently with a Bunsen burner until the crystals begin to appear. Put the dish to one side and allow it to cool. The salt will crystallise.

4   Separate the crystals by suction filtration and place in a desiccator for at least 24 hours to dry.

5   Determine the actual yield of the salt obtained by weighing the product.

6   Calculate the theoretical yield.

7   Estimate the cost of making the salt by finding the prices of reactants in a chemical supplier's catalogue.

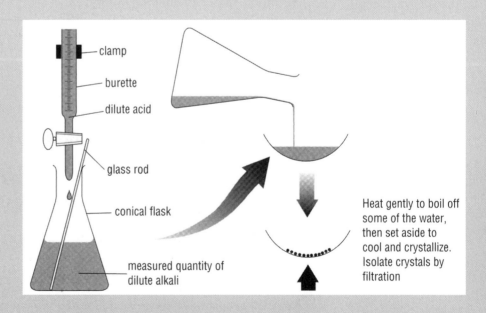

clamp
burette
dilute acid
glass rod
conical flask
measured quantity of dilute alkali

Heat gently to boil off some of the water, then set aside to cool and crystallize. Isolate crystals by filtration

technique

MAKING SALTS BY PRECIPITATION REACTIONS

USE

Insoluble salts can be prepared by precipitation reactions. Aqueous solutions of two soluble salts are mixed. One contains the appropriate metal ion and the other contains the appropriate anion. The insoluble salt forms as a precipitate.

EQUIPMENT AND MATERIALS

- Centrifuge tube
- Dropping pipette
- Glass rod
- Centrifuge
- Oven
- Some possible reactants:

Insoluble salt	Reactants
silver chloride	silver nitrate + any soluble chloride
silver bromide	silver nitrate + any soluble bromide
silver iodide	silver nitrate + any soluble iodide
lead chloride	lead nitrate + any soluble chloride
lead bromide	lead nitrate + any soluble bromide
lead iodide	lead nitrate + any soluble iodide
barium sulphate	barium chloride + any soluble sulphate
lead sulphate	lead nitrate + any soluble sulphate
metal carbonates	soluble metal salt + sodium carbonate or sodium hydrogen carbonate
	(**Note:** This is not always straightforward as sometimes a 'basic carbonate' – a mixed carbonated and hydroxide – is precipitated; this is less likely with sodium hydrogen carbonate.)

HEALTH AND SAFETY

Wear eye protection (goggles for corrosive substances).

In general, many soluble metal salts are toxic or harmful (depending upon their concentration). Always use low hazard salts where possible, for example, sodium chloride, sodium bromide, sodium iodide and sodium sulfate.

Solutions of silver nitrate greater than 0.5 mol dm^{-3} are CORROSIVE; between 0.5 and 0.2 mol dm^{-3} they are IRRITANT.

Solutions of lead nitrate greater than 0.01 mol dm^{-3} are TOXIC.

Solutions of barium chloride greater than 0.2 mol dm^{-3} are TOXIC.

technique

METHOD
1   Place a solution of the salt containing the required metal ion in a centrifuge tube.

2   Use a dropping pipette to add a solution of the salt containing the required anion (e.g. SO_4^{2-} (aq), Cl^- (aq)). Continue adding until no more precipitate appears to be forming.

3   Centrifuge the mixture. Now add 1 drop of the solution of the salt containing the required anion to check that precipitation is complete. If a precipitate forms, continue to add the solution until no more appears. Centrifuge and test again.

4   When all the insoluble salt has precipitated, centrifuge once more. Carefully remove the clear solution above the precipitate using a dropping pipette. Now add half a test tube of water, stir well and centrifuge. Repeat this process one more time to ensure that the solid has been thoroughly washed.

5   Place the test tube in an oven at 110 °C for 2–3 hours to dry. Remove it from the oven, using tongs, and place in a desiccator to cool.

6   Determine the actual yield of the salt obtained by weighing the product.

7   Calculate the theoretical yield.

8   Estimate the cost of making the salt by finding the prices of reactants in a chemical supplier's catalogue.

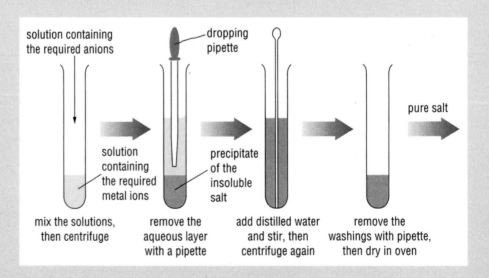

technique

MAKING SOLUBLE SALTS FROM AN ACID AND A METAL

USE This technique can be used to make soluble salts from an acid and a reactive metal. The chemical reaction that takes place is a redox reaction. Just like metal displacement reactions, electrons are transferred. This time electrons are transferred from the metal, leaving positive metal ions, to hydrogen ions from the acid. The hydrogen ions combine with the electrons to form hydrogen gas, which is given off in the reaction.

EQUIPMENT AND MATERIALS

- Beaker

- Glass rod

- Tripod, gauze and Bunsen burner

- Evaporating basin

- Filtration apparatus (both normal and suction)

Some possible reactants:

(The quantity of metal used should be 10–20% more than quantity given below; this is to make sure there is a sufficient excess.)

Name of metal	Mass of metal	Name of acid	Quantity of acid
magnesium	2.4 g	hydrochloric acid	50 cm^3
		nitric acid	50 cm^3
		sulfuric acid	
zinc	6.5 g	hydrochloric acid	50 cm^3
		nitric acid	50 cm^3
		sulfuric acid	25 cm^3

Notes: In each case the concentration of the acid is 2 mol dm^{-3}. Other quantities can be used provided they are in the same proportions. 2 mol dm^{-3} hydrochloric acid is HARMFUL; 2 mol dm^{-3} solutions of the other acids are CORROSIVE

HEALTH AND SAFETY Wear eye protection (goggles for corrosive substances).

METHOD The method is the same as for 'Making soluble salts from an acid and an insoluble base or carbonate' (see page 277–79).

technique

OBTAINING METALS: REDUCTION OF A METAL OXIDE BY CARBON

USE

The oxygen can be removed from some metal oxides by heating the oxide with carbon, usually in the form of charcoal. Carbon dioxide is also formed. This reaction is used industrially to extract iron, zinc and lead from their ores.

EQUIPMENT AND MATERIALS

- Lead oxide   TOXIC

- Copper oxide   HARMFUL

- Charcoal powder

HEALTH AND SAFETY

Wear eye protection (goggles for corrosive substances).

Good ventilation is necessary.

METHOD

Lead oxide

1   Add one spatula measure of lead oxide to a crucible.

2   Add one spatula measure of charcoal powder.

3   Mix the two solids together using a wooden spill.

4   Strongly heat the mixture for five minutes in a roaring Bunsen burner flame.

5   Allow the mixture to cool and tip it onto a heatproof mat.

6   Test to see if the mixture conducts electricity.

Copper oxide

1   Add one spatula measure of copper oxide to a crucible.

2   Carefully add one spatula measure of charcoal powder on top without any mixing.

3   Strongly heat for five minutes in a roaring Bunsen burner flame.

4   Allow the mixture to cool and tip it onto a heatproof mat.

5   Test to see if the mixture conducts electricity.

technique

OBTAINING METALS: DISPLACEMENT REACTIONS FROM SOLUTION OF SALTS

USE   Metals can be obtained from solutions of their salts by displacing them with a more reactive metal.

EQUIPMENT AND MATERIALS

Lead from reaction of lead nitrate with zinc:
lead nitrate 3.3 g   zinc 0.6 g

Copper from copper(II) sulfate and zinc:
copper(II) sulfate 2.5 g   zinc 0.6 g

Silver from silver nitrate and copper:
silver nitrate 1.7 g   copper 0.6 g

Note: Other quantities can be used provided they are in the same proportions.

Lead nitrate is a TOXIC solid.
Copper(II) sulfate is a HARMFUL solid.
Silver nitrate is a CORROSIVE solid.

HEALTH AND SAFETY   Wear eye protection (goggles for corrosive substances).

METHOD   Note: In the method described below **X** is the metal that is being made. **Y** is a more reactive metal.

1   Dissolve a salt of **X** in distilled water. Add the required quantity of metal **Y**. This quantity is calculated so that it is just less than that needed to completely displace metal **X**.

2   Stir the reaction mixture for 10 minutes or so. Some mixtures may need warming (check with your teacher).

3   Separate metal **X** from the reaction mixture by filtration or centrifuging. Wash it well with distilled water.

4   Dry it in an oven at about 110 °C for 2 hours.

5   Determine the actual yield of the metal obtained by weighing the product.

6   Calculate the theoretical yield.

7   Estimate the cost of making the salt by finding the prices of reactants in a chemical supplier's catalogue.

3.3 Instruments and machines

Instruments and machines are everywhere in the workplace. All scientists use them. However, scientists do not take this equipment for granted. They think about the equipment's usefulness and its limitations. They have to determine its suitability for particular tasks. Things like precision, reliability and portability are considered. Modern analytical instruments, for example, are expensive, sometimes very expensive. If an analysis will only be done once or twice, buying expensive equipment is probably not the answer. A cheaper method, even if it takes longer, or sub-contracting the work out may be better. Scientists work with fixed budgets. Money needs to be well spent.

Electrical and electronic devices

The usefulness of electrical devices

You need to:
- *describe the use of electrical or electronic devices for:*
  - *sensing, monitoring and controlling electro-mechanical devices or machines*
  - *generating pulses of light that are transmitted through optical fibres in communication*
  - *controlling movement*
  - *monitoring and controlling physical conditions.*

Scientists use electrical and electronic devices in their work. These are particularly useful for:
- sensing, monitoring and controlling electro-mechanical devices or machines
- generating pulses of light that are transmitted through optical fibres in communication
- controlling movement
- monitoring and controlling physical conditions.

Controlling

Electronic devices (such as computers) excel at controlling machinery and complex systems. Computers control railway switching networks and manufacturing lines in factories. They control washing machines,

Computers and other electronic devices help this pilot to fly the aircraft. They enable the plane to be controlled and the pilot to communicate with airport staff and pilots in other planes. They even allow the plane to 'fly itself'.

central heating systems and microwave ovens. And this is only the tip of the iceberg. You will find out more about sensors, monitoring and control later when you read about the components of electronic devices.

Communication

Electricity can be used to allow people to communicate with each other. The mobile telephone is a good example of this. Telephones allow two-way communication. E-mail is a good way of communicating. It can be two-way, but there is a time delay! Radios and televisions allow one-way communication. One of the key modern technologies is optic fibres. These allow pulses of light to be transmitted through them. The pulses contain far more data than can be sent down an electrical wire. They are generated electrically.

Electricity can be used to allow people to communicate with each other.

Movement

Electricity can be used to move things. Many machines contain electric motors. Some are powered by batteries and other by mains electricity. They can be turned on and off by switches. Their speeds can also be controlled. Examples that you might find in the laboratory are fans,

This robot explored the surface of Mars. It was powered by electricity from solar cells. Each wheel was driven by a different motor. By turning these on and off, and varying the speed, the operators had great control over its movement.

stirrers, pumps (for example, for aerating aquariums) and dishwashers for laboratory glassware. You can probably make a very long list of others that you come across daily.

Monitoring and controlling physical conditions

Electronic devices are used to measure many things. Electronic thermometers are used to measure temperature. Light levels are measured with light meters. Probes are used to measure the quantities of chemicals in soil, water and the air. But as well as being able to measure, they can control the conditions. Using a system of feedback (page 299), certain changes in the quantity being measured can be used to trigger a response. For example, if the humidity in a greenhouse gets too low, a spray of water can be switched on. Electrical devices can warn people of danger. Burglar alarms tell us about intruders in our homes. Electronic systems are routinely used in hospitals to monitor patients and set off alarm signals if anything goes wrong.

Hand-held stopwatches are rarely used in top class sports events these days. Electronic timers are always used at major meetings.

Components of electronic devices

You need to:

- *explain the functions of the following components in an electrical or electronic device:*
  - *power source*
  - *processor*
  - *input components*
  - *output components.*

There are four main parts in any electronic device. Once you can identify them and know what they do, complicated looking electronic devices become much simpler to understand. The four main parts are the power supply, input devices, processor and output devices. The difference between an electrical device and an electronic device is the processor. A simple electrical device doesn't have one.

The power source in a calculator is either a tiny battery or a solar cell. The keys are the input devices. The processor is an integrated circuit inside the calculator. It processes signals from the keys and activates the liquid-crystal display (the output device).

Power supply

The **power supply** provides energy for all parts of the device. You have a choice of what might be used. Each has advantages and disadvantages, as shown in the table.

Power supply	Advantages	Disadvantages
Mains power supplies	• always available and doesn't 'run out' • device may not be very portable	• can be large and heavy • need a cable connected to the mains power supply • contain (dangerously) high voltages.
Batteries	• portable	• expensive to replace • can be large and heavy if large amounts of electricity are needed • problems with disposal • run out after time
Rechargeable batteries	• portable • can be re-used after charging	• very expensive to buy
Solar cells	• long-lasting	• expensive • need a source of light • can't provide much electricity

Input and output devices

Input devices get information about the system being controlled by an electronic device. They convert non-electrical forms of energy such as heat, light and sound into electrical energy. These are often called sensors or probes. Output devices convert electrical energy into other forms of energy.

Input device	What it senses
switch	pressure
LDR (light-dependent resistor)	light
thermistor	heat
microphone	sound
aerial	radio waves

Output device	What it does
lamp	emits light
buzzer	makes a noise
motor	spins round
loudspeaker	emits sounds
heater	makes heat energy

REMEMBER

In an electrical/electronic device the flow of electricity does two things

• it provides each part of the device with the power it needs

• it carries information between parts of the device

Processors

Processors take electrical information from the input devices, use it to work out what needs to be done and send electrical messages telling the output devices what to do. In modern electronic devices they are integrated circuits. They have enabled amazing miniaturisation and devices are being made smaller and smaller.

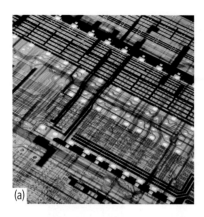

(a) Integrated circuits contain large numbers of electronic switches (transistors) built onto a small piece of silicon. They are usually enclosed in black plastic boxes for protection.
(b) An integrated circuit package has a number of integrated circuits. Metal pins stick out from the black plastic boxes and enable electrical connections to be made between them.

Assembling and testing electrical and electronic devices

You need to:

- *assemble and assess the effectiveness of one electrical or electronic device by:*

  - *selecting the components you need*

  - *safely assembling them to build the device*

  - *testing the assembled device under conditions of normal use*

  - *evaluating the performance of the device and commenting on its fitness for purpose*

Describing the device

An electrical or electronic device consists of a number of parts (usually called components) connected so that an electric current can flow between them. A **block diagram** is a useful way to show how energy and information flow through the device. It shows what types of power supply, input devices, processors and output devices are used.

The way in which components are connected so is shown in an **electrical circuit**. A **circuit diagram** shows this. It's a map of the electrical circuit. There are British Standard symbols for the components and these are used when drawing circuit diagrams. It means that you can select the correct components by looking at the circuit diagram. The circuit diagram also shows you how to connect the components in the correct sequence. The connections may be made in a number of ways and we'll look at this later.

REMEMBER

A **block diagram** shows how energy and information flow through the device. It's a useful way of picturing the whole device. It shows what types of power supply, input devices, processors and output devices are used.

A **circuit diagram** shows how the components have to be connected to one another. It's a map of the device. If you study a circuit diagram you will be able to select the correct components for the device.

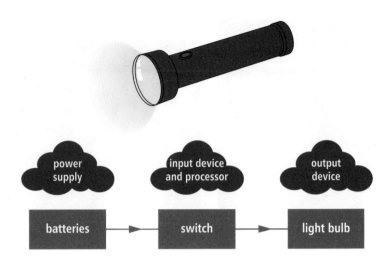

Block diagram of a torch system.

Selecting the components

The circuit diagram contains the information you need to select the correct components, so this is always your starting point.

Circuit symbols			
cell		capacitor	
battery		microphone	
variable power supply	0 – 12V + dc –	motor	
lamps		loudspeaker	
resistor		transformer	
switches		bell	
LED		buzzer	
variable resistor		ammeter	
voltage divider		voltmeter	

You need to be able to recognise what these symbols represent when used in electric circuit diagrams

Power supply

You might use a variable power supply or a fixed one (one or more cells in a battery). If you use a battery, its size depends on how much work it has to do. The **capacity** of a cell is given in **ampere hours** (**Ah**). If a cell has a capacity of 1 Ah it can supply (in theory at least):

1 amp	for	1 hour
0.1 amps	for	10 hours
0.01 amps	for	100 hours

A battery is made up of one or more cells. So you need to know the voltage and current required and how long the battery needs to last. The more current a device needs to make it work, the more quickly it will drain a battery.

(a)
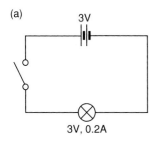
3V

3V, 0.2A

(b)
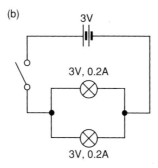
3V

3V, 0.2A

3V, 0.2A

(c)
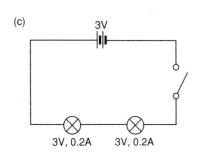
3V

3V, 0.2A   3V, 0.2A

(d)
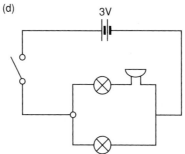
3V

The circuit diagram shows that you need the following components:
- Power supply: 3 V d.c. supply
- Input device: switch
- Output device: light bulb.

However, in each case there are still decisions to be made. For example, what could be used to supply 3 V d.c.? A battery? If so, what type – normal or rechargeable? You also need to decide how to connect the components and what to put them in.

REMEMBER

Three important relationships when you are working with electrical circuits:

E = VIt

where E = electrical energy, or work done by an electric current on a device (like a light bulb or an electric motor) in joules (J)

V = voltage in volts (V)
I = current in amps (A)
t = time in seconds (s)

P = VI

where P = power (W)
V = voltage in volts (V)
I = current in amps (A)

V = IR

where R = resistance (Ω)
V = voltage in volts (V)
I = current in amps (A)

Input and output devices

There are several input and output devices you might use:

- input devices: switch, LDR (light-dependent resistor), thermistor, microphone, aerial
- output device: lamp, buzzer, motor, loudspeaker, heater.

The choice of actual input or output device depends on what energy conversion is needed (for example, a lamp converts electrical energy into light and a LDR converts light into electrical energy). The other thing to consider is how much energy is being converted. For example, do you want a small light bulb or a large one?

Other components

As well as power supplies, input devices and output devices most circuits contain other components. These include resistors, capacitors, integrated circuits, LEDs and diodes.

Resistors. These control the magnitude of the current flowing in a circuit (remember: $V = IR$). They have coloured bands that tell you what their resistance is. Each colour represents a number from 0 to 9.

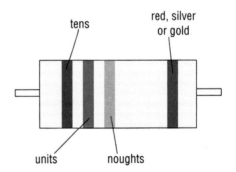

The band on the right will be red, gold or silver. This tells you how accurately the resistor was manufactured (red is best, silver is the least good). The first two bands on the left give you a number between 10 and 99. The next band tells you how many 0s to put after this number. Now you have the resistance in ohms (Ω). For example, brown, green, yellow would be 150 000 Ω or 150 kΩ. If the band on the far right were red, you would know that this value was very accurate.

The resistor colour code:

black	brown	red	orange	yellow	green	blue	Purple	grey	white
0	1	2	3	4	5	6	7	8	9

Capacitors. These store electrical energy. The energy can be stored or discharged almost instantly, unlike a battery. Some capacitors have positive and negative terminals (they are polarised). They must be connected the right way round. Those with a capacitance of less than 1 μF are not usually polarised and can be connected either way round.

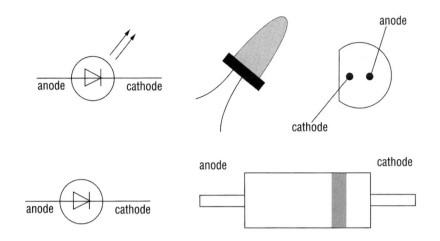

anode — cathode

anode — cathode

The cathode of a diode is nearest the band painted on its body. The direction of flow of current is shown in its symbol by an arrowhead.

Diodes. Diodes allow current to flow in one direction, from anode to cathode.

Integrated circuits (ICs). These are found in most processors. They consist of many electronic switches (called **transistors**) built on to a piece of silicon – the well known 'silicon chip'. The IC is usually housed in a protective box that has metal pins sticking out of it. These are used to make the electrical connections.

Components: in series or parallel?

Components can be arranged in a circuit in **series** or in **parallel**. When components are in series you can calculate their total resistance by simply adding the resistances of each component. However, if they are in parallel the total resistance is lower. This is why two light bulbs in series are dimmer than two arranged in parallel (assuming all other things remain the same).

The metal pins to make connections are not actually numbered. To find pin 1 lay the IC flat with the D-shaped cut-out on the left. Pin 1 is then on the bottom left-hand corner. Sometimes there is a dot impressed in the plastic next to pin 1.

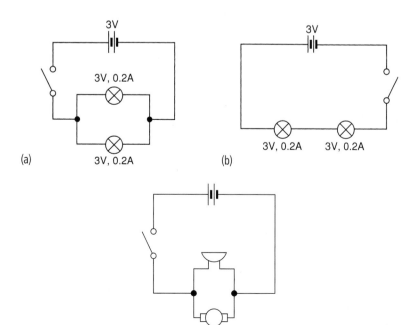

(a) two light bulbs in series, (b) two light bulbs in parallel.

More than one device can be operated in the same circuit. For example, you could design a circuit for an electric motor so that a warning light comes on and a buzzer sounds when the motor is working.

Measuring instruments

Many measuring instruments both in the laboratory and elsewhere contain a sensor. For example, instruments such as electronic thermometers, light meters and colorimeters all contain censors. Sensors convert one form of energy into electrical energy. You read about sensors on page 46.

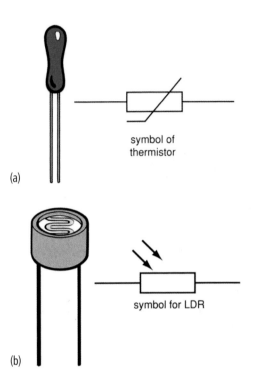

Temperature and light sensors, in particular, are cheap and easy to get hold of. Diagram (a) shows a thermistor (a temperature dependent resistor) and (b) shows a light-dependent resistor (LDR).

Potential divider

A potential divider can be used to control voltage. It's a variable resistor. Potential dividers are used, for example, for volume control in music systems. By changing the resistance you can increase or decrease the voltage input to the amplifier. It's simply Ohm's law in action. The sound becomes louder or quieter.

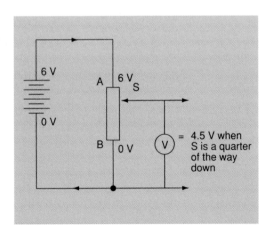

Using a potential divider. By moving the position of the contact on the resistor the resistance changes and this, in turn, changes the size of the voltage.

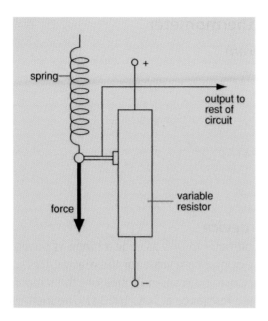

The contact arm on a potential divider can be attached to a spring. As the spring stretches and contracts the resistance of the variable resistor increases and decreases, respectively. You could use this idea to make a measuring instrument to monitor a force.

Sensor as an input device

If a sensor is going to be used as an input device, it must be part of a potential divider. One resistor is fixed and the sensor is the second resistor. It is, of course, a variable resistor as its resistance depends on the conditions. For example, the hotter a thermistor gets, the lower its resistance becomes.

The output device

The output device for measuring instruments might be a voltmeter (analogue or digital). This displays the electrical output from the sensor as a voltage. The block diagram for such a device is:

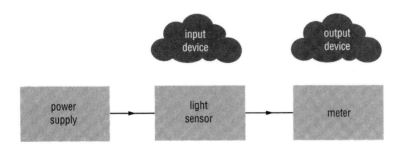

Here are circuit diagrams for two measuring devices, a light meter and an electronic thermometer. You could try constructing one of them and calibrating it. You may even try to make working instruments based upon these circuits.

Electronic thermometer

Circuit diagram

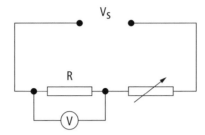

Making the device

You want the voltmeter to give as wide a range as possible. So you need to find the appropriate value for the resistor. This is done by experiment. Suppose you wanted to measure the temperature of water. You would set the resistance at, say, 1000 Ω. The thermistor is put into:

- very hot water (just below boiling)
- cold water.

The voltage in each case is measured. This is repeated for several other values of resistance until one is found that gives the biggest range of values of output voltage. This is the resistor to use in the instrument.

Calibration

The next stage is to calibrate the device. Put the thermistor and an accurate thermometer into a beaker of near-boiling water. Measure the voltage as the temperature falls. Record it for every 5° C fall in temperature. Plotting temperature/°C (*x*-axis) against voltage across resistor/V (*y*-axis) gives you a calibration graph.

Light meter

Circuit diagram

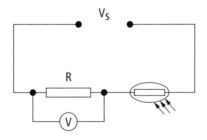

This is the same principle as the electronic thermometer. You need to do some trial experiments to select the value for the resistor. It will depend on the range of light intensities you want to measure.

Controlling a device

You usually need to control a device. You may want to simply switch it on or off. Or you may want to adjust (for example, turning the volume up on a radio). You may want it to 'adjust itself'.

REMEMBER

All electronic devices must be calibrated. You take readings with the device on samples where you already know the answer (see standard reference materials on page 21). Usually you plot a calibration graph and use this to convert the instrument reading into the quantity you are measuring.

Remember an electronic device has four main parts: power supply, input devices, processor and output devices. It's the processor that enables the device to be controlled. There are several ways this might be done.

Open-loop control. Once the device has been started it continues no matter what's happening to the output. It's the crudest form of control. Think about an electric motor. The speed can be set using a speed controller. However, when it's loaded, for example, it has to operate a hoist to lift something, its speed decreases. With open-loop control no steps are taken to get the speed back to its original value. Another example might be a simple electric fire or an electric light. Once they are switched on they give the same output no matter what happens around them. Even if the room gets very hot the fire still stays on. A light turned on at night doesn't go out when it's daylight again.

Closed-loop control. This uses the idea of **feedback**. The circuit has a device to measure the output. If it strays from what it's meant to be, a processor sends a message back to the controller. The controller reacts to correct the error. Think about the electric motor again. In closed-loop control, the processor detects that the speed has changed. It sends an electrical message back to the controller and it responds by adjusting the speed of the motor. This is an example of **negative feedback**.

Looking at this picture might help you understand the idea of feedback. The brain is the processor. It receives messages from the nerve endings in the left hand (the input device) and sends messages to the right hand to adjust the tap (the output device) if the water is too hot or too cold.

On-off feedback control. Unlike closed-loop control, there are no subtle adjustments here. The feedback message is simple: turn off the device or turn it on again. A good example is an electrical fan heater. It has a thermostat that senses when the temperature gets too hot. The thermostat is a processor. It sends a signal to the **comparator** to turn off the heater. If the room cools below the temperature set, the heater is turned on again.

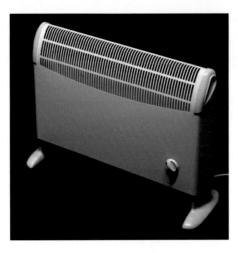

An electric heater without a thermostat stays on until you turn it off. The room gets hotter and hotter. It's an example of open-loop control. On the other hand, a heater fitted with a thermostat turns itself on and off to maintain a fairly constant temperature in the room it's heating. This is an example of on–off feedback control.

> **REMEMBER**
>
> When you are going to build an electrical or electronic device, study the circuit diagram and write down a list of components needed.

Safely assembling

Once you have the circuit diagram and have selected the components needed, there are two stages in making an electrical device:

- choosing a suitable container and working out how to fit the components and connections into it
- connecting the components.

The device must be checked by your teacher before you test it.

The container

The device needs to be housed in a container. Boxes are readily available for mounting small electronic circuits. They are made of a polymer that is tough, light and an electrical insulator. They can be easily cut and drilled with hand tools.

Boxes that can be used to house electronic circuits

Connecting the components

Connections can be made in various ways. You have probably used crocodile clips and leads with plugs and sockets. You may also have used a screwed terminal (for example, in an electric plug). However, these are bulky. They would take up a lot of room in the container for the device.

A neater method for electronic devices that need to be compact is to make connections by **soldering**. **Printed circuit boards** (pcbs) can be used rather than wiring. The metal pins of components are pushed through holes in the board. They are soldered to the copper tracks (which take the place of wires) that have been etched on the underside of the board. Again, this reduces the size of the device. Techniques for soldering and for making a **pcb** are given below.

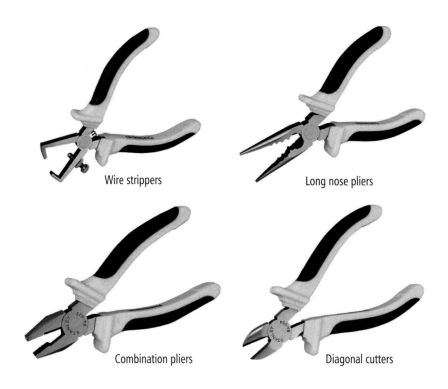

Wire strippers

Long nose pliers

Combination pliers

Diagonal cutters

The insulating sheath on wiring must be removed using wire strippers. Do not try cutting through the sheathing with a sharp knife. Different types of pliers are available for you to use when constructing the device.

MAKING A PCB

technique

A one-sided pcb has one side coated with copper. This is covered by a light-sensitive polymer called photoresist. It's protected from the light by a black plastic film.

EQUIPMENT AND MATERIALS		
	One-sided pcb	
	UV exposure box	HAZARD
	Plastic trays and tongs	
	0.5 mol dm^{-3} sodium hydroxide solution	CORROSIVE
	0.5 mol dm^{-3} iron(III) chloride solution	HARMFUL
	Plastic film with pcb transfers	
	Drill with 1 mm bit	

SAFETY Protective clothing and eye protection must be worn. A risk assessment must be done before starting work.

METHOD

1 Cut the pcb to the size and shape you want.

2 On a piece of graph paper, make a full scale drawing of the copper tracks that will connect the circuit. Copy it in black on to transparent plastic film. You should use transfers and black rubber strips if possible. This is the mask.

technique

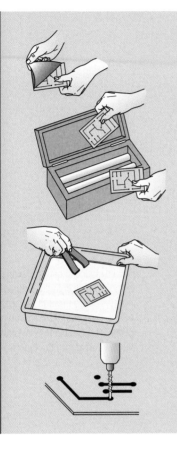

3   Carefully remove the black plastic film from the pcb. This will expose the photoresist. Place the mask on the photoresist and put both in a UV light box. The top surface of the mask must touch the photoresist.

4   Expose the pcb to UV light for about 4–5 minutes (the exact time will depend on the UV exposure box and the pcb; some trials may be necessary).

5   Take it out of the UV exposure box and remove the mask. Place it in a shallow tray containing 0.5 mol dm^{-3} sodium hydroxide solution for a few minutes. Make sure the pcb is covered with the solution.

6   Rinse it with cold water and place it in a shallow tray containing 0.5 mol dm^{-3} iron(III) chloride solution for a few minutes. Again, make sure the pcb is covered with the solution. Agitate occasionally and leave until all the copper that was exposed to UV has gone.

7   Rinse the pcb with water and leave it to dry.

8   Starting from the underside, drill holes at the end of each copper track. This is where the component pins will be pushed through and soldered to the tracks.

technique

SOLDERING

Components and wires must often be soldered in place, for example, on a pcb.

A soldering iron must be handled with care and with skill.

EQUIPMENT AND MATERIALS

- Soldering iron.
- Resin-free flux cored solder.
- Side cutters to trim the soldered joints.

SAFETY   Soldering irons get very hot and can burn. Handle them with care. Protective clothing and eye protection must be worn. A risk assessment must be done before starting work.

METHOD   The soldering iron must be hot. It should be cleaned at intervals on a damp sponge.

Before using the soldering iron bit make sure that its surface is coated with a thin film of fresh solder.

1   Make sure both the component and track are hot before applying solder.

2   Make sure that you have a comfortable working position. If right-handed, the soldering iron should be on your right and you should use a soldering iron stand if possible.

3   Push the pins of the components (or bared wires) through the holes.

4   Hold the hot bit of the soldering iron against a pin and the copper.

5   Push the solder against the pin and let a small amount melt.

6   Remove the bit when the solder has flowed over the pin and the copper track. The joint should be smooth and shiny. If it is rough, apply the bit and fresh solder again.

7   Use side cutters to remove surplus copper wire poking through the board.

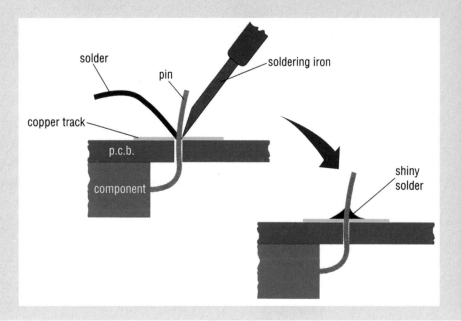

Testing and evaluating performance

If you look at the paperwork that comes with equipment in the laboratory, for example, you will find there are specifications for the device. These tell you what the device is supposed to be able to do.

You should make your own list of specifications for the device you made. These are the things you might be looking for. Some will be more important than others for a particular device. You might not

REMEMBER

When you are evaluating a device, think carefully about what you want it to do. Make a list of specifications for the device. Then write a list of questions about your device that you want to answer so hat you can evaluate it.

even have to consider some for certain devices. You might want to design tests to check the following features of your device:

- effectiveness
- reliability
- accuracy
- sensitivity
- robustness
- portability.

Some ideas for you to think about are given below.

Effectiveness

Basically, does it do the job it was designed for? Is it useful? Do the outputs achieve what they are intended to? For example, does a heater switch on in response to messages from the processor that the temperature is too low?

Reliability

The first question you might ask, of course, is 'does the device work?' Hopefully the answer is 'yes'. But will it continue working under normal operating conditions? How often does it need repairing? How long will it last for? It's often good to 'test to destruction', in other words until the device will not work any longer. That way you can find out just what its limitations are!

Accuracy

If the device is measuring a property how accurately does it do so? For example, if its purpose was to monitor and respond to temperature changes, can it measure temperature accurately? You may consider using a standard reference material to check the accuracy (see page 000). How precise are the readings? For example, can the temperature be measured to the nearest 1 °C, 0.1 °C or 0.01 °C?

Sensitivity

How good is the device at picking up signals as its input? Can it respond to a range of signals, from weak ones to strong ones? For example, if it's measuring temperature, does it work over a wide range of temperatures?

Robustness

How rugged is the device? If it's intended to be used in a harsh environment can it withstand extreme conditions? For example, will it work outside in the rain? Will it work in an environment where the temperature is very high? Is it strong enough to be moved from place to place without too much care?

Portability

What is the size and weight of the device? Is it easy to carry? Does it depend on mains electricity? If it uses batteries, how long will they last? Can spare ones be taken?

Machines

You need to:

- *identify a range of components in mechanical machines used in the workplace, explain how they work, and be able to:*

  - *measure the applied force and the force produced by the machine*

  - *calculate the amount by which the machine multiplies force*

  - *calculate the work done by the machine and its efficiency*

  - *understand the advantages and disadvantages of friction in machines.*

What is a machine?

Machines are everywhere. They all have one thing in common – they are used to move things. Some are very simple, like a screwdriver. Some are more complicated, like a bicycle. Others are even more sophisticated and complicated, like Formula 1 racing cars.

Most machines are made of a number of simple machines like levers, pulleys and gears. In a bicycle, the pedals are connected to the back wheel by a pulley (the chain). Gear wheels change the size of the force needed. You can make cycling easier or harder. But you will notice that when riding in a lower gear you have to pedal faster compared to the speed at which the bicycle moves. The brakes use levers.

It takes effort to move a load

Machines are designed to move things. An **effort** is needed to move a **load**. Efforts and loads are both forces and so their units are newtons (N). The effort is the applied force and the load is the force produced by the machine. Machines change the size and direction of a force.

Let's look at the simplest machine, a **lever**, to see how it works. Think about a wheelbarrow. The pivot is the axle of the wheel. The load is put in the barrow and you lift the handles. You can lift and move quite

Like all machines, a bicycle changes the size and direction of a force. When you press down on the pedals you are exerting a force. The bicycle is designed to change this force into a smaller one that moves the bicycle forward.

REMEMBER

The effort is the applied force and the load is the force produced by the machine.

The wheelbarrow is a simple lever machine.

heavy things this way. It requires less effort to lift a wheelbarrow full of sand and push it along than it does to lift the sand in a bag and carry it. The wheelbarrow converts a small force into a large one.

Mechanical advantage

The **mechanical advantage** (MA) of a machine tells you how big the load is compared with the effort, or how much a machine multiplies a force.

$$\text{mechanical advantage (MA)} = \frac{\text{load}}{\text{effort}}$$

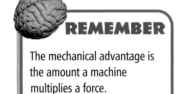

REMEMBER

The mechanical advantage is the amount a machine multiplies a force.

So if the load in our imaginary wheelbarrow is 500 N and the effort to lift it is 250 N, the mechanical advantage = 500/250 = 2. You would expect the load to always be twice the effort. This means that to lift 1000 N you would expect to need an effort of 500 N.

But you never get something for nothing. Look at the diagram below. The small force has to move a larger distance than the larger one does.

When you lift a wheelbarrow the handles move more than the load carried in the barrow.

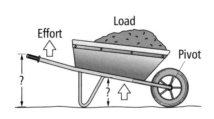
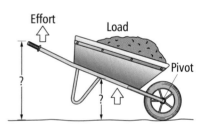

Velocity ratio

This means that the effort and load move at different speeds. The term **velocity ratio** (VR) is used to tell us about this aspect of the machine's performance.

$$\text{velocity ratio (VR)} = \frac{\text{distance moved by effort}}{\text{distance moved by load}}$$

In the case of the wheelbarrow:

- the distance moved by the effort is proportional to the distance from the axle to the effort

and

- the distance moved by the load is proportional to the distance from the axle to the load

(Think about right-angled triangles!).

Therefore:

$$\text{velocity ratio (VR)} = \frac{\text{distance from axle to effort}}{\text{distance from axle to load}}$$

So if the effort is twice as far from the axle as the load, the velocity ratio is 2.

Work done

The work done (in joules, J) by a machine is the load (in newtons, N) times the distance (in metres, m) it moves. So, if a load of 200 N is moved 4 m, the work done is $(200 \times 4) = 800$ J.

REMEMBER

work done = load × distance moved by load

Efficiency

The **efficiency** of a machine is the ratio of the mechanical advantage to the velocity ratio.

efficiency = $\dfrac{\text{mechanical advantage}}{\text{velocity ratio}} \times 100$ % or $\dfrac{\text{MA}}{\text{VR}} \times 100$%

REMEMBER

You saw in Unit 2 (page 229) that efficiency is defined as:

efficiency = $\dfrac{\text{load} \times \text{distance moved by load}}{\text{effort} \times \text{distance moved by effort}} \times 100$%

Now we have said that the efficiency of a machine is given by:

efficiency = $\dfrac{\text{mechanical advantage}}{\text{velocity ratio}} \times 100$ %

At first you may think these two are different. But try replacing mechanical advantage by its formula:

mechanical advantage (MA) = $\dfrac{\text{load}}{\text{effort}}$

and velocity ratio by its formula:

velocity ratio (VR) = $\dfrac{\text{distance moved by effort}}{\text{distance moved by load}}$

You should end up with the definition you met in Unit 2!

The perfect machine?

What do you notice about the values for the MA and the VR of our imaginary wheelbarrow? They are the same, both 2. It's a perfect machine, 100% efficient. But in reality no machine is 100% efficient. The velocity ratio is always fixed by the positions of the effort and load. However, the mechanical advantage depends on the efficiency of the machine.

The reason is that energy changes are involved. It takes energy to move a force. You know from Unit 2 (page 227) that when energy is changed from one form to another, energy is conserved but tends to spread out and become less useful.

Suppose a real wheelbarrow has MA = 2.4 and VR = 3.

efficiency = $\dfrac{\text{MA}}{\text{VR}} \times 100 = \dfrac{2.4}{3} \times 100 = 80\%$

REMEMBER

Energy is used when a force is moved.

$E = F \times d$

where

E = energy change when work is done in joules (J)

F = force in newtons (N)

d = distance moved in the direction of the force in metres (m)

This means that for every 100 J of energy put into the effort, only 80 J of useful energy is obtained. The remainder is wasted energy, mostly in the form of heat energy. The diagram below summarises this.

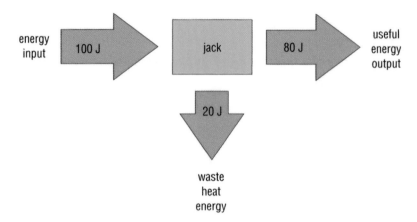

The most common problem is **friction**. Whenever two parts move in contact with one another, friction causes them to heat up. In the case of the wheelbarrow it's the axle and the wheel. In general the disadvantage of friction in machines is that it decreases their efficiency. It can also cause moving parts to wear out. However, as you will see later, friction is often very useful.

More levers

Crowbars, wheelbarrows, scissors, pliers, barbeque tongs, and nutcrackers are just some examples of simple machines that are levers. In any lever the velocity ratio is fixed by the distance of the effort and the load from the pivot. The efficiency, and therefore the mechanical advantage, depends on how much energy is wasted by the machine.

Three machines that are simple levers. Energy is wasted through friction. How could friction be reduced in these machines?

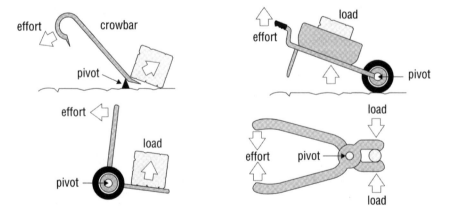

Two possible investigations are described here. If you try them remember to wear protective clothing and eye protection. Be careful when using heavy masses. And remember that a risk assessment must be carried out before starting work. Make a plan and discuss it with your teacher before starting.

Modelling a wheelbarrow

You can model a wheelbarrow using a metre ruler with holes drilled at regular intervals, mass pans or mass hangers, and a Newton meter.

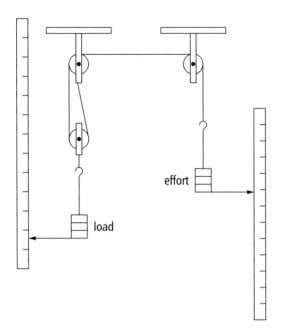

1   Pivot the ruler on a metal rod in the hole nearest one end. This is the 'axle' of the wheelbarrow.

2   Hang a mass somewhere along the length of the metre rule. This is the load. You can calculate the load from the mass using load (N) = mass (kg) × 9.8 (N kg^{-1}).

3   Attach a Newton meter to the other end of the ruler. This is the effort.

4   Investigate how the mechanical advantage, velocity ratio, work done and efficiency vary with the positions of the load and effort.

5   Compare various designs of wheelbarrows. Use your experimental results to help you explain how their design makes them fit their purpose. Try to find other machines that work in the same way as a wheelbarrow.

Modelling a pair of pliers

You can model a pair of pliers using a metre ruler with holes drilled at regular intervals, mass pans or mass hangers, and a Newton meter.

1   Pivot the ruler on a metal rod in a hole somewhere along the length of the ruler. This is the pivot of the pliers.

2   Hang a mass at one end of the metre rule. This is the load. You can calculate the load from the mass using load (N) = mass (kg) × 9.8 (N kg^{-1}).

3   Hang at mass at some point on the other side of the pivot. This is the effort.

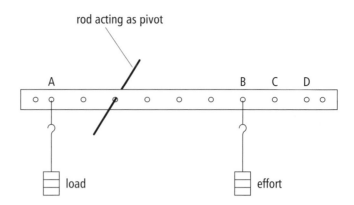

rod acting as pivot

A   B   C   D

load   effort

4   Investigate how the mechanical advantage, velocity ratio, work done and efficiency vary with the positions of the load and effort.

5   Compare various pliers, shears and scissors. Use your experimental results to help you explain how their design makes them fit their purpose. For example, why are some scissors much longer than others?

Pulleys

Pulleys are machines that have wheels connected by belts, cord or chains. The velocity ratio is determined by the diameters of the pulley wheels. As with levers, the efficiency, and therefore the mechanical advantage, depends on how much energy is wasted by the machine. Friction is a problem and a salvation. The more friction there is between the moving parts (for example, between the belts, cord or chains and the pulley wheels), the less efficient the pulley will be. However, if there were no friction a belt, for example, would slip and would not turn the pulley wheel.

A hoist is a pulley system that can be used to lift heavy weights. The pulley wheels are connected by chains.

Investigating a pulley system

You will need a pulley system, mass pans or mass hangers and masses. Wear protective clothing and eye protection. Be careful when using heavy masses. Remember that a risk assessment must be carried out before starting work. Make a plan and discuss it with your teacher before starting.

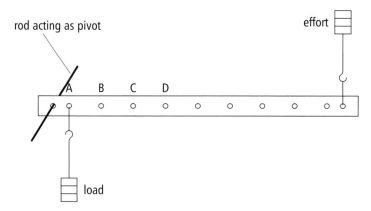

You should determine the velocity ratio, mechanical advantage and efficiency of the pulley system.

1. Determine the velocity ratio by measuring the diameters of the input and output pulleys.

$$VR = \frac{\text{diameter of output pulley}}{\text{diameter of input pulley}}$$

2. Suppose the pulleys are hidden from view (for example, hidden in a safety cage). Devise and try out another way of measuring the velocity ratio.

3. Determine the mechanical advantage (MA) by putting a 50 g mass on the load pan or hanger. Pull the effort pan or hanger until it is taut and then add masses until the load begins to rise slowly and steadily. Repeat for a number of other masses and, in each case, calculate the mechanical advantage.

4. Calculate the work done and the efficiency at each load.

5. Plot graphs of (a) *mechanical advantage* (*y*-axis) against *load*/N (*x*-axis) and (b) *efficiency*/% (*y*-axis) against *load*/N (*x*-axis). Your machine is doing useful work by lifting the load, but it's also doing 'useless' work by lifting parts of the machine itself and in overcoming friction. Explain the shape of your graphs.

Gears

A simple gear train is a series of interlocking cogs of different diameter. When one cog turns, it makes another turn, but in the opposite

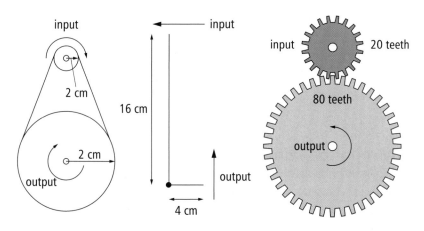

These cog wheels have a velocity ratio of 4. This is the ratio of the number of teeth on each of the two cogs. The machine has the same velocity as both the two-wheeled pulley and the lever shown in the diagram.

direction. The cogs are fixed to shafts (not axles because they are not free to turn).

The velocity ratio is determined by the number of teeth on the cogs. The efficiency, and therefore the mechanical advantage, depends on how much energy is wasted by the machine. There is no problem of slipping as there was with pulleys. The cogs link through interlocking teeth. Friction is a problem. It reduces efficiency and it wears the cogs.

3.4 Monitoring living organisms

You need to:

- *select an organism for a particular purpose, which you can monitor*

- *produce a plan for your investigation that includes information about:*

  - *the type of organism*

  - *the purpose of your monitoring activity*

  - *how you have considered the welfare of the organism, where appropriate, and taken into account any ethical issues*

  - *the conditions you will be providing and controlling*

  - *how you intend to monitor the organism's growth/development/responses*

  - *a monitoring schedule for the duration of your investigation*

  - *how you will evaluate the results of your investigation*

- *carry out the investigation, recording relevant data*

- *analyse your results and explain what they show*

- *evaluate your investigation.*

Why monitor living organisms?

We grow and nurture living organisms for many purposes. Many useful products can be obtained from them (see page 126) and, as you have seen, agriculture and horticulture are important industries.

Whether growing **plants** or **micro-organisms** or rearing **animals**, it's essential to know the conditions that promote healthy growth. And the best way to do this is to use what we know and to try some carefully controlled experiments. Of course, we are working with living organisms so it's essential that:

- appropriate care and consideration is shown during this work
- procedures are followed that are ethical.

People working in agriculture and horticulture must try to get maximum yields of products for least cost. But it isn't hit and miss. The conditions that promote healthy growth can be found by controlled experiments.

We also monitor the health and behaviour of **people**. Nurses and doctors monitor patients to see how they are responding to treatment. The performance of sports people can be improved through training and coaching. Skills are learned and developed; strength and fitness is improved.

Structured fitness programmes depend on a thorough understanding of how physical and mental performance is affected. The trainer needs to understand physiology (how the body works) and psychology (how the mind works).

What could you study?

In Unit 1 you found out about some important techniques scientists use. You learned about:

- microscopy
- aseptic techniques for working with micro-organisms.

In Unit 2 you learned about some aspects of:

- useful products that can be obtained from living organisms
- cells, organs and organisms
- growing healthy plants
- inheritance, selective breeding and genetic engineering
- agriculture and horticulture
- micro-organisms
- the human body.

In this section of Unit 3 you can bring these ideas together and investigate a living organism. There is no restriction on what you study, though your school may limit the choice because of the equipment, materials and laboratory space available. It makes sense, however, to investigate something that you have developed some background understanding of already when working on Units 1 and 2.

The GCSE in Applied Science says you must *'investigate the growth and/or development and/or responses of an organism under controlled conditions'*. In this section we will look at how you could monitor the effect of differing conditions on:

- the growth of a plant

Tomatoes are an important commercial fruit. How can we learn more about the factors that affect their growth?

- the growth of a micro-organism

Yeasts are used in the brewing industry and the baking industry. There are many different types. How can we learn about which are best to use and under what conditions?

- the performance of a person in a physical or mental activity

The biathlon requires strength, endurance and skill. The mental attitude of the biathlete must be right. How can we devise a training programme to prepare such an athlete for the Olympic Games?

Plants, micro-organisms or people?

Your first decision is which type of organism you would like to investigate: plants, micro-organisms or people. Then you need to select an actual organism to study for a particular purpose. The sections that follow will give you some ideas. Each section also gives some techniques you might use. You will need to write one or more procedures based on these techniques. Remember that a procedure must give sufficient information for somebody else to repeat your experiment.

Keeping records and writing the report

Whatever you decide to investigate you must keep full records of what you did, the results you obtained and what you think they told you. You should write a report that summarises all of this.

Planning

Once you have agreed the plan for the investigation with your teacher, put it in your file. Make sure you keep a note of any sources of information you used. It's rare that any scientific investigation goes completely to plan. If you change your plan during the course of the investigation make a note of what you did differently and why.

Making measurements and collecting data

Remember that all practical work must have a risk assessment before it's carried out. In the laboratory you should always wear protective clothing and eye protection.

You should record relevant data directly into your laboratory notebook. Never write information on scraps of paper, even if you intend copying them into your laboratory notebook later. If some of the data is produced by an instrument (for example, in the form of a graph or print out), keep the output (graph or print out) in your laboratory note book.

Analysis and evaluation of data

Read pages 57–61 to remind you about analysing and evaluating data.

Writing your report

Your report should be accurate and concise. It does not need to contain all your experimental results, but these should be cross-referenced to your laboratory notebook.

Micro-organisms

Links to units 1 and 2

Unit 1: Micro-organisms, page 72–82

Unit 2: Micro-organisms, page 151–156

REMEMBER

Make sure you know about aseptic technique (page 000) before undertaking any work with micro-organisms. Remember also that all micro-organisms are BIOHAZARDS. You must know about the precautions to be taken when working with micro-organisms.

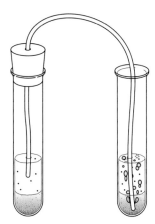

The rate of fermentation can be determined by measuring how quickly carbon dioxide is given off.

REMEMBER

The idea of a standard procedure is that it provides enough information for somebody else to repeat the experiment.

What to monitor?

You need to choose something that can be studied within the time available and using the equipment and materials available to you. You might get some ideas from local science-based organisations such as environmental health departments, hospital pathology laboratories, dairy product manufacturers or breweries. It will help if you know something about micro-organisms and how they multiply.

Here are suggestions for two broad areas you might investigate. There is plenty of scope to set up your own individual investigation within either of them.

The growth of yeast during fermentation

Sugars ferment to make alcohol and carbon dioxide. Yeast is needed for the process. The conditions for fermentation are chosen so that the yeast grows during the process. The purpose of this investigation is to see how conditions affect the growth of yeast during fermentation.

What to do

Selecting the variable

The growth of yeast during fermentation is affected by many things (you might remember that we call these variables). Make a list of them. Decide which variable you want to study and which ones you will keep constant. These might include one or more of the following:

- type of yeast used
- initial quantity of yeast
- glucose concentration (or other sugars)
- temperature
- type and quantity of nutrients.

Planning

Plan a series of experiments to investigate how what you chose to vary affects the growth of yeast when you keep the other variables the same in each experiment.

1   Whatever you decide to vary you will need to find a suitable technique for carrying out a fermentation. (A technique for the fermentation of glucose to make ethanol is given on page 81.) Write a standard procedure based on this technique. The procedure must make it clear what you kept constant and what you varied from one experiment to another. Check the procedure with your teacher.

2   You will also need to find a suitable technique for monitoring the growth of yeast. (Some possible techniques are given on page 80.) Write a standard procedure based on this technique. It must include how and how often you will take samples to monitor the growth of yeast. Check the procedure with your teacher.

3   The plan must also say how you will evaluate the results of the investigation.

Making measurements and collecting data

Carry out the experiments recording all the relevant data. You may want to repeat some of the measurements. Before starting work a risk assessment must be carried out and checked by an authorised person.

All data from the experiment should be accurately recorded directly into your laboratory notebook.

Analysis and evaluation of data

Finally, analyse your results, explain what they show and evaluate your investigation. On pages 50–54 you can read about presenting data, carrying out calculations, analysing and interpreting results and evaluating investigations.

The response of bacteria to different conditions

Bacteria thrive and grow under certain conditions. Under other conditions they die. The purpose of this investigation is to study the conditions that affect the growth of bacteria.

What to do

Selecting the variable

The growth of bacteria is affected by a number of things, including temperature and availability of nutrients. Bacteria can also be killed or stopped from growing by disinfectants and antiseptics. Decide exactly what you would like to study. For example, you might choose a particular bacterium (check with your teacher about what is available) and find out under what conditions it multiplies most quickly.

Planning

1   Plan a series of experiments to investigate how the condition you decide to vary affects the growth of the bacterium. You could investigate the effect of:

    • type and quantity of nutrient used
    • incubation temperature

REMEMBER

The investigation of micro-organisms might look quite complicated. Just remember to think through all the variables and that you must only vary one condition at a time. All others must be the same.

You could compare the effectiveness of different disinfectants.

REMEMBER

Again, the idea of a standard procedure is that it allows somebody else to repeat the experiment. There must be no doubt about what to use, how much and how to carry out the experiment.

or the effectiveness of:

- different methods of sterilisation
- disinfectants (type, brand, concentration, temperature and time)
- antiseptics (type, brand, concentration, temperature and time).

2   Whatever you decide to vary you will need to find a suitable technique for culturing the bacteria. Select a suitable technique and write a standard procedure based on it. The procedure should state the fixed conditions and the variable. Check the procedure with your teacher.

3   You will also need to find a suitable technique for monitoring the growth of bacteria. A technique for monitoring anti-microbial action is given on page 78. Write a standard procedure based on this technique. It must include how and how often you will take samples to monitor the growth of yeast. Check the procedure with your teacher.

4   The plan must also say how you will evaluate the results of the investigation.

Making measurements and collecting data

Carry out the experiments recording all the relevant data. You may want to repeat some of the measurements. Before starting work a risk assessment must be carried out and checked by an authorised person.

Analysing and evaluating data

Finally, analyse your results, explain what they show and evaluate your investigation. On pages 50–54 you can read about presenting data, carrying out calculations, analysing and interpreting results and evaluating investigations.

DETERMINING THE GROWTH OF MICRO-ORGANISMS

SAFETY   Wear protective clothing and eye protection.

Micro-organisms   BIOHAZARD

A **risk assessment** must be carried out before starting work.

METHOD   *Micro-organisms growing on the surface of a solid*
To determine the growth of micro-organisms on the surface of a solid substrate such as agar in a Petri dish:

Measure the area covered by the colony of micro-organisms. You could do this by tracing the area of the colony by putting a sheet of tracing paper over the dish. Use a fine-tipped pencil or pen to trace the outline of the colony. Put the tracing paper over a sheet of graph paper and count the number of 1 mm by 1 mm squares covered by the colony. The units are 'mm^2 of colony'.

Measuring the area covered by a colony of micro-organisms. The traced outline can be stuck into your laboratory notebook.

Micro-organisms growing in a liquid medium
To determine the growth of micro-organisms in a liquid medium (for example, a culture medium in a fermenter) there are three techniques you could use.

(a) Take a small sample and place it on a microscope slide. Cover with a coverslip and place it under a light microscope. Count the number of individual cells that can be seen. The units are 'number of cells per mm^2 of microscope slide'.

(b) Using a graduated pipette, take a small sample of known volume and put it onto a haemocytometer slide. Count the number of cells under a light microscope. The units are 'number of cells per mm^3 of culture'.

technique

technique

(c) Use a colorimeter to measure the cloudiness (opacity or turbidity) of the suspension, in other words how difficult it is for light to pass through. The more cells there are, the cloudier the suspension because the more difficult it is for light to pass through. The units are 'percentage of light absorbed'.

Using a colorimeter to measure the cloudiness caused by micro-organisms in a liquid medium. As always, experimental results are written straight into a laboratory notebook.

Plants

Links to units 1 and 2
Unit 1: Microscopy, pages 66–71

Unit 2: Useful products that can be obtained from living organisms (page 126), Cells, organs and organisms (page 128), Growing healthy plants (page 136), Inheritance, selective breeding and genetic engineering (page 143), Agriculture and horticulture (page 148).

What to monitor?
You need to choose something that can be studied within the time available and using the equipment and materials available to you. You might get some ideas from local garden centres, market gardens, farms and so on. It will help if you know something about seeds and germination, and about how plants can be propagated. Gardening books are a good source of information.

Here are suggestions for two broad areas you might investigate. There is plenty of scope to set up your own individual investigation within either of them.

REMEMBER

Seeds, plants, soil and compost are BIOHAZARDS. You must take the necessary precautions when handling them.

Growing plants from seeds
Many plants are grown from seeds. These are usually bought in packets, but many can be collected from the previous year's plants (and this is much cheaper!). There are two parts to growing plants from seeds:

- how well the seeds germinate (in other words, how many seeds actually produce plants)
- how well the seedlings grow.

What to do

Choosing the seeds and what to investigate

1 Choose which seeds to investigate. They might be different types of vegetables, fruit and flowers, or different cultivars of one particular plant (for example, different types of lettuces). Read the instructions on the label carefully.

2 Both the germination of seeds and the growth of seedlings are affected by many things. Decide which you want to study and, therefore, which you will need to keep constant. These might include one or more of the following:

- pre-treatment of seeds, e.g. soaking them overnight in water
- growing medium, e.g. soil and different types of compost
- light
- temperature
- carbon dioxide in the atmosphere
- water content of the growing medium
- humidity
- nutrients.

Planning

Plan a series of experiments to investigate how the condition you chose to vary affects seed germination and secondly seedling growth. Remember, the other variables must be kept the same from one experiment to another.

You can measure seed germination by counting how many seedlings are produced from the seeds you sow.

1   Whatever you decide to vary you will need to find a suitable technique for sowing seeds and growing on the seedlings (including, for example, thinning out and pricking out). One technique is given on page 323. Write a standard procedure based on this technique. The procedure should state the fixed conditions and the variable. Remember, a standard procedure should provide enough information for somebody else to be able to repeat the experiment. Check the procedure with your teacher.

2   Choose a suitable technique for measuring the growth of seedlings. Some possible techniques are given on page 323. Write a standard procedure based on one of them. It must include how and how often you will take samples to monitor the growth of seedlings. Check the procedure with your teacher.

3   The plan must also say how you will evaluate the results of the investigation.

You can measure plant growth by counting the number of leaves, measuring their mass, measuring their height and measuring the length of their roots.

Making measurements and collecting data

Carry out the experiments recording all the relevant data. You may want to repeat some of the measurements. Before starting work a risk assessment must be carried out and checked by an authorised person.

Analysis and evaluation of data

Finally, analyse your results, explain what they show and evaluate your investigation. On pages 50–54 you can read about presenting data, carrying out calculations, analysing and interpreting results, and evaluating investigations.

technique

OBTAINING PLANTS FROM SEEDS

METHOD

1 Pre-treat the seeds if needed, for example, soak them in water overnight.

2 Fill the seed tray with seed compost. Tap the sides of the tray briskly so that the compost settles. Spread the compost evenly in the tray and firm it gently.

3 Sow the seeds and lightly cover them with seed compost.

4 Water well with a fine rose. Leave to stand until any excess water has drained away.

5 Place the tray in a suitable place (this will depend on the variables you are monitoring).

6 Once the seedlings are about 2 cm high, count how many have germinated.

7 Depending on what you intend to do you could:

- remove every other seedling in each row and allow the others to grow on
- prick out seedlings and re-plant them in a fresh growing medium (remember to hold them gently by their leaves and not by their roots).

8 After a suitable time, collect seedlings, measure their length and count the number of leaves.

9 Carefully wash any compost from the seedlings and dry them by dabbing with absorbent paper towel. Weigh each seedling. You might also want to measure the mass of seedlings above the ground and the mass of the roots.

CALCULATIONS

- Calculate the percentage of seeds that germinated.

$$\text{Percentage germination} = \frac{\text{number of seeds that germinated}}{\text{number of seeds that were sown}} \times 100\%$$

There is no uncertainty in this value.

- You have measured the growth of each seedling by: (a) measuring their length, (b) counting the number of leaves and (c) weighing the seedling. You must decide how to present these data. Assess the accuracy, precision and uncertainty of the measurements (see pages 62–63).

Growing plants from cuttings

Many plants are grown from cuttings taken from established plants. Different types of cuttings can be taken, such as softwood and hardwood cuttings, stem cuttings and leaf cuttings. Each requires a slightly different technique. There are two aspects to growing plants from cuttings: how well cuttings take (in other words, how well new root systems form from the cutting) and how well the plant grows once established.

What to do

Choosing the cutting and what to investigate

Choose the plant that you want to propagate from cuttings. Decide which type of cutting needs to be taken.

How well the cutting takes is affected by many things. Decide which variable you want to study and which ones you will keep constant. These might include one or more of the following: pre-treatment of cuttings (for example, dipping the cutting in rooting powder), growing medium (for example, soil and different types of compost), light, temperature, carbon dioxide in atmosphere, water content of growing medium, humidity, nutrients.

Planning

1   Plan a series of experiments to investigate how the condition you decide to vary affects the growth of a new plant from a cutting when you provide constant conditions for all the other variables.

2   Whatever you decide to vary you will need to find a suitable technique for taking the cuttings and growing on the plants. Some techniques are given on page 325. Write a standard procedure based on your chosen technique. The procedure should state the fixed conditions and the variable. Check the procedure with your teacher.

3   Choose a suitable technique for determining how well the cuttings take, for example, measuring the length and mass of

The percentage of cuttings that take can be counted by seeing how many of them survive and do not simply die.

their roots. Some possible techniques are given on page 326. Write a standard procedure based on one of these techniques. It must include how and how often you will take samples to monitor the growth of the cuttings. Check the procedure with your teacher.

4 The plan must also say how you will evaluate the results of the investigation.

> **REMEMBER**
>
> A standard procedure must give enough information for somebody else to repeat the experiment.

Making measurements and collecting data

Carry out the experiments recording all the relevant data. You may want to repeat some of the measurements. Before starting work a risk assessment must be carried out and checked by an authorised person.

Analysis and evaluation of data

Finally, analyse your results, explain what they show and evaluate your investigation. On pages 50–54 you can read about presenting data, carrying out calculations, analysing and interpreting results and evaluating investigations.

OBTAINING PLANTS FROM CUTTINGS

technique

There are various types of cuttings you can take. The methods below outline some of the techniques used. More detail can be obtained from a good gardening book. Softwood cuttings are probably the most successful and commonly used type of cutting.

METHOD **Softwood cuttings** (for example, clematis, but try anything)

1 Choose young, green, healthy stems.

2 Take 5–10 cm long cuttings in early spring just after new growth has started. Cut just below a node (growing/branching point). Keep the cuttings in a plastic bag to keep them moist.

3 Remove the lower leaves so that the cutting has three remaining leaves.

4 Dip the cut stem into rooting powder and put it into a hole pushed in cutting compost.

Taking a softwood cutting.

technique

5 Keep the cuttings in an incubator at 18–21 °C until they have grown roots, then separate them out and pot them on.

6 If the cuttings have large leaves, cut the leaves in half to reduce water loss.

Root cuttings (for example, phlox, oriental poppies)

1 Select young healthy plants in early autumn and label for later use.

2 Dig the plant up in late winter and wash off the soil.

3 Choose thick fleshy, not woody, roots and cut them into 5–10 cm lengths.

4 Put the roots upright, with their ends just below the surface, into pots of cutting compost. Leave about 2 cm between cuttings. Make sure the top of the root is the part of the root that was originally nearest the surface.

5 Place the pot in an incubator set at 18°C. Shoots should be visible after a month or so, then plant on the cuttings.

Leaf cuttings (for example, Streptocarpus, Sansevieria)

1 Either cut the leaf off at the stem and put the leave petiole (leaf-stem) into the cutting compost, with the leaf laying on the compost or cut across the leaf every 2 cm with a sharp knife, and bury the leaf sections, with the edge nearest the petiole below. *Begonia rex* leaves can be cut into 1 cm squares. Each square can be buried or left pushed against the compost surface.

2 Place cuttings in an incubator at 18–21 °C.

MEASURING GROWTH

Carefully wash any compost from the cuttings and dry them by dabbing with absorbent paper towel. Measure the length of the roots. Now cut the roots and measure their mass.

CALCULATIONS

- Calculate the percentage of cuttings that take.

$$\text{Percentage} = \frac{\text{number of cuttings that take}}{\text{number of cuttings planted}} \times 100\%$$

There is no uncertainty in this value.

- You have measured the growth of each cutting by measuring the length and mass of their roots. You must decide how to present these data. Assess the accuracy, precision and uncertainty of the measurements (see pages 62–63).

USING FERTILISERS

There is a wide variety of commercial fertilisers to choose from. Alternatively you could make one in the laboratory and test its effectiveness.

METHOD

1 Decide what fertiliser you are going to use.

2 Read the instructions on the pack carefully. Decide how you are going to modify them to investigate the effect of the fertiliser on plant growth.

Some fertilisers have to be diluted before use. Follow the instructions on the label.

3 If necessary prepare any fertiliser solutions you are going to use by following the instructions on the pack. Alternatively you may want to modify these and write your own procedure.

4 Decide how you will grow your plants and how to add the fertiliser.

5 Grow samples of plants using differing amounts of fertiliser or using different fertilisers (depending upon the purpose of your investigation), and monitor their growth.

CONTROLLING THE GROWING ENVIRONMENT

MEASURING AND CONTROLLING SOIL/ COMPOST TEMPERATURES

1 Use a soil thermometer to measure the temperatures in the compost. Push the bulb-end of the thermometer into the middle depth of the tray or pot. Be careful not to bend the metal case of the thermometer and break the glass thermometer inside. You could use an electronic thermometer. With data logging equipment this would allow the temperature to be measured and recorded continuously.

technique

2   For seedlings or cuttings in a propagator or on a heat mat, adjust the propagator or heater thermostat to maintain a soil temperature of 20–25 °C.

3   The soil temperature is also controlled indirectly by controlling the air temperature.

In commercial greenhouses factors like soil and air temperature, humidity and moisture, and light are monitored and controlled

MEASURING AND CONTROLLING AIR TEMPERATURE

1   Use a maximum–minimum thermometer to check the air temperatures or use an electronic thermometer connected to a data-logger to track the air temperature. A maximum–minimum thermometer must be read and re-set daily. Keep a record of the maximum and minimum temperatures.

2   In winter, most plants will survive if they are kept frost-free. Thermostats are usually set to about 5 °C. If the greenhouse or room has a source of heat, adjust general heating thermostats to give a minimum (night-time) air temperature of 5 °C, or a little more if plants are very sensitive.

3   In summer too much heat can be the problem. Reduce heat by: (a) shading, (b) increasing ventilation and (c) watering the floors and walls (in the case of a greenhouse). Control one or more of these to give a maximum summer daytime temperature of 25–30 °C.

MEASURING AND CONTROLLING HUMIDITY/MOISTURE

1   Place the hygrometer where the plants are growing, wait for a couple of minutes and take a reading. The relative humidity for any plant, except cactus, should be kept in the region of 70%. In a propagator it should be about 80–90%.

2   Increase the humidity by misting the air, spraying water on the greenhouse floor and matting, and reducing ventilation. Remember that these will also affect the temperature. Be careful not to over-water the plant compost or growing medium.

3 If the relative humidity is at about 100% there is a danger of fungal growth damaging the plants, so increase ventilation to reduce the humidity.

4 Take another relative humidity reading about 10 minutes after you have taken your actions to check that the humidity has changed.

Note: Relative humidity can vary over a short distance, being about 80% from just above the soil below a plant to perhaps 60% in the air above a plant, so it may be necessary to take a few readings and average them.

A plastic bag held up by small sticks can be used to keep the atmosphere humid. You can measure the humidity using a hygrometer.

MEASURING AND CONTROLLING LIGHT

Extra light can be provided using electric lighting. This is useful in winter and can lengthen the growing period. Usually plants need only fairly low light levels for photosynthesis. Plants grown on a windowsill, in a greenhouse or outside between April and October are more likely to need shading than extra light.

Greenhouse windows are often painted with white lime-wash during the summer to prevent excess light and heat.

MEASURING AND CONTROLLING CARBON DIOXIDE

This is done commercially but cannot be done easily in somebody's greenhouse. However, you could investigate the effect in the laboratory by using a seed propagator with:

- either sodium hydroxide pellets (you should get an experienced person to help you as these are EXTREMELY CORROSIVE) to remove carbon dioxide from the atmosphere
- or a mixture of sodium carbonate and citric acid made slightly wet with water (the chemicals react to give off carbon dioxide)/

People

Links to units 1 and 2
Unit 2: The human body, pages 157–166

What to monitor?
You need to choose something that can be studied within the time available and using equipment and materials available to you. You might get some ideas from local hospitals, sports clinics, fitness centres, sports clubs and so on. It will help if you know something about the underlying scientific principles.

We all **move** things and **lift** things. Moving includes walking, running and swimming. You might lift objects and yourself. How effectively you do it depends on many factors, such as the load, fitness, psychology and skill.

Load
Not surprisingly the heavier the weight carried (in other words, the load), the poorer our performance in moving and lifting it. This why athletes compete using equipment and clothing made from the lightest materials.

The more weight something carries, the more energy is needed and the more it affects performance. That's why the best horses are made to carry extra weights in handicap races.

Fitness
The fitter you are, the easier you will be able to move or lift things. But fitness is not straightforward. There are three main aspects: stamina, strength and suppleness.

Nothing comes easy. If you take up a new physical activity, you can expect several weeks to pass before there is any significant improvement in your fitness. And for the improvement to last you will probably need to do the activity at least three times a week for more than 15 minutes each time.

• = no real benefit •• = beneficial effect ••• = very beneficial effect
•••• = excellent effect

Activity	Stamina score	Strength score	Suppleness score
Badminton	••	••	•••
Canoeing	•••	•••	••
Climbing stairs	•••	••	•
Cricket	•	•	••
Cycling (hard)	•••	•••	••
Digging	•••	••••	••
Football	•••	•••	•••
Golf	•	•	••
Gymnastics	••	•••	••••
Hill walking	•••	••	•
Jogging	••••	••	••
Judo	••	••	••••
Rowing	••••	••••	••
Sailing	•	••	••
Squash	•••	••	•••
Swimming (hard)	••••	••••	••••
Tennis	••	•••	•••
Walking (briskly)	••	•	•
Weightlifting	•	••••	•
Yoga	•	•	••••

Psychology

Your 'mind set' will often affect how well you perform at a physical task. You have may have heard about 'getting in the zone'. It's when a sportsperson doesn't have to think about what they are doing. It comes automatically. They are completely focused. Top-class sports people increasingly make use of sports psychologists. Sports psychologists identify the psychological factors that contribute to success. They teach sports people the mental skills that allow them to perform to the peak of their potential. And they help sports people overcome psychological problems, such as a crisis of confidence.

Psychologists have analysed Beckham's actions and conclude that he was completely 'in the zone' when scoring from a free kick to ensure that England made it to the World Cup finals in 2002.

Skill

The way you move or lift something is important. Think about any sport. You can be taught how to do something properly and if you learn the skill you will do it better. For example, throwing, kicking or hitting a ball. To develop a new skill you need a good teacher and plenty of practice.

This ice skater can lift his partner more easily and more safely if he does it in the correct way. It's a skill and it takes practice.

Here are suggestions for two investigations you might undertake. There is plenty of scope to set up your own individual investigation.

Improving performance

The ability of somebody to move or lift things can be improved. You could investigate different training and coaching regimes aimed at improving people's fitness and skill. Monitoring psychological factors is fascinating, but not something for an untrained person to undertake.

What to do

Choosing 'who, what and why' to monitor

Choose which moving or lifting activity to monitor and the person or people who will be doing it. Your choice will depend on the techniques you have for monitoring the people's performance. You might want to investigate how accurately somebody can throw a ball and how far he or she can throw it. You would need to decide which tests to use to measure performance and what training or coaching programmes you might put people through to improve this performance.

The performance of a task can be monitored by measuring a person's:

- speed
- strength
- stamina
- suppleness
- reaction time
- recovery rate
- physical skill.

A 400 m hurdler needs suppleness, speed, strength and stamina. All of these can be improved using the right training programme and a coach who understands the athlete and the demands of the sport. Each training programme is different and is chosen to match the needs of the athlete.

The ability to move or lift something depends on many factors. Decide which of these you want to build into the programme and monitor its effect on performance. Remember that you can only vary one of these at a time. Keep the others constant and investigate the effect on performance of changing the variable factor.

Planning

Plan a series of experiments to investigate how the condition you decide to vary affects the chosen moving or lifting task when you provide constant conditions for all the other variables. Whatever you decide to vary you will need to choose a suitable technique for measuring the moving or lifting performance. Some possible techniques are given on page 335. Write a standard procedure based on one of them. It must include how and how often you will take samples to monitor the performance. Check the procedure with your teacher.

The plan must also say how you will evaluate the results of the investigation.

Making measurements and collecting data

Carry out the experiments recording all the relevant data. You may want to repeat some of the measurements. Before starting work a risk assessment must be carried out and checked by an authorised person.

Analysis and evaluation of data

Finally, analyse your results, explain what they show and evaluate your investigation. On pages 50–54 you can read about presenting data, carrying out calculations, analysing and interpreting results and evaluating investigations.

technique

DETERMINING SPEED

The speed with which someone can carry out a task is a measure of his or her performance at it. Of course, he or she needs to carry out the task correctly. A professional secretary, for example, can type ten times faster, and more accurately, than someone who has spent a few hours at a typewriter or word processor. The world record for 100 m is 9.77 s. The British record is 9.87 s. Even the fastest people of your age can only run 100 m in around 11–12 seconds.

METHOD

To determine speed all that's needed is to measure the time it takes to complete a task. For example, how long it takes to walk, run or swim a particular distance.

CALCULATIONS

$s = d/t$

where s = speed/m s^{-1}

d = distance covered/m

t = time taken/m

WORKED EXAMPLE

How fast does the world record holder for 100 m run?

$d = 100$ m

$t = 9.77$ s

$s = 100/9.77 = 10.23$ m s^{-1}

SAFETY

- You should warm up thoroughly before undertaking strenuous exercise.

- Weight training can lead to serious injury unless you are careful. A qualified person should be in attendance when such equipment is being used.

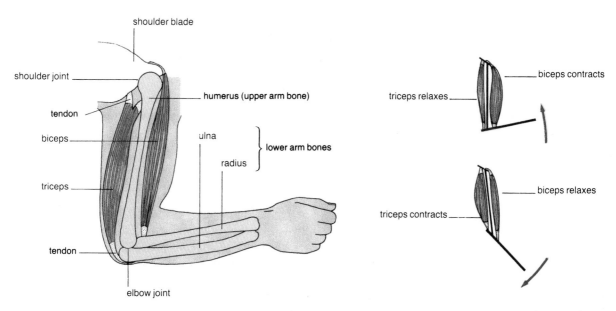

Somebody's strength is a measure of how much force their muscles have. This picture shows how the biceps and triceps muscles move the arm at the elbow joint. Closer examination of a muscle shows that it is made up of large numbers of muscle fibres. Training to increase strength, for example, weight training, has little effect on the number of muscle fibres. However, it does increase:

- the number and size of the fibrils that make up each muscle fibre
- the amount of protein in the muscle
- the strength of tendons (which attach muscles to bones) and ligaments (which attach bones to bones at a joint)
- the blood supply to the muscles.

STRENGTH

technique

Not many tasks need strength alone. However, all moving or lifting needs some strength. There are many ways of measuring strength, for example:

- the maximum mass moved in a leg press
- the maximum mass lifted in a bench press
- the length of time a lateral hang lasts
- the length of time a mass can be held at arm's length
- the maximum force exerted in a grip test.

Note: if you visit a local gym or fitness centre you will find other equipment and methods you could use.

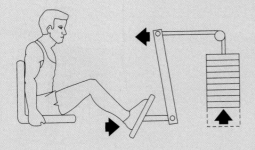

Leg press
Sit with your back firmly against the seat with an angle at your knee joints of 90°. Hold the seat rails and straighten your legs. Record the maximum mass you can move. You may need to try a number of masses until you find there is one you can't move. If you do this, remember that your performance will decrease as you get tired. You must leave enough time to recover before going on to a greater mass.

technique

Bench press

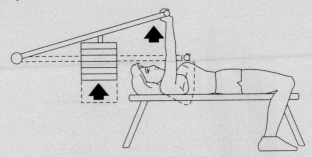

Lie face up on a bench with your head nearest the weights. Keep your feet flat on the ground. Make sure your hips are always in contact with the bench. Extend your arms fully. Record the maximum mass you can move. You may need to try a number of masses until you find there is one you can't move. If you do this, remember that your performance will decrease as you get tired. You must leave enough time to recover before going on to a greater mass.

Lateral hang
Pull yourself up on a bar so that your chin is level with it. Without making any other movements record how long you can hold this position.

Extended arm hold
Hold a small dumbbell at arm's length (you will need to decide what weight to use; it might be between 0.5 and 3 kg). Record how long you can hold it at arm's length.

technique

Dynamometer
Make sure the needle is adjusted to the zero mark. Keep your arms well away from your body and squeeze as hard as possible. Record the best of three attempts. Repeat with your other hand.

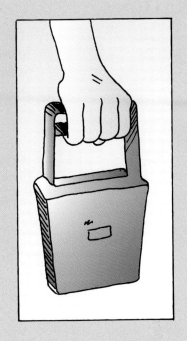

METHOD

1 Choose which way of measuring strength you will use. You may decide to use more than one way.

2 Record the measurements of strength before and after a period of training or coaching. Compare the results to see whether strength has increased.

CALCULATIONS

For each measurement, calculate the percentage change from the previous measurement.

$$\% \text{ change} = \frac{y - x}{x} \times 100\%$$

where x = first measurement
        y = second measurement

WORKED EXAMPLE

A person holds a 1 kg mass at arms length for 100 s (x). After one week of training she is tested again. This time she can hold it for 120 s (y).

$$\% \text{ change} = \frac{120 - 100}{100} \times 100 = 20 \%$$

technique

STAMINA

The time it takes to run 2400 m (about 1$\frac{1}{2}$ miles) is a good measure of stamina. Unless you are reasonably fit, you may not be able to run this far. Run 800 m instead and multiply how long this takes by three. This gives an estimate of how long it would take you to run 2400 m. Of course, this will be an underestimate.

From the National Coaching Foundation: stamina by measuring how long it takes a 17–29 year old to run 2400 m

Stamina	Time for a woman	Time for a man
Superb	Under 9 min	Under 7 min 30 s
Excellent	9 min – 9 min 53 s	7 min 30 s – 8 min 14 s
Very good	9 min 54 s – 12 min 17 s	8 min 15 s – 10 min 14 s
Good	12 min 18 s – 14 min 23 s	10 min 15 s – 11 min 59 s
Fail	14 min 24 s – 17 min 23 s	12 min – 14 min 29 s
Poor	17 min 24 s – 19 min 47 s	14 min 30 s – 16 min 29 s
Very poor	Over 19 min 48 s	Over 16 min 30 s

METHOD

1   Record the time is takes for a person to run 2400 m. Use a stopwatch. If the person is not very fit, reduce the distance they have to run, for example, to 1200 m or 800 m and use this to estimate how long it would take for this person to run 2400 m.

2   Record the measurements of strength before and after a period of training or coaching. Compare the results to see whether time has decreased or increased.

technique

SUPPLENESS

Suppleness is the same thing as flexibility. The easiest way to measure your suppleness is to try to touch your toes. Be careful. You should not strain, otherwise you risk injuring yourself.

METHOD

1 Stand on a bench or chair. Make sure there is somebody to hold you should you start to fall.

2 Bend over slowly and reach down to your toes. If you cannot touch your toes, ask a friend to measure how far short you are. If you can touch your toes easily ask a friend to see how far beneath your toes you can reach.

3 Record your results. A distance short of your toes should be written as a negative distance, and a distance below your toes as a positive distance.

4 Record the measurements of strength before and after a period of training or coaching. Compare the results to see whether suppleness has decreased or increased.

Measuring suppleness

technique

REACTION TIME

If you play electronic games you will know about the importance of reaction times. A sprinter also knows about the importance of reacting to the starter's gun. Reaction times are important. Your reaction time is a measure of how long it takes for you to register a signal (such as a noise or a flash of light), process it in your brain and react by contracting certain muscles. With practice, a person can improve their reaction time.

METHODS

a) Reaction times can be measured with great precision using a computer. Software that records the time between the signal on the screen and your response to it.

Many computer games require fast reaction times.

b) If you do not have access to this equipment, you can find your reaction time like this:

1 Ask somebody to hold a ruler vertically.

2 Almost clasp the end nearer the floor with your thumb and index finger.

3 The person should then drop the ruler without your knowing when.

4 Clasp the ruler as soon as you can.

5 Record the distance, d, the ruler has fallen in metres. Use the formula $t = d/4.9$ to calculate your response time, t, in seconds.

WORKED EXAMPLE

The ruler dropped 14.7 cm before the person grasped it.

14.7 cm = 0.147 m

therefore response time, $t = 0.147/4.9 = 0.173$ s

RECOVERY RATE

One measure of fitness is that the fitter someone is, the quicker they recover after undertaking a task. The easiest way to determine a person's recovery time is to measure their heart rate and see how long it takes to return to normal. You can measure heart rate by taking the person's pulse.

METHOD

1 Ask the person to sit down quietly for 5 minutes. Take their pulse for 30 seconds and multiplying by 2. This is the heart rate per minute.

2 Wait 30 seconds and measure the pulse again.

3 Ask the person to undertake a fixed task such as 100 step-ups. If you intend to compare the recovery rates of different people, make sure they undertake the same task, and take the same amount of time to complete it.

4 Ask the person to sit down and rest.

5 Thirty seconds after the end of the task, take their pulse.

6 Take the pulse every 30 seconds until it returns to normal.

CALCULATIONS

1 Plot a graph of heart rate against time.

2 Find out from your graph approximately how long it takes from the end of the exercise for the person's heart rate to return to normal.

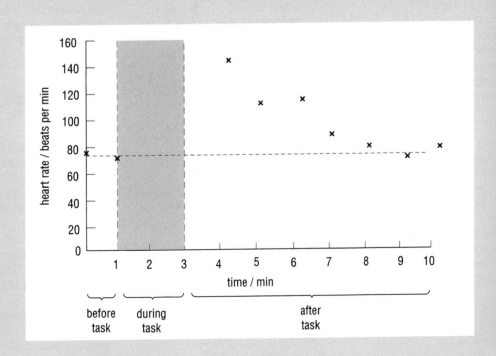

Index

accidents 4–5
accuracy 63, 304
acid-base chemical reactions 267–8, 277
acid-base titrations 102–8
acid-carbonate chemical reactions 277
acids 102
actual yields 261
advantage, mechanical 306
aerobic respiration 162
agents, anti-microbial 78–9
agriculture 149–51
alkalis 102–3
alleles 143
ammeters 45, 112
amounts and quantities 33–4
anabolism 131
anaerobic respiration 164
analogue meters 28–9, 45
analysis
    chemical 83–109
    data 57–61
    in workplace 244
animals
    cells 129–30
    growth monitoring 313
    useful products 127
anti-microbial action 78–9
antibiotics 156
antibodies 155
antigens 155
antiseptics 155
arteries 157
aseptic techniques 73
asexual reproduction 136
assembly, electrical and electronic devices 291–304
assessments of risk 5, 7–9
atomic mass 33
atomic particles 183–4
atoms
    compounds 201–2
    electrons in 186–7
    elements 184
averages 58–61

bacteria 152–3, 156, 317–19
balances 30–3
bar charts 50
bases 102–3

biohazards 67
biological catalysts (enzymes) 131, 258
block diagrams 291, 292
blood 158, 159–61
body temperature maintenance 165
bonding
    ceramics 207
    chemical 187, 190–3
    covalent 189–90, 201, 207
    ionic 187–9, 207
    metals 195, 202–4
    polymers 205–6
British Pharmacopoeia (BP) 20, 95
British Standards (BS) kitemark 5
bulk chemicals 178–9
Bunsen burners 27
burns 13

calculations 55–6
calibration 32
calibration graphs 53
callipers 37
capacitors 294–5
catabolism 131
catalysts 131, 258–9
cells 128–9
    animal 129–30
    chemical reactions 131–6
    plants 129–30, 141
centrifuging technique 271, 276
ceramics 194, 207, 208
changes to raw materials 172
charts 50, 52
chemical analysis 83–109
chemical bonding 187, 190–3
chemical changes 172
chemical reactions
    acid–base 267–8, 277
    acid–carbonate 277
    breaking and making 190–3
    cells 131–6
    rates 255–66
    reversible 264–5
    temperature 257
    types 267–71
chemical reduction 174–5
chemical tests 88, 90–2, 93
chemicals
    costs of making 265–6
    injury from swallowing 14

metal ore reduction 174–5
    obtaining useful 167–93
    types 176–9
chlorophyll 137, 141–2, 213
chromatography 88, 89
chromosomes 143
circuits
    components 294–5
    diagrams 291, 292–3, 298
    integrated 295
    printed circuit boards 300, 301–3
    relationships 293
circulatory system 157–8, 159–61
climate 149, 217
cloning 147
closed-loop control 299
clothing materials 199
communication devices 287
comparators 299
components
    circuit 294–5
    connecting 300
    selection 292
    series or parallel 295
composites 194–5, 208
compounds 170, 176–7, 201–2
compressive strength 121
concentration 260
concrete 208
conductance 115
conduction
    electrical 195, 203, 206, 208
    thermal 115, 196, 203, 206, 208
conductivities 116–18
construction materials 198–9
control
    devices 286–7, 289, 298–300
    growing environment 327–9
    types 299, 300
Control of Substances Hazardous to Health Regulations 7
costs 198, 224–5, 265–6
covalent bonding 189–90, 201, 207
crystallisation technique 271, 272
cultivars 148
culturing micro-organisms 72–4
cuttings, plants from 324–9

data
    analysis 57–61
    collection 315
    interpretation 57–61
    loggers 46
    presentation 50–4
    types 57–8
decantation technique 271, 273
density 40, 118–20, 195, 204
derived products 127
development, scientific 243
diagrams
    block 291, 292
    circuit 291, 292–3, 298
diffusion 131–2
digital meters 29
diodes 295
diploid number 136
direct weighing 98–9
diseases
    micro-organisms 152–3
    plants 149, 150–1
displacement cans 40
displacement reactions 285
distillation 87–8, 173–4, 271, 277
dough making 80
drawing 50, 51, 54
dynamometers 337

education through science 244–5
effectiveness 304
efficiency 227–34, 307
effort 305
electric current measurement 45–7
electric shock 14
electrical appliances 229
electrical circuits see circuits
electrical conduction 195, 203,
    206, 208
electrical and electronic devices
    286–8, 291–304
electrical energy 239
electrical power 235–7
electrical properties 109–14
electrical resistance 110–14
electrical resistivity 114
electricity
    fossil fuels 215–16
    generation 222–4, 232
    mains 224–5
    nuclear power 222–5
electrochemical series 270–1
electron transfer 270
electronic balances 31–3
electronic devices 286–8,
    289–304
electronic thermometers 298

electrons 186–7
elements 168–70, 184, 185–6
endothermic reactions 191, 193
energy
    costs 224–5
    efficiency 227–34
    importance 211–39
    plants 213–14
    recycling 232
    resources 212
    sources 214
    transferring 221–2
enzymes 131, 258
equations
    balanced 100–1
    ionic 268–9, 271
equipment 23–48, 199–200, 266
errors 62
ethanol 81
European safety standard 5
evaluation 49, 62–5, 303–4
evaporation 85–7
exothermic reactions 191, 193
extinguishers, fire 15, 16
eye injuries 14

farming methods 148–51
feedback systems 164–5, 299
fermenters 152
fertilisers 327
filtration techniques 173, 271,
    273–5
fine chemicals 178–9
fire prevention 15–17
first aid 4–5, 12–15
fitness 330–1, 341
flame 27, 94
formula mass 33–4
formulae use 55–6
formulations 180
fossil fuels 214–18, 222–4
fractional distillation 173–4
fumes 14
fungi 152–3

gases 43, 93, 181–2, 224–5
gears 311–12
genes 143
genetic engineering 145–7, 150
genetically modified (GM) foods
    145–7, 150–1
germs 153, 155
giant structures 201–3
glass reinforced plastic 209
glassware 26, 41–3
global warming 217
glucose 162, 166

GM foods 145–7, 150–1
graduated glassware precision
    41–3
graphs 50, 52–4, 55–6
ground
    substances from 171
    see also soil
growing environment, plants
    327–9
growth factors, plants 148–51
growth monitoring
    living organisms 312–29
    micro-organisms 315–20
    plants 313, 320–9

handling equipment and materials
    23–48
haploid number 136
hardness 196–7, 204, 208, 209
hazards 5, 6, 67
health education 244–5
Health and Safety regulations 7
heart 158–9
heat
    energy 238–9
    fossil fuels 215–16
    loss reduction 230–1
heating systems 234–9
heating techniques 27
high efficiency devices 229–30
histograms 52
horticulture 149–51
human body 157–66
hydroelectric power 219

ICs see integrated circuits
immunisation 155
incubating plates 77
indicators 103
industrial fermenters 152
infection protection 153–6
inheritance 143–4
injuries 13–15
inorganic chemicals 128
inorganic compounds 176–7
input devices 290–1, 294, 297
integrated circuits (ICs) 295
intensive farming 150–1
International Standard (ISO) 20
interpretation of data 57–61
investigating materials
    109–23
ionic bonding 187–9, 207
ionic equations 268–9, 271
ions 90–2, 141
ISO see International Standard
isotopes 185

kinetic energy 212, 238
kitemark 5

labour costs 266
laws of thermodynamics 221
length measurement 35–9
levers 305–6, 308–12
light meters 298
light microscopes 66–7
liquids 25, 41–3, 180–1, 182
living organisms 66–82, 126–66,
        312–41
load 305, 330
looking at slides 70–1
lungs 161, 162–4

machines 228–9, 305–12
magnesium ions 141
malleability 203
Management of Health and Safety at
        Work Regulations 7
mass measurement 30–5
materials
    classification 194–5
    costs 198
    handling scientific 23–48
    investigating 109–23
    for making things 194–210
    properties 115–22, 198, 201–9
    raw 167–8, 171, 172–3, 265
matter, states of 172
mean average 59
measurement 28–35
    electric current 45–7
    instruments 296
    length 35–9
    living organisms 315
    mass 30–5
    microscope 36
    precision 36–8, 41–3, 63
    temperature 44–5
    time 45
    voltage 45–7
    volume 39–43
mechanical advantage 306
mechanical machines 228–9
median 59, 60–1
medicines 20
meiosis 134–6
melting point, ceramics 208
metabolism 130
metallic bonding 202–3
metals
    bonding 195, 202–4
    conduction 203
    electrochemical series 270–1
    elements 169

giant structures 201–3
    obtaining 284–5
    ores 174–5
    properties 202–4
methods 21
micro-organisms 72–82, 127, 151–6,
        313, 315–20
micrometer screw gauges 38
microscopes 36, 51
microscopy 66–71
mitosis 134–6
mixing techniques 26
mixtures 170–1, 172, 180–1, 182
mode 59, 60
molecular structures 201–2, 205–6
monitoring
    devices 288
    living organisms 312–41
    people 313, 315, 330–41
    plant growth 320–229
movement devices 287–8
multimeters 45, 110, 111

natural gas supply 224–5
natural products 127
nitrates 140–1
non-metals 169
nuclear energy 220, 222–5
nutrients, plants 137–8, 141, 150–1

oil 214–15, 216
on-off feedback control 299
open-loop control 299, 300
ores 174–5
organic chemicals 129
organic compounds 176–7
organic farming 150–1
osmosis 133
output devices 290–1, 294, 297
ovens 27
oxygen gain or loss 269–70

paper chromatography 89, 142
pathogens 152
pcbs see printed circuit boards
people monitoring 313, 315, 330–41
performance
    evaluation 303–4
    improvement (people) 332–4
    testing 303–4
periodic table 185–6
pests and diseases, plant 149, 150–1
pH of soil 29, 139, 149
photographs 50
photosynthesis 137
physical changes 172
physical conditions monitoring 288

pie charts 50, 52
planning 315
plants
    cells 129–30, 141
    energy 213–14
    from cuttings 324–9
    growth monitoring 313, 315,
        320–9
    healthy growth 136–42, 148–51
    nutrients 137–8, 141, 150–1
    pests and diseases 149, 150–1
    useful products 126–7
plastic
    glass reinforced 209
    see also polymers
pliers modelling 309–10
polymers 195, 204–6, 209
portability 304
potential divider 296–7
potential energy 211–12, 238
power
    alternative sources 219
    electrical 235–7
    electronic devices 289–90, 292–3
    hydroelectric 219
    natural gas 224–5
    nuclear 222–5
    work and 237–9
    see also energy
practical tasks 18–23
precipitation 268–9, 281–2
precision 36–8, 41–3, 63
presenting data 50–4
printed circuit boards (pcbs) 300,
        301–3
probes 46, 139, 141
procedures see standard procedures
processors, electronic 290–1
production 243
products see useful products
properties
    electrical 109–14
    materials 115–22, 198, 200–9
proteins, plant growth 140
psychology 331
pulleys 310–11
pulse 158, 159

qualifications in science 253
qualitative chemical analysis 83,
        85–95
qualitative data 57
quantitative chemical analysis 83,
        95–100
quantitative chemical tests 88
quantitative data 58
quantities and amounts 33–4

radioactive material 9–10
range 59
rates
    chemical reactions 255–66
    recovery (human) 341
raw materials 167–8, 171, 172–3, 265
reactants 256–7
reaction times (human) 340
reactions see chemical reactions
reading rulers 36
record keeping 315
recovery rates 341
recycling energy 232
redox reactions 269–71
reference materials, standard 21–2
reinforced concrete 208
relative atomic mass 33
relative formula mass 33–4
reliability 62, 304
repeatability 41, 62
report writing 315
reproducibility 41, 62
research, scientific 242–3
resistance 110–14
resistivity 114
resistors 294
resources, energy 212–20
respiration 162–4, 244–5
results evaluation 49, 61, 62–3
reversible reactions 264–5
risk assessments 5, 7–9
robustness 304

safety 4–17, 300
salts 277–85
samples for analysis 83–5
science
    businesses 246–8, 250–1
    energy needs 226–7
    jobs 249–50, 251–4
scientific research 242–3
screw gauges 38
secondary sources 61
seeds growth monitoring 320–3
selective breeding 144, 243
sensitivity 304
sensors 29, 46, 296, 297
separation
    chlorophyll 142
    raw materials 172–3
shock 14
simple distillation 173

skills 252, 332
slides 51, 69–71
soil 29, 139, 141, 149, 327–8
    see also ground
solar energy 213, 218–19, 232
soldering 302–3
solids
    conductivities 116–18
    mixtures of 180–1
    surface area 39, 257–8
    transferring 25
    volume measurement 39–40
soluble salts 277–80, 283
sources
    risk assessment information 8–9
    secondary 61
speed determination 334
spread plates 76–7
sprinklers 17
stamina 338
standard procedures 18–20, 22–3, 49
standard reference materials 21–2
standard solutions 95–100
states of matter 172
stiffness 196–7, 206, 208
stirring techniques 26
storage techniques 24, 25
straight line graphs 52–3, 55–6
streak plates 74–5
strength
    human 335–7
    materials 204, 206, 208
    types 121–2, 196–7
structure 201–2, 205–6, 207
suction filtration technique 274–5
Sun 213
    see also solar energy
suppleness 339
surface area 39, 257–8, 260
swallowed chemicals 14

tables 50
techniques 21, 23–4
temperature 260, 298
    body 165
    chemical reactions 257
    measurement 44–5
    polymers 206
temporary slides 69–70
tensile strength 121–2, 196–7
testing electrical and electronic devices 291–304

tests, chemical 88, 90–2, 93
theoretical yields 261, 262–4
thermal conduction 115, 196, 203, 206, 208
thermal conductivities 116–18
thermodynamics, laws of 221
thermometers 298
thermoplastic polymers 206
thermosetting polymers 206
thin layer chromatography 89
thorax 161–2
tidal power 219
time measurement 45
titrations 100–8
toughness 197, 203, 206, 208
transferring
    energy 221–2
    substances and materials 25

uncertainty 62–3
useful products
    animals 127
    genetic engineering 145
    living organisms 126–8
    making 254–85
    micro-organisms 79–82, 127, 151–2
    plants 126–7

veins 157
velocity ratio 306
Vernier callipers 37
videotapes 50
viruses 149, 152–3, 156
voltage measurement 45–7
voltmeters 45–6, 112
volume measurement 39–43
volumetric analysis and titrations 100–8

waste disposal 10–12, 217, 220
wave power 219
weeds 149
weighing 32, 96–9
wheelbarrow 305–8, 309
wind power 219
work done 307
work and power formulae 237–9
workplace science 242–54

yeast growth 316–17
yields 261, 262–4
yoghurt making 82